ABOUT THE BOOK:

Wrapped In Blue is Donna Rose's deeply personal memoir of self-discovery. Hers is a coming-of-age story with an unusual twist. By exploring the thoughts and emotions of an every-day person facing a unique midlife dilemma, Donna forces herself to question even the most basic aspects of her life. This is the story of her courageous and difficult journey across the gender line in hopes of finding true peace and contentment.

Although being transsexual is integral to the story, *Wrapped In Blue* explains this journey in universally human terms that can be appreciated and understood by all. It provides a rare glimpse at the emotional, physical and spiritual upheaval that transsexuals, or anyone facing a dramatic midlife transition, must face and overcome. It challenges the reader to consider life, love and gender in a new and insightful way. And, it provides a unique, intriguing, and sometimes humorous view of the differences between men and women that only someone who has lived successfully on both sides of the gender line can provide.

Free from prejudice and sensationalism, *Wrapped In Blue* is an uplifting, universal story about the power of the human spirit.

WRAPPED IN BLUE

~

A Journey of Discovery

a memoir

Donna Rose

Inquiries should be addressed to:
Living Legacy Press
603 Louis Henna Boulevard
Suite B-170, #122
Round Rock, TX 78664
www.Living-Legacy.Press.com

Library of Congress Cataloging-in-Publication Data

Rose, Donna
Wrapped In Blue: A Journey of Discovery

    p.   cm.

ISBN 0-9729553-1-3 HDBK
ISBN 0-9729553-0-5 PBK

1. Transgender—United States   2. Gender identity—biology   3. Self-actualization
4. Women—gender identity   5. Sex change—United States   6. Gender—United
States—social aspects   7. Rose, Donna—memoir

HQ 77.8R39   305.3 RO

Cover Photograph: Brenda Ladd Photography
Cover Design and photo design: Kimberly A. Selber
Page Design: Terry Sherrell

Printed in the United States of America
at Morgan Printing in Austin, Texas

It is better to be hated for what you are
than loved for what you are not.

— ANDRE GIDE

Dedication:

To the Human Spirit

ACKNOWLEDGEMENT

There have times over these past several years when I had no place to turn, had no idea where to go, or thought that I had reached my limit. Almost as if on cue, somebody incredible would enter my life, would help me to find my bearings, and would help me on my way.

I'd like to thank a very special group of people. Their support, inspiration, courage, and vision have helped me survive some incredibly difficult times. They have all touched my life in a special way, and each has earned my eternal gratitude.

Michelle
Cyndi
Dona
Dori and Rob
Julie Treiber
Deborah Netti
Sandra
Maria DiNicola
Dr. Sheila Dickson
Dr. Ken Fisher and the entire staff at First Family Medical Group
Mike
Kate
Sally and Ray
Dan, Lois, JoElyn and Danny
Dr. Douglas Ousterhout and Mira

Dr. Becky Allison
Sally and Nancy
Cassie

~

I'd like to give extra special thanks to my family. They have somehow found the ability to welcome this new person into their lives without pause or reservation. They have enveloped me with unconditional love and support, and have been my safest of havens. They are a truly amazing group of people.

My mom, Patsy.

My sister Judy, her husband Ralph, and my nieces Rachel, Rhiannon and Kyrié.

My brother Jay, his wife Melissa, and their children Ben and Corinne.

And my dad. I know you're watching…

~

This book would never have been possible without the vision and tireless support of my editor, Mindy Reed. Her boundless energy, contagious enthusiasm, patient guidance and general love for books have helped mold a capable writer with an important story into a publishable author.

~

Finally, I'd like to acknowledge two very special people. The first is my ex-wife. She did not ask to be a part of this journey. I am sorry for bringing her along, and for being unable to be what she expected me to be. And finally, I'd like to thank my son. His ability to love and accept unconditionally is truly extraordinary.

PREFACE

It takes courage to grow up and turn out to be who you really are.

(ANONYMOUS)

The author of the quotation above must have assumed that each one of us actually knows ourselves well enough to be able to define who, or what, we *really* are.

I have done that. I *have* turned out to be who I really am. Some people consider that accomplishment to be courageous. Others seem to consider it to be the epitome of weakness. Some, in fact, consider what I have achieved to be a sin against God, against nature, and against humankind. But to me, it's none of those things. It's just my life.

Today, I'm happy to report that my life is an *ordinary* life. My typical days are the normal routine that most people tend to take for granted. Normal is all I ever really wanted, but there have been times when I seriously doubted that such a life was possible for me.

What makes me unique is not necessarily who, or what, I am. It is the journey that has led me here.

I am a transsexual. More accurately, I'm a transsexual woman. I spent the first forty years of my life as a man in a man's world. I have lived life as a world-class athlete, as a husband, as a father, and as a successful businessman.

I had earned all the *toys* that society equates with success. I bought nice cars. I owned multiple homes. We had money. We traveled. By the time I was forty years old I had reached a level of achievement that so many seem to strive for, but so few seem fortunate enough to achieve.

Ultimately, that world imploded under the weight of my need to explore nagging questions that had plagued me for much of my life. My struggle to accept things about myself that I initially did not want to be true, and to express my true self in ways that I never dared to share, eventually turned that tidy, comfortable little world upside down.

The end result was a desperate but relentless attempt to storm and breach a barrier that many feel to be impenetrable and secure. The gender barrier stands alone as a line that cannot be crossed, a wall that cannot be climbed, and a concept that cannot be tested. Its defenses are many and mighty, and our society has reserved harsh punishments for those that would dare to test them. I am proud to report that I survived my successful assault, and this is my story.

Over time, I have come to realize that a transsexual is merely one form of explorer; a self-explorer. In many ways, true self-explorers are not unlike explorers of old, setting sail on uncharted seas; seduced by the call and the promise of a New World. Very few hardy souls could hear the faint, beckoning whispers of promise, and fewer still dared to answer it. Those who did sailed in constant fear of imminent destruction in the foaming jaws of some giant snarling creature, or of tumbling into the abyss that marks the end of the Earth. But still they persevered, not knowing exactly what they were looking for, but hoping they'd know it when they found it.

A transsexual's journey into the uncharted unknown is a test of commitment and character, fraught with perils and poisons that would surely cause the weak of spirit among us to turn back in terror. We risk all we have ever known and loved in hopes that the fates will provide safe passage for tormented souls through the churning black storm-filled seas that buffet our fragile hulls. We seek nothing more than to be ourselves, and our journey of discovery is the test we endure to get there.

It is hard to determine if forward momentum is fueled by promising winds of hope and freedom, or by desperation to free ourselves from exile in self-imposed prisons. Whether pushed or pulled, this mysterious spiritual force will not be denied, relinquishing its rock-solid grip on our mind and soul when and only when we have found and achieved our true destiny, or perished trying.

What could possibly make a person want to change their gender? To most people such a thought is unimaginable...unthinkable... unbearable. The fact that someone would even consider such seeming sacrilege often produces strong responses at a variety of levels. And this emotional disconnect often creates substantial communication barriers when trying to explain or understand.

While many people seem to view transsexuals as freakish novelties or curiosities, there are those who consider us to be dangerous perverts, criminals, deviates, or worse. Their reaction is often one of anger, fear, hate, and violence. As a result of this undeserved negative perception, some may feel that there is no need to read any further; as though my disclosure alone is indictment of anything I have to say. I urge these people to read on because, as odd as this may sound, I suspect that as they read my story they will realize that it contains universally *human* elements that *all* readers will be able to relate to and apply in their own lives.

In its purest form, free from sensationalism and prejudice, my story is a very human odyssey of self-discovery, and the changes that we each face inside ourselves on that path. It features the darkest and murkiest of human emotions...confusion, fear, anger, guilt, frustration, and shame. At the same time, it exhibits elements of our society's highest and most noble of qualities...courage, honesty, integrity, and dignity.

Our culture seems hell-bent on simplifying the incredible diversities of our complex world by reducing them to polar absolutes: good or bad, right or wrong, truth or lie, boy or girl. Things are rarely that simple. The breadth of the human condition cannot be appreciated when viewed through a prism that separates the entire spectrum of life into only two or three or four colors. My journey is a celebration of

11

that spectrum, and an invitation to others to explore there, as well.

My story's message is universal and simple: The search for inner-peace through the freedoms of self-knowledge and self-expression, earned on the stormy seas of self-discovery. To be, or not to be. That truly is the question.

All of the rest is just the "details."

Other than changing certain names and places to protect the privacy of others, everything in this book is an honest account of my journey, from my perspective. Much of it has been culled from journal entries and correspondences documenting a very difficult two-year period in my life. My intention in publishing it is not to argue or convince. I am not here to preach, or plead, or persuade. Rather, I strive only to share some of my most personal experiences and observations in the hope that others can use them in their own personal struggles.

This book is not a step-by-step guide for self-discovery. I do not pretend to know all the answers, or even all of the questions. I do not say that everything I have done was the "right" thing or the best thing to do. I can, however, say with confidence and conviction that I did the best I could at the time. When sailing uncharted waters there are no guides or guarantees. I somehow survived my many mistakes and miscalculations, learning firsthand that oftentimes we need to do things wrong in order to know what's right.

This book is not an attempt to explain all there is to know about transsexuals. While this sensitive subject is certainly integral to my story, it is not *the* story. Those who want that will find that other books, and other sites on the Internet, already do a thorough and admirable job in tackling this very difficult issue.

Rather, this book is about my journey. For those who want to take it at face value, I think you will find it interesting, intriguing, and thought-provoking. For those who look deeper, the ultimate value will be in your own personal interpretations.

Lord Thomas Dewar once wrote, "Minds are like parachutes; they work best when open." As you read, I would ask that you please put your preconceptions and judgments aside, at least for the duration of reading this book. If your only point of reference for transsexuals comes from sensational daytime television talk shows with titles like, "A Tranny Bitch Stole My Husband," or if you believe that the career path for a transsexual is limited to either prostitution or pornography, this may be a difficult request. Please try.

I also urge you to break free from the constraints and constrictions of popular paradigms, as self-discovery cannot be confined by such arbitrary boundaries. To do so would mean that common notions and models are the only tools you have to understand or analyze things that seem to have no explanation. I fear that such limitations doom our efforts to examine, to learn and to grow, to a point where the end result is little more than commonly acceptable confusion. Think free, be free.

Whether you agree with what I have done or not, the fact that I have accomplished it is living proof that we, as simple everyday ordinary human beings, have far more control of our own lives, our own destinies, and our own happiness than we dare to imagine. All we need to do is to maintain our faith, make a commitment, and to try.

H.L. Mencken once defined faith as "an illogical belief in the occurrence of the improbable." This allows me to chuckle at both its simplicity and its ironic wisdom. Throughout history it has been proven that this simple concept has been the source of *miracles*, so I urge you to embrace it as you read my story and live your lives. Have faith that things will be better, have faith in others, but most importantly, have faith in yourself and the things you know to be true. Once you have that, you will be well on the way to making your own miracles happen.

A Metaphor

Courage is the price that Life exacts for granting peace.
—Amelia Earhart

Imagine you are on a crowded train platform, standing within a crowd of others waiting for a train as it pulls into the station. As the train comes to a stop, the doors open, and a stream of passengers pours out onto the platform. You are deep within the waiting throng and it carries you as it surges forward, anxious to board the waiting train. You wander to the last car, climb into the corner seat, and as the train pulls away from the station, you fall asleep.

You wake up when you feel the conductor tapping you on the shoulder. The train has reached the end of the line, and the few remaining passengers gather their belongings. Bleary-eyed, you leave the train.

Standing there, alone on the platform, you realize that you are in the wrong city! As you think about it you realize, with growing anxiety, that you have no idea *where* you are! You start to get concerned and scared.

What if there were no signs to help you find out where you are? What if you asked for directions, but no one in the city spoke your language? What if the people you encountered eyed you cautiously with some mixture of distrust and outright contempt, seemingly aware of your awkward distress? You're not quite sure what to do...how to act...how to ask for help.

How would you find your way back home? How resourceful could you be? As your efforts to determine how this had happened and how to get back to "normal" yielded no results, how desperate would you become?

You feel as though you must be stuck in some sort of bad dream, but your distress is all too real. Although you appear to be in no immediate danger, you just don't feel comfortable; you just don't feel right. In fact, you struggle to contain the growing sense of panic as it wells in your stomach.

Wouldn't you give anything for that unexplainable sense of peace and comfort we find in being comfortable with our surroundings, and with our place in the world? Wouldn't you give anything to flee this place of discomfort and confusion? Wouldn't you give anything to find some answers? Wouldn't you give anything to go "home"?

Part I

Life Paths

CHAPTER ONE

MY REFLECTION

Q: What is the difference between a caterpillar and a butterfly?
A: Everything.

It was late and I was tired. The nurse had finally decided to leave me alone and let me rest. My roommate had long since drifted off to a morphine-induced sleep. I suddenly realized that twenty-four hours later, I would be in a similar situation…surrounded by machines and wires and drips hissing and bleeping at me, interrupted every couple of hours by the pokings and proddings of the night nurse on her quest to take my blood pressure or my temperature.

The last eight hours had been spent prepping me for the major surgery scheduled for early the next morning. I had been warned many times that the "prep" process was more unpleasant than the surgery itself, although considering the nature of it all I was naturally skeptical that this was possible. I had had to drink a full gallon of nasty liquid to clean out my insides, and had spent a good deal of the night stumbling back and forth from my bed to the small hospital bathroom just a few steps away. My insides were sloshing with each step, bent over from the cramps and shivering from the loss of body heat. Compared to other things I had endured over the previous couple of years, though, it really wasn't all that bad.

My mom had been there with me for much of the evening. I wondered what she thought as she watched what was happening to her firstborn. With my blessing, she eventually decided that she didn't need to watch me in my discomfort any more and had retreated back to her hotel room.

My feelings about her being here with me at this time and at this place had come full circle, from excitement, to nervousness, to doubt, and then back to excitement again. The previous night we had shared a deeply intimate talk about the nature of parents and children, and I realized that she had come to her own personal sense of peace with what I was doing. In fact, I had noticed in her luggage that she had a box of pink bubble-gum cigars with "It's a Girl!" printed on the ribbon, ready to give to anybody who would take one after the symbolic rebirth that was to come. I was so proud of her.

In fact, I was *filled* with pride. Proud of the people I had met, of the courage that they had given me, and of just how far I had come on my journey of self-discovery. I was proud to have maintained my sense of integrity and dignity through very difficult times. I had learned first-hand that the level of satisfaction in achieving something is directly proportional to the difficulty in achieving it, and by that measure I felt lucky to have even survived.

It was astounding to realize that pride was the emotion that had filled the gaping hole left where fear, guilt, shame and despair once plotted to direct my life and my destiny, now banished to the nether-regions of my soul. However, this was not a time to dwell on the pain or the negative emotions so I let my mind drift to other thoughts.

I had been prepped, shaved, painted with Betadine, and given a pill to help me sleep. I wondered to myself, "How the heck did I get here? How the heck did I unravel myself from the tightly bound ball of my entire life, start a brand new life, and work myself to be here, at this holy place? How did I overcome all the barriers, all the fears, and all of the defenses that our society brings to bear towards anyone who dares to wander too close to the gender barrier? Surely this must be a dream."

Sex. Gender. They are not one and the same. While most people rarely find a need to consider the fine points that differentiate the two, or the significant impact that each has on their lives, transsexuals can often think of little else. In fact, it was my own need to understand the complex distinction and interaction between the two that had perplexed me for much of my life.

In its most basic form, the concept of a person's *sex* was relatively simple for me to define. Sex is a "body" thing. It is the mere presence or absence of a Y chromosome, causing a body to develop the physical attributes that define a human body male, or female.

What, then, is gender? That is the question I had struggled to answer for as long as I could remember. The Merriam-Webster dictionary defines gender as "the behavioral, cultural, or psychological traits typically associated with one sex." It is the complete set of culturally based roles, expectations, and expression assigned to each person based solely on whether they have a penis or not.

Gender is **not** specifically a *body* thing. It's **not** a *sexuality* thing. It is a *culture* thing. It is a *mind* thing. It is a *self* thing. Usually, mind and body are so closely aligned that most people consider sex and gender to be one in the same. Those of us who are considered to be "gender gifted" know otherwise. *That* was the big revelation.

Anthropologists know that some Native American cultures labeled people using three categories of gender, not just two. There were, of course, male and female. However, a third group that exhibited traits that were considered to be both masculine and feminine, were identified as *dual-spirited*. They believed that God surely felt these people were special, to bestow such a precious gift upon them. These people were honored and revered, and were often asked to teach the children of the tribe in hopes that their wisdom and insight would be transferred to the future tribal leaders. In that society, people had to actually *prove* that they truly were gender gifted.

Now, it is something that is considered to be so heinous that we have to seek surgery to *correct* it. I had struggled with that for so long.

Could it be that I truly was a transsexual? Was I one of *them*? How could that be? I felt so…so…*normal*.

A transsexual is a person whose physical sex, and whose sense of gender identity, do not match. They are people who become increasingly uncomfortable and unhappy in the roles that society assigns to them based on their physical sex. Their brain and *soul* tells them one thing, but their body and the rest of society tells them something else. It is a very difficult and confusing existence.

We are all born into this world with infinite possibilities. We have the potential to speak any and all languages. We can adapt to any and all cultures. We have an arsenal of talents and skills just waiting to be discovered and developed. Our boundaries are only those physical limitations we inherit by being *human*.

From the moment we are born, however, our lives are spent narrowing those possibilities. As we learn a culture, and a language, and as we face the realities of our socioeconomic world, our potential is continually narrowed. As time passes we build mental barriers that are as constricting and as limiting as anything imposed on us in the physical world. Unexplored horizons remain uncharted. Untapped skills go undetected and undeveloped. Sadly, by the time we reach adulthood, that once unlimited potential has become a mere sliver of its original promise.

Although I doubt most people stop to think about it, the determination of a person's gender is the first and ultimately most significant limit imposed on a child. This seemingly obvious proclamation, based solely on a visual inspection of a newborn baby's genitals, is the single, most defining moment of any child's life. The implications reverberate in everything a child does from the moment of birth, forward. It will affect how others view and treat a person throughout his or her entire life, as well as how they feel about themselves.

As I lay in my hospital bed, considering it all, I knew that I had already changed *gender*. I had crossed the gender divide, and had adopted the roles, the expectations, and the limitations that our culture reserves specifically for women. I had lived successfully in that world for nearly a year, and few people who met me had any indication of my unique pedigree.

Now, I was about to change my *sex*. The next night I would not have a penis. It would be gone…reshaped and reborn into something more appropriate for my new life. Would a real *man* allow such a thing to happen? Would a *man* allow the very thing that our society uses to define him *as* a man to be taken? I had male friends who would, literally, rather die than have anything happen to their precious jewels.

I thought of the words that some people used to describe the surgery: "Sex Change," and I smiled. It just sounded so dramatic, so "out there." A nip here, a tuck there, and it would all be over. Would that change my life significantly? At that point, I doubted it. Certainly, it was the pinnacle of my physical transformation; a point of no return. The thought of it filled me with a calm sense of peace and satisfaction, and that's what seems to have been missing from my psyche for so long.

Self-mutilation? My own mother had once used those words! How come others feel so free to judge my motives like that? They had not endured what I had. They did not know what I knew. They were comfortable in their skin, and couldn't begin to imagine that others might not be. They were not ready to die to get to this point, as I was. No, this was not self-mutilation. It was self-preservation.

With a sense of sadness, my mind wandered to thoughts of my wife and son, home in bed a thousand miles away, unaware of what was about to happen. I had not seen my wife since the day, 14 months before, that she forced me to make a choice…. "Be what your son and I expect you to be or leave!"…and I made the one that led me here to the brink of my new life.

I had been married for nearly 20 years. Although the marriage had still not legally ended, spiritually and emotionally it had flat-lined a long time ago. I still loved my wife. She, on the other hand, loved a person that she felt had died, or perhaps never even really existed. He had seemed almost to good to be true. A mirage. The fact that our marriage and our bond had imploded was a tragedy of *Romeo and Juliet* proportions; our love a casualty of cruel irony, circumstance and fate.

She completely rejected me, which I could initially understand and accept, but it ultimately made me frustrated and angry. I had come to feel that her tactics were little more than emotional blackmail to get me to go home again. However, in calmer moments I realized that it was all probably for the best. I considered the difficulty I would have mixing my many conflicting roles: Dave and Donna, man and woman, husband and father vs. selfish home-wrecker. I could never again be the person that she wanted and expected. Perhaps it was better to make a clean break rather than continue to tantalize and torture each other with things that could never be.

At one point I had promised myself that the last words on my dying lips would be my wife's name, symbolically demonstrating my love and devotion to her, hoping the depth of my feeling would somehow make it from my heart to hers. Each time I went into surgery I would repeat her name over and over and over as the warmth of the anesthesia washed over me, just in case I never woke up. In the face of her continued painful rejection, I felt it was fitting, at this threshold, to finally break my vow and my link to her.

It is rare in our lives that we arrive at a milestone where one chapter abruptly ends, and another begins. As I lay there in my hospital bed, comfortable and relaxed, I knew I was at that place. I knew that the dawn of the next day would start on a blank page of a brand new chapter, but wasn't a whole new book. Rather it was the sequel of the life and the spirit inside me, continuing like a thread that changes colors midway through the spool. Penis or no penis, I was still me. I reached down to touch it one last time…and to wish it a peaceful voyage, as the caterpillar enters its cocoon and transforms into a butterfly.

As I slowly drifted off to sleep, I couldn't help but feel that this was like dying. I could see the pages of the previous chapters of my life turn slowly through my mind, viewed as if by a stranger at the cinema…wondering how the hero would escape the clutches of fate this time… .

CHAPTER TWO

BOYHOOD

As soon as a child realizes there is something wrong with the way the world looks at them and the way they perceive themselves and how they fit in they do their best to cope in a world in which they feel uncomfortable and alone.

— JOURNAL ENTRY

I was born into this world at 6:54 a.m. on February 22, 1959, at the Chicago Lying-In Hospital in Chicago, Illinois. From all indications, the birth was routine, and without complication.

The name on the birth certificate read DAVID GUY ROSE. I am told that my parents had considered several names, including Billy Bob and Jimmy John, before mercy and common sense got the better of them and they settled on David, a strong biblical name meaning beloved. Ironically, my middle name was Guy, a shortened version of my mother's maiden name, Guinand, and *not* a subliminal reference having anything to do with sex or gender.

My sex, according to the original birth record, was MALE.

My mom had been an army nurse before moving to Chicago, and she had decided to retire to be a stay-at-home mom. My dad, on the other hand, was attending the University of Chicago, studying to earn his Ph.D. in mathematical biophysics. For many years I could not even pronounce that, much less understand what one of those actually did. Other kids would explain that their fathers were dentists or lawyers. Mine was a theoretical biophysicist (whatever that was). Dad once explained that he was a scientist, which conjured visions of test tubes and white lab coats, but I never saw any indication of that, so I was skeptical from an early age.

My inauspicious arrival was followed a year and a half later by a younger sister, Judith, and then two years later my brother Jacob was born. The five of us lived in a small apartment near the university. As far as I can recall, my early childhood was an uneventful and generally happy one.

At an early age, children do not innately understand the differences between being a boy and being a girl. If we accept that expression of one's gender is culturally based, then indeed many of these behaviors must be taught and learned. As parents, we often begin this process immediately. Based on the sex of the child, we assign a gender-appropriate name. Often, girl babies are wrapped in a pink blanket, and boys are wrapped in blue. We take the child home to a bedroom or a nursery that has often been painted and decorated based on the sex of the baby. As we take our still gender-neutral looking baby into the world we want to communicate that the child is a boy or a girl. In fact, I have even seen newborn baby girls decorated with a big pink bow wrapped around their heads in an effort to preempt admiring onlookers who would dare to ask, "Look how cute! What is *his* name?"

As a child develops and begins to socialize, whether we realize it or not we constantly steer our children towards gender-appropriate behaviors. Boys play with cars and trucks, play army, while girls play with dolls. Boys wear pants and shirts; girls wear dresses and skirts. Boys keep short hair; girls can grow their hair and wear barrettes or bows. It is okay for boys to roughhouse, wrestle and play sports; girls have tea parties, take dance lessons, and learn gymnastics. Although these are certainly generalizations, there can be no denying that socialization of our children is very much dictated by the sex of the child. This is accepted as normal and natural to the point that the child, and perhaps even the parent, is often unaware of this very powerful gender-directed disposition.

From a young age, various forms of punishment and reward are used to steer children and teach them proper and acceptable behavior. Not surprisingly, children who begin to express themselves in ways that are considered inappropriate for their sex are often gently corrected. If open-minded parents are unwilling to provide this correction, then peers and playmates will certainly do it, although their tactics are usually much more aggressive and hurtful.

For transsexuals, the realization that something is not right often begins early in life. As young children, I doubt most of us can explain exactly what this mysterious feeling is. I find that many of us remember the corrections given to us more than the specifics of how we felt or what we thought at four or five years of age. In either case, we can usually recall things that, in retrospect, indicate that the seeds of our gender issues had already been planted.

My own earliest memories that something was not right were when I was five or six years old. It was certainly not an overpowering feeling, but it was there nonetheless. I somehow expected that socialization bestowed upon girls in our society, would come to me too. Instead, these female rights-of-passage were not forthcoming, and that confused me more than anything.

School is where gender-specific training becomes formalized. As important as any formal education that we receive, it is where we essentially start learning to be boys and girls, and what happens to kids who can't or won't conform.

For example, young boys are often taken into the ladies restrooms with their mothers. It is never questioned. Once the child begins school, though, they learn that there are BOYS bathrooms and GIRLS bathrooms. We are taught that boys do not go into the girls' bathroom, and that anyone using a girls' bathroom must be a girl. From that point forward, I remember how uncomfortable it made me feel when my mom dragged me into the ladies restroom with her. Real boys just don't *do* that.

I remember math classes where the teacher would arrange a competition between teams to see who could answer simple flash card math problems the fastest. It was always the boys against the girls. For some reason, the girls always seemed to win, and I wished I was on their team.

Some gender-disposed training is far more obvious and direct. In fact, it is sometimes so formal that there are gender-specific schools for boys or girls. Other schools may enforce a specific dress code where boys wear a white shirt, blue pants, and a tie, and girls wear a white blouse, a sweater, and a skirt. There's a school where boys who break the dress code are punished by being forced to wear a pair of pink sweatpants for the day. Those forced to endure this humiliation rarely transgress a second time.

As I started school, my sister was my best playmate. It was not long before I learned that boys don't play with girls. All one needed to do was to look at the playground during recess, where the boys gravitated with the boys, and the girls went off into their own little groups. Any boy that broke this unwritten rule was a "fem," and *nobody* wanted to be one of those! This made sense to my young mind, because more than anything, I wanted to fit in, so I stopped playing with my little sister. She had not yet learned the real-boys-don't-play-with-girls rule, and was crushed by my newfound independence. I did my best to do what I had been told that boys were supposed to do, so I ignored her. My mom was horrified by this, and tried to steer me back to play with her, which put me in a confusing place. Apparently, my boorish behavior was not very long-lived, and I was back playing with her before too long.

In the middle of the first grade we moved to a small suburb just outside of Buffalo, New York. Kenmore was a wonderful place to grow up, an older neighborhood full of tidy tree-lined streets with well-kept houses. Kids still ride their bikes along its calm streets, and play football in front of Lindberg Elementary School today, just as we did in the mid-1960s.

The house we lived in was white, with red shutters and a black door. It has changed colors several times since then, but to me it always looks that way when I close my eyes and visualize it.

I remember how it looks during the summer, with sun poking through the canopy of huge maple trees that line the street. I remember how it looked in the winter, with gray skies and cold winter air; shoveled piles of snow lining each side of the driveway. The boys in our neighborhood would play hockey on the driveway until late in the evening.

My mom was not a shy woman. After we moved in, she took us up and down the street in search of potential playmates. We went door to door, and Mom rang every doorbell and introduced us to everyone on the street. It was unmercifully embarrassing.

One of my friends from down the street was a girl named Rachel. I remember playing house with her, and we both took turns being the mom. We both used the hand and face creams that she kept in her bedroom. Her mom checked on us one day, and said that I should check to see whether my mom felt that this game was appropriate. Neither of us understood what we were doing "wrong," but socialization based on gender can be an insidious thing.

My dad was a brilliant man. Whereas some people know a lot about a few things, he seemed to know a lot about *everything*…history, geography, math, science, music, philosophy; he even knew five or six languages well enough to get by. Our entire family took much pride in the fact that my dad was our very own walking set of encyclopedias.

Growing up in Brooklyn, he was a bookworm, which he said worried his parents, who fretted that he should be spending more time outside. They worried that he was not fitting in with the other kids of his tough Brownsville neighborhood, so they took away all of his books in order to encourage him to get out more. The only book he had left was a dictionary, so he spent his nights memorizing it.

My dad realized early in his life that his brains, and not his brawn, would be his ticket out of Brooklyn. During high school he won the prestigious Westinghouse National High School Science award, which provided a certain level of notoriety including a trip to Washington, D.C. to meet the president

Bathroom reading material at our house was not the typical fare one might expect to find; no weekly magazines or out-of-date newspapers. You were more likely to find *Rise and Fall of the Third Reich*, a book on Einstein or on Oppenheimer, and an occasional book of *Peanuts* cartoons.

Although my dad's intellectual horsepower was never questioned, I think he felt a little awkward being a parent. We rarely did father/son bonding activities. I don't know if that's because there were five of us in the house and finding an opportunity to get away for some privacy was rare, perhaps it just made him uncomfortable.

When I was nine or ten years old, he took me to see the movie *2001—A Space Odyssey*. Movie excursions were usually mom's job and consisted of taking the entire group of us to a Saturday or Sunday Disney matinee. This was my first nighttime movie, and that alone made me feel grown-up and special. I must admit that the film totally confused me, although it seemed to be some sort of amazing experience for him. I did my best to act like I understood it all, but to this day my favorite parts are when the monkeys get agitated at the beginning, and when the computer sings near the end. Dad told me I should have read the book.

Another time, he took me to a Buffalo Bills game. It was midwinter, and the War Memorial in downtown Buffalo was buried under a foot of snow. The Bills played the Dolphins, and won, but the game is not my main memory of that day. I remember being cold… no, I remember being frozen! My small hands, feet and nose were ice cubes by the time the game was over. To top the day off, my dad had decided to park the family station wagon in a lot that had a sign that read Vehicles with chains only. Of course, we got stuck and had to be towed out.

My mom was the one who made our family tick. She was the practical one. She was our taxi when we needed to be driven somewhere. If something needed to be fixed, she fixed it, or she made the arrangements to have it fixed. She did all of the yard work. She did all of the decorating. She often did the work of both parents, so I suppose I couldn't begrudge her the weekly Saturday afternoon off when she left to be on her own for a few hours. Of course, the thought that she wouldn't come back, or might be involved in a terrible accident, crossed my mind more than once and filled me with a sense of anxiety. But to her credit, she always came back.

Mom was our Cub Scout den mother. I remember her planning a skit about Indians, and painting my face with bright red lipstick. Even at that young age, I remember wishing I could put it on my lips and not just as war paint streaks across my cheeks.

My mom always had a plan, or a list. She knew what was what, and where to find it. She made sure we went to piano lessons. She took us to horseback riding lessons. She made sure we did our homework and that we didn't take more than three cookies for our bedtime snack. She punished us, and she rewarded us. She taught me how to drive. She taught me how to balance the checkbook. She felt it was important for us to develop a spiritual foundation, so she insisted that we go to Sunday school each week. Despite my protests, she made sure that I took typing in high school, and to this day it remains the class that has proven most useful of any during those years.

Mom's literary tastes were in stark contrast to Dad's. She became addicted to cheesy romance novels. My most vivid memories are of her sitting on her end of the couch, near the lamp, reading. She had hundreds, maybe even thousands, of them, and it seemed that she could read an entire book in an hour or two. She had her favorites, which she read over and over again, and the very thought that she would *want* to read any of them more than once still makes me smile.

Once she settled into her reading, getting her attention was next to impossible. A blood-curdling shriek could pass unnoticed as she sped through the lines of her book, too engrossed to notice. Dozens

31

of times a day we would stand in the living room yelling, "Mom. Mom. *MOM*!" in an attempt to get her attention. She sat, still reading, oblivious to our presence until we physically shook her back to the here and now.

My sister, Judy (Jude), is 18 months younger than I am. When she was seven years old I remember her wanting to grow her hair out, and I was terribly jealous of her for that. At the same time, my mom decided to give my brother and me a buzz-cut. I actually cried as she sheared off my already short blonde hair, right down to the nubs. I wore a winter hat on my head for days in an attempt to hide it, not wanting to be seen with a head that felt like a tennis ball.

Jude liked to wear dresses. Any dress she wore was only as good as its ability to twirl. She would put on the dress, and spin round and round, watching the dress as it spun elegantly with her. If a dress could not twirl properly, my sister had no interest in it. At the time it seemed ridiculously pointless and stupid to me.

Perhaps more than anything, though, I remember my sister for our inability to connect, on any level whatsoever. We were the personification of what John Gray would call Venus and Mars, and as I look back on much of our relationship as we grew up together, I feel a sense of remorse and regret at having been such an egotistical, self-centered ass.

I considered myself to be a fairly intelligent, logical person. My sister, on the other hand, seemed, to me, completely and irresponsibly *illogical*, and that frustrated the heck out of me. It was the source of many an argument, and led to a very tenuous love/hate relationship that we struggled with throughout our teenage years. It got so bad that my mom asked the school to assign us lockers that were located on opposite ends of the campus.

For example, I started a stamp collection when I was eight or nine years old. I especially sought old stamps, because they were worth more money, and *money* was a magic word for me. My sister, however, only had interest in "pretty" stamps with animals on them; horses in particular. I taunted her by saying that these stamps would never be worth anything, but she didn't care. She just liked the stamps. And that kind of *irrational* thinking was absolutely foreign to me. It drove me bonkers, and I teased her unmercifully for it.

The fact that I did not understand her in no way tainted my feelings of protection for her. I was not scared to get into a scuffle if the need should present itself. She recalls a time once, when some bullies were taunting her from across the street, when I crossed the street to confront them, and ended up punching somebody out. Perhaps I felt that I, as her older brother, was the only one with the right to cause her grief. My sister used to joke that I suffered from testosterone poisoning, and I sometimes wonder if she was right.

My brother Jacob (Jay), on the other hand, was my buddy and my best pal. We played with trucks together. We played army. We played football, and hockey, and basketball, and we wrestled. We collected sports cards. We played soldier. We played board games. We did all those brotherly *guy* things. I had no interest in playing with dolls. Oh, no. Not me. Boy toys were much more fun, and having a younger brother to share them with was the best.

I don't remember being all that tough on Jay, but I think if you ask him he will remember otherwise. A younger brother is usually the one that gets hurt, or pushed, or bruised. I used to get him in wrestling holds and asked him if they hurt, knowing by his screaming and yelling that they did.

My sister, however, wanted Jay as a pal, too. So we fought over him. I think in retrospect, that the two of them had an empathy, which never involved me. One time, when we were all very young, Judy was crying about something. My brother started to cry for no other reason than because she was crying. The two of them were baw56 ling together and I sat there, dumbfounded. "What the heck was that all about?" Whatever it was, I was pretty sure it had to do with emotion and even at that young age I think my emotional barriers were fairly solid, and kept me from understanding.

I would get so angry when the two of them would go off and do stuff without me. I was probably afraid that she would contaminate the poor, young, impressionable boy with her illogical ways. There was a time that Jude was interested in Yoga, and seemed to be getting Jay interested in it, too. I was appalled! But in the end, I knew that he would come back. He always came back. I knew that he could not resist the guy games, and as we grew older, and Jude went off to play with her own friends, an uneasy truce for him took hold.

CHAPTER THREE

THE PUBERTY MACHINE

Many of the roles that you are allowed to play and many of
the expectations for you in our society are associated with
your gender. This becomes painfully apparent as a child
enters and exits the puberty machine.

— JOURNAL ENTRY

As I neared puberty, questions that had been rumbling around in my head for a while started to take some sort of definitive shape. They began to play an active role in my life. This sense of something not being right slowly solidified into something clear and unmistakable. I was twelve years old, and we had moved to Santa Barbara, California for a year.

Puberty is a time of many changes, even in the best of circumstances. As my own son neared this portion in his own life, I visualized puberty as a thick, dense fog laying just on the horizon. We watch our children enter it, as if engulfed and swallowed whole. We agonize and wait for years in the hope that a healthy, happy adult will emerge on the other side of the haze. Of course, there are no guarantees. This is the puberty machine.

Puberty is the time when a child becomes a young adult, and struggles with their sense of self-identity. It is a time when hormones seize control of the mind and of the body, causing tremendous conflict and confusion. It is the time when secondary sex characteristics kick in. It is the time when many rights of passage for boys and for girls are realized.

Because of our unique situation, puberty is often especially difficult for transsexuals. It is a time when the onslaught of permanent physical changes begins to mold our bodies indelibly into something that we know does not reflect who we understand ourselves to be. We are unable to communicate about or stop that process. It is like being awake and aware on an operating table, feeling every incision, every suture, but being unable to open your mouth to alert the doctor of your distress. I think many of us realize, in retrospect, that puberty was actually an especially lonely time for us, as we did our best to internalize our struggle and deal with our issues alone.

I remember enduring changes to my voice that made my sweet boyish tenor suddenly much deeper. I remember watching the hair begin to grow on my chest and around my penis, and feeling helpless to stop it. I remember the scraggly stubble on my face growing to a point where my dad dutifully gave me my first shaving lesson. The fact that I was indeed trapped in the wrong world, and was getting pushed deeper and deeper into it, started to become painfully obvious.

In my still childish innocence, I saw nothing wrong with voicing my confusion and concern. I remember asking my sister when I would be old enough to be able to shave my increasingly hairy legs. "Boys don't shave their legs, stupid," she told me. How the heck could I stop this train and get off? It was headed down the wrong track.

My questioning, and some of my innocence, ended at Halloween. I had decided that I wanted to go trick-or-treating dressed as a girl. My request was simple, and innocent.

Apparently, my mom thought otherwise. She said, "No."

"Why not?"

"No," she said.

"Pleeeaaase. I really want to."

"No," she said.

"Come on," I pleaded. "I think it would be fun."

"ABSOLUTELY NOT! It's absolutely inappropriate!" she yelled.

Her response was loud, firm and final. I was shocked by its intensity and by the implications that it would have on my sensitive, confused mind.

This seemingly trivial event was a defining moment in my life. It was my first attempt to actively explore anything even remotely having to do with my gender confusion. Her reaction exploded on me like a bucket of ice water in the face. How could my mom know that my questions were about something so much deeper and more important to me than a silly costume? I was crushed.

Today, my mom has no memory of this incident. However, it is indelibly burned into my memory. As far as I was concerned, this was Groundhog Day, and David, now thirteen, was the groundhog. As I tried to peep my already anxious head out of my safe little hole, I suddenly saw an angry black shadow that was so horrifically terrifying, that it sent me scurrying for the deep, dark warmth of my burrow for a long time to come.

I made several important decisions in the weeks that followed.

I decided that if I had to be a boy, I would work my hardest be the best boy I could be.

I decided I needed to keep my feelings buried and hidden, away from prying eyes and closed minds. My mom's reaction showed me that such thoughts and feelings were absolutely unacceptable, and I found it unthinkable to face her disappointment or her disapproval. I felt a strong pressure to live up to my parents' expectations of me, and this gender bewilderment was not firmly formed enough in my mind to run the risk of disappointing them.

At the same time, I decided to start actively exploring this confusion. I realized that I had a feminine side to my personality. I didn't know why and I didn't know how. But it was becoming ever more apparent that it was active, and it was healthy, and it was demanding attention.

In the months after Halloween, I began to experiment and explore. I would wake up at two o'clock in the morning and tip-toe into the small bathroom that separated the master bedroom from the one we three kids shared. I locked the doors on both sides, hoping to conduct my late night experiments without being disturbed.

With a mixture of excitement and terror, I began to experiment with my mom's cosmetics. These first attempts were clumsy and awkward. I'm not even sure what I was hoping to accomplish; it just made me happy to have some quality time to finally express my feminine self. Once finished, I cleaned up and put everything back exactly as I found it before sneaking back to bed undetected.

My experiments were totally innocent. There was absolutely nothing sexual, or erotic, about them. In fact, I hadn't even matured at that point. I really wasn't doing anything terribly wrong. Why, then, did it make me feel so guilty and ashamed when it was all over? And what made me keep going back for more?

That year I was in seventh grade. The walk home from school each afternoon was a long one. It took me over an hour to trudge up the hills that line the Santa Barbara coastline, to get from the junior high school to the house we were renting, which was precariously balanced overlooking the city and the coast. Whereas most boys probably daydreamed about being sports heroes, or astronauts, I used to spend much of my walking time fantasizing about a life much different from the one I was apparently destined to live. I dreamed of being a girl.

I remember one particular daydream about a sensational procedure whereby a scientist could miraculously switch the personalities between two people. I, of course, volunteered to change brains with a girl, secretly hoping that nobody would realize that I had ulterior motives. As the plot unfolded, the switch was only supposed to be for a short time, but apparently the girl's brain was so happy to be in the strong, boy's body, she that did not want to trade back. Of course, it was actually *me* that didn't want to change back, but I did my best to hide that. These fantasies filled my walks, and I would sometimes continue them day after day.

Although I had fantasies and experimented, I was not outwardly effeminate in any sense of the word. I participated in neighborhood pick-up games of football, hockey, or basketball. I built models of World War II airplanes and tanks, and studied the great battles and generals of that war. For some reason, I became interested in the events surrounding the mutiny on the HMS Bounty, and bought all the stamps I could find from tiny Pitcairn Island. My favorite author was Alexander Dumas, who penned swashbuckling stories such as *The Three Musketeers* and *The Man in the Iron Mask*.

Eventually, my natural curiosity spread to this vexing, unnamed problem. I knew that I couldn't be the only one in the entire world feeling perplexed; there had to be others. There had to be a name or a label for it somewhere. There had to be a way to treat it. I expected that if I found out what it was called, I could learn more about it.

Here I was a thirteen-year-old child who needed to do research about something that I couldn't even name. I went to the library in hopes of finding books. I scoured the old *Time* magazines in the basement. I searched the encyclopedias, looking for clues and answers.

The only point of reference that I had to start with was a word that I had heard, with sex in it: Homosexual. I did a little research and learned that homosexuals, or gays, were attracted to members of their same sex. Although some homosexual men may express themselves in ways that are considered feminine, most of them had absolutely no desire to change genders. Homosexuality is a sexuality issue, not a gender identity issue, and even at that point in my life I knew that the two were not the same thing.

I learned that transvestites (or cross-dressers) are typically heterosexual men who find that dressing or appearing as a woman provides a sense of excitement, relief, or satisfaction. There is often a fetishistic aspect to these adventures, whether it is with female clothes, or makeup, or pretending to be in a female role for a short while. These people do not want to actually be women, however. I did not think I was one of these.

I learned that drag queens were typically flamboyant homosexual men who dress as women. Often, they are entertainers, known for their flamboyant costumes and behavior. Again, these people had no desire to become physically female. I *knew* I was not one of these.

Finally, I learned about a group of people that were labeled as transsexuals. This group suffered from an in-born affliction that was not sexuality based, and was not based on specific items such as clothes or shoes. These people felt that they had been mis-cast in life; that they had been born into a body that that indicated one gender but had the self-identity of the other. The result was often a life-long struggle to either maintain the façade of trying to live out their lives as their physical gender, or to change their physical form to match their self-image (a "sex change" operation). Suddenly, it all seemed to make sense. This was me!

The following year Dad moved our family to East Lansing, Michigan for another one-year assignment. That year I decided to join the junior high wrestling team. The fact that I had never even seen a wrestling match was of little consequence. Subconsciously, I saw this as the *manliest* sport I could find, so I wanted to participate to prove to myself just how manly I could be.

Over the next nine years, wrestling sculpted my body, taught me mental and physical discipline, fueled my competitive nature, and developed a sense of confidence, all of which would prove invaluable to me in later years. Although I couldn't explain why I did it, joining wrestling turned out to be one of the best decisions that I ever made.

It was also at this time that my interest in girls finally blossomed. Up to that time I used to explain that I was allergic to two thing, cats and girls. My cat allergy continues to this day. But my girl allergy seemed to clear up as I entered the eighth grade. I suddenly noticed just how nice girls really looked, and smelled. I noticed how soft their hands were. I had my first girlfriend, and kissed a girl for the first time. As the year progressed, I was tremendously relieved to realize that my gender issues did not seem to have clouded my budding sexuality.

During that year I participated in two school plays. In the first, I played the role of Mercutio in *Romeo and Juliet*. I was killed in a sword duel during each performance. What could be more manly than that? During the second semester I was somehow chosen to play the male romantic lead in *You Can't Take it With You*. As luck would have it, the girl chosen to play the female lead was a pretty blonde girl who rode our bus.

The highlight of my thespian career was nothing that happened on-stage, or even the nightly curtain call to the standing ovations we received after each performance. It was the fact that I needed a face full of stage make-up for each show. Backstage as the make-up girl applied the heavy doses of eye shadow, eyeliner, blush, mascara, and lipstick that comprised my stage face, I struggled to remain calm and to act nonchalant, not wanting to seem too eager or excited. My time in the make-up chair was pure heaven.

My budding heterosexuality, along with my growing masculine presence, confused me. Never having ever met a transsexual, or even seen one (as far as I knew), my only points of reference were the common stereotypes that I had heard: that transsexuals were at least somewhat effeminate, and that they were somehow homosexual. I wondered how I could truly be transsexual if these depictions were accurate, and neither was true in my case. It was an apparent paradox that would trouble me for many years.

During my middle teenage years, my gender issues never neared a point where they became overwhelming for me. Rather, they were constant "companions." Sometimes they lay dormant in the background, like a dull toothache that just won't go away. I think what bothered me most, though, was the gnawing sense of shame and guilt that I felt in harboring my secret life, and the constant fear of being discovered.

Although I am told that many transsexuals cross-dress extensively throughout their lives, I did not. However, I was not always successful in denying myself this simple pleasure. I discovered a trunk in the attic full of my mom's old army uniforms, but there was usually little time or opportunity in our house to play dress-up even if I wanted to. And, I was scared to death of getting caught.

What I did know, however, is that my cross-dressing adventures really had very little to do with the clothes, or with the makeup. Some people find significant excitement, or relief, from wearing female clothes. In my case, it was not the clothes that gave me that sense of relief that I needed. Instead, I found wearing the clothes or putting on the makeup to be simple and innocent opportunities for self-expression for the feminine side of my personality. They were symbolic of a feminine world that I could not live in, and my brief visits there provided an effective outlet for the pressures that were building up inside me. Expressing this feminine side was a double-edged sword. The more I visited it, the more I wanted to continue to live there. This led to feelings of guilt and shame.

My periodic outlets were very important to me. Like a steam engine needing to release pressure that has built to dangerous levels, attempts to totally cap and control this part of my personality for any length of time inevitably led to an increase in pressure, tension, and frustration. Once vented, the pressure would dissipate and things would go back to normal.

By the time I turned 17, my body had been sculpted into a buff young man. To my daily amazement, I had become quite the budding jock. My sister's friends ooh'd and aah'd over me, and I think Jude felt some pride in the fact that they lusted after her big brother. Although I was flattered, and it was very good for my male ego, I had very little interest in most of them. It's not that I had any interest in boys, either. Rather, being sexual was not a big deal to me at the time.

How many post-pubescent teenage boys can say that? At a time when many kids seem to be able to think of little else, sex really wasn't important to me. I remember how nervous I felt as I prepared to buy my first *Penthouse* magazine. I half expected alarms and sirens to go off, and for police to descend on the small drugstore to shackle this shameful underage delinquent who dared to buy such filthy pornography. Thankfully, I survived my magazine purchase experience, and escaped the store with both my booty and my pride.

I remember those adventures more as attempts to fit in than anything having to do with sex.

Although very few people who knew me would have described me as shy, I knew that to be true about myself. I was successful at hiding it. While I appeared to be assertive and confident on the outside, I felt passive and awkward when it came to meeting new people, and especially when it came to boy/girl type relationships. Most of the dates I did have resulted from me being the ask-ee rather than the ask-er. I just did not feel comfortable in the typical male role as the pursuer and conqueror. I found that being put into situations where I felt I was supposed to know what to do made me uncomfortable, and I ultimately felt inadequate and frustrated. So I avoided them.

One day I was with a girlfriend at her parents' house. Her mom and dad were out of town, and we had been necking on the couch. One thing started to lead to another, and to another…pretty soon we were lying down and I was on top of her. My hands were starting to explore places that they had never been before. We stopped for a moment, and she looked deep into my eyes. I could sense that she was waiting for me to make a move. A *big* move. But taking that initiative made me uncomfortable, and so I did nothing, eventually letting the moment pass. While relieved on one level, I kicked myself about it for weeks.

Although certainly not one of the popular kids, I enjoyed school. I was selected as editor of the school newspaper and I wrote poetry that was included in the student literary anthology. Although my mental horsepower was certainly no threat to my dad, my internal drive to be successful pushed me to expect and achieve A's and high B's in all of my subjects, so I was considered a brain.

I did my best to fit into things that "cool" kids did. As far as I was concerned, the easiest way to do that was through athletics. I enjoyed watching football, so I tried out for the team. I survived the brutal late-summer two-a-day practices, and the anxious days leading to final cuts, and was selected to be the second string middle linebacker, calling our defensive plays in the huddle. Although some of the defensive players on the team wore relatively little padding, I had far too much respect for my body to let it get beat up like that. I padded myself from head to toe; shoulder pads, elbow pads, forearm pads, hand pads. Once you tape it all up, it's like playing football while wrapped in a mattress. The highlight of my football career occurred when I turned around in the middle of a play (I was out of position, I think), I saw the ball on the ground, and fell onto a fumble.

During one of our late-season practices I split open and broke my nose. Although it didn't really hurt, it was re-injured every time I hit someone, sending an impressive stream of blood down the front of my face and dripping off my chinstrap. The doctor urged me to stop playing until it healed, so I decided to retire from football indefinitely. I was a far better wrestler than I was a football player anyways, so it gave me an opportunity to devote my full athletic attentions to grappling.

As I proceeded through the rest of high school, and especially into college, there came to be two distinct seasons in my life: wrestling season, and getting-ready-for-wrestling season. Wrestling offered the best of both worlds as far as a I was concerned: the self-determination freedoms of an individual sport, along with the camaraderie and spirit of a team sport.

Our team really wasn't very good, and in the beginning I probably lost as many matches as I won. That really didn't dampen my enthusiasm or optimism, as the bitterness of my losses pushed me to get better, and the sweetness of my victories pushed me to want more. I spent the off-season honing my skills, building my strength and endurance, and attending summer wrestling camp, all in preparation for my six minutes on the mat.

Wrestlers are unique creatures. To casual observers, wrestling is a tough, brutal sport, and I think we take some sort of primal pride in that perception. However, to those who participate, it is as beautiful as a ballet: move, counter move, speed, agility, strength. I like to think of it as a brotherhood based on shared suffering and hardship.

My first coach told me that being a successful wrestler was not about watching what was happening in your match at any point in time. Those who waited to react, or who thought about a match one move at a time, lost. Good wrestlers predict what is going to happen, and like in chess, think one, two, three, four moves ahead, so that is the skill that I tried to develop in myself.

One of the unique aspects of wrestling is the difficulty that many of us have maintaining our wrestling weight. Wrestlers compete with others in their same weight range, and depending on the lineup of the team, a wrestler can compete at 10 or 20 pounds below their natural, comfortable weight. I spent many a lunch hour running up and down the stairs of the school, or sitting in the boys' locker room showers in a plastic suit, the hot water to turning it into a steamy sauna, so I could sweat off excess weight. In college I would spend hours spitting into a cup, trying to lose a few ounces any way that I could.

Although one could debate the healthfulness of such a regimen, one could never argue that being a successful wrestler doesn't require a tremendous amount of discipline and dedication. It requires a certain mental toughness, a drive to succeed, and a will to win. All of these qualities would be key for me throughout the rest of my life. In fact, I attribute many of the successes I experienced throughout my life directly to the things I developed and learned about myself in wrestling.

My family moved to Nova Scotia after my junior year in high school. I did not want to go. The prospect of being plucked from my comfortable little world in Buffalo, as I was heading into my senior year of high school, seemed cruel and unreasonable to me. My grades were probably good enough to get me a scholarship. I was poised to have a great year in wrestling, and I finally had lots of friends. My protests about how this wasn't fair, and how this would ruin my life fell on deaf ears, as my mom dragged me kicking and screaming to Halifax. I made up my mind to hate everything about moving there, and once I got there I did my best to be miserable.

I was in no mood to appreciate the Maritime charms or the beauty of Nova Scotia. I found that a very thin line divided picturesque and peaceful, from boring. I had decided before I even got there that Halifax was no place for a disgruntled high school senior, mourning a year of stolen experiences and rights of passage. Instead of captaining the wrestling team, I found myself defending the honor of my home country in Social Studies class, arguing that the United States Revolutionary War patriots were not motivated by pure greed, power and lust. Instead of learning "real" French, I was forced to endure a year with a teacher whose thick French-Canadian accent obscured the fact that there may not have actually been any French under there at all. To top it all off, they don't even get to wear real caps and gowns when they graduate from high school! I had looked forward to that my entire life! The culture…the pace of life…just the plain fact that it wasn't home, all made for a very long and unpleasant year.

As I had very few friends to distract me, I trained hard. I lifted weights. I ran. I climbed the stairs at the university ice rink with 50-pound bags of cement on my shoulders. My 145-pound physique bulked up to 170 pounds, and by the time I graduated I was bench-pressing over 300 pounds. My sudden muscular explosion was so dramatic that my father pulled me aside one day to ask if I was taking steroids. I almost laughed in his face. How could I tell him that I wouldn't have done that even if my life had depended on it?

Time and maturity have helped me to realize that my time in Halifax really wasn't all that bad. I fell in love for the first time. I got my first job. I earned enough money to buy my first car.

My one year there turned into two, and then into three. I hadn't set a direction for life yet, so rather than cast my sails to see where the winds would take me I stayed close to home. College there was cheap. Living expenses were nil. I was working and saving money. Plus, there was my wrestling.

During my second year of college I won the tournament to become the collegiate champion for all the Canadian Maritime provinces. I was featured on Canadian Network Television. I was chosen to compete against other elite collegiate wrestlers in CIAA (Canadian Intercollegiate Athletic Association) wrestling championships at the Olympic Village in Montreal. It was the pinnacle, and the end, of my wrestling career.

CHAPTER FOUR:

MY MANHOOD

*Years ago, manhood was an opportunity for achievement,
and now it is a problem to be overcome.*

— GARRISON KEILLOR

The year was 1979. I was twenty and suddenly my childhood was gone. I applied to Syracuse University as a Television/Radio production major, and had been accepted to begin there in the fall. I was excited to be leaving home and going back to upstate New York. I looked forward to living in a dormitory and finally being able to experience college life at its lusty, alcohol-drenched, gregarious best.

A month after the school year started, Halloween arrived. Anyone who has ever felt the need to cross-dress will appreciate the freedom we feel on that day, and I exploited that as much as I could. Every year for the previous several years I had gone out on Halloween in drag. One year, a friend and I even rented 1920s-style flapper costumes from a costume store. Despite outward appearances, I remained confident that my defenses were secure enough to ensure that nobody would suspect that my motives were deeper than they appeared to be.

As I waited in line for our dorm Halloween "Get Lei'd" party, I met Elizabeth. She approached me to ask how much tickets cost for non-residents. My life would never be the same again.

Within a week we were seeing each other exclusively. Within a month we were using the "L" word. And within six months, we were engaged.

Elizabeth had the most incredible eyes I had ever seen. Deep, brown and sparkling with life, they were absolutely intoxicating. With a happy round face framed by dark shoulder length hair, a cute little nose, and lips as full and supple as any I had ever seen, she was a natural beauty. She rarely, if ever, wore makeup and her skin still seemed like porcelain to me.

Elizabeth considered herself to be a tomboy, an only daughter with three older brothers. She never carried a purse. She couldn't fathom the value of a relaxing day in a spa. Rather than pay a salon to style her hair, she preferred to trim it herself. She felt far more comfortable hanging around with the guys than being with other women. She could throw a football or softball as well as any guy I knew.

In a cruel twist of irony, the thing that initially mde me attractive to her was my physique. She *loved* my muscles. She loved the way they felt. She enjoyed the fact that, when we walked through a bar, people got out of my way. She reveled in the respect that I was given by the guys in my dorm.

I rarely felt the need to actually use my muscle. I had learned early on that being a guy was 90% appearance and attitude, and 10% substance. I knew for a fact that I had the attitude thing down pat. I used to feel that going into a bar was like being a ram, looking for other rams to butt heads with to determine who would rule the herd. With my chest puffed and my muscles bulging, I felt up to any challenge.

One evening Elizabeth and I went to a dance club with some friends. When we returned to our table after dancing, someone else had taken our seats. Elizabeth was not a shy woman, and she stepped right up to the intruders to indicate that they would need to move, as we had only left the table to go to the dance floor. The leader of the group did not seem to want to relinquish his newly taken turf.

"I don't see your name on it," he replied, challenging her.

Elizabeth was never one to back down easily. "Yeah. I guess you're right. My name isn't on it." She paused.

"But *his* is," she said, pulling me forward to confront this challenger as her champion. She said that if they didn't move they could take it up with me, implying that if they didn't retreat, we'd take it back by force. A bar table turf-war gauntlet had been thrown, and a battle for control appeared imminent. As we stood there, toe to toe, one ram to another, posturing and staring menacingly at each other, our friends all stepped back expecting there to be trouble.

After a few moments, the guy backed down. He realized that I was ready to accept his challenge, and he did not have the nerve to follow it through. He turned, collected his stuff and left the table.

"You've got balls," he said to Elizabeth as he shuffled away. He was right.

Elizabeth had warned me that one of her older brothers had a habit of scaring off her boyfriends. She said that he sometimes tended to be a bit of a hothead, and seemed to go out of his way to intimidate and discourage her beaus. The very first time I met him, I saw what she meant. We had barely even made our initial introductions when he approached me.

"Hey. Wanna arm wrestle?" he challenged.

At that time I was still lifting weights quite a bit and was very strong, so I viewed his challenge with a mixture of amusement and skepticism. I had expected to be challenged somehow, at some point, but something as blatant as this had never even crossed my mind. I quickly accepted. We went into the basement followed by a group of eager spectators.

I had arm wrestled before, and knew that winning this seemingly simple competition takes a combination of technique and strength. I was confident that I had the advantage in the strength department, so unless he had some special super-duper-wrist-bending technique up his sleeve, I figured that he was a goner.

The match was over in just a few seconds. He never really stood a chance. I won a second match. He challenged my left arm, and I beat him with that, too. I did not like to lose.

Over the years, my memories of our earliest days together have developed an almost fairy-tale like sheen. It was as though I was thunderstruck by the flood of emotion that had suddenly been awakened in me, and carried me to new heights of joy and happiness. I had never experienced anything like it before. The fact that I could love someone like Elizabeth, and be loved in return, absolutely astounded me.

I finally realized what the big deal was…all of this time and energy that people spent throughout the ages proclaiming the joys and wonders of this mythical beast called love. I had seen it with my own eyes, and suddenly, I was a believer, a convert, a disciple at Cupid's temple. I had been sucked in, heart first, and I had no intentions of making even the feeblest of struggles to resist or escape.

We were young. We were deeply in love. We were ready to spend the rest of our lives together.

We graduated from college in May 1981, and we were married six weeks later.

Many women feel that total and complete sharing is the ultimate form of intimacy. It is a freedom, almost an expectation, for women in our society that does not transcend gender barriers. Whereas women freely share personal thoughts and feelings amongst friends and family, men do not enjoy that freedom. This communication gap, the heart of the Venus/Mars conundrum, is often the largest single issue in a marriage where intimacy does not mean the same thing to both parties involved.

Often, self-disclosure does not come easily for men. They are taught from an early age to repress feelings and emotions. As a result, most efforts of self-disclosure are usually pretty shallow and superficial when compared to the full and complete disclosure women seem to be able to achieve. Even when a man lets his guard down, the resulting levels of self-exploration cannot match what a woman is capable of doing, and often expects in return. It's not just that men are trying to hide things nearly so much as they just don't view sharing and self-disclosure in the same way.

I saw no need to explain all of my bad habits or personal insecurities to Elizabeth prior to our marriage, or even afterwards. To be perfectly honest, she would be the *last* person that I'd want to share them with. After all, I had an image to maintain. I had expectations to live up to. It's not that I consciously made a decision to hide my gender issues from her. Rather, the thought of needing to confess it never even entered my mind. Did that make me a fraud?

I had always been successful at handling the issues in my life, and saw no reason why that would not continue. Would I allow a small and seemingly insignificant blemish in an otherwise fine person interfere with the wonderful life that Elizabeth and I were planning? Hardly. In fact, loving Elizabeth made me happier than I had ever been before, and I was more than a little optimistic that our love and our new life together would banish those thoughts completely.

Denial is an easy world to live in. It would be many more years before I would able to come to any semblance of self-acceptance of my true situation. How can anyone expect somebody to be honest with others when they can't even be honest with themselves? Self-acceptance can be a very painful and frightening process, and at 21 I was far too immature, arrogant, shortsighted, and intoxicated by love to realize that I was building a trap for my own demise. I would learn the hard way that the key ingredient in the struggle for my soul was not courage or strength; it was patience, and it was a battle that I could not win.

Our first years of marriage were wonderful, almost storybook-like, as we watched our plans for the future bear the fruits of success. It didn't take long to realize that television production really wasn't the career for me, so I changed directions and got a job as a computer programmer, where it soon became obvious that my logical skills, creativity and my drive to achieve, would make me successful.

In two short years I found myself making more money than I had ever imagined. We bought a two-story colonial home in upstate New York, and immediately embarked upon the yuppie lifestyle: we bought a Volvo, we traveled, and we had money in the bank. After four years of marriage, we took the biggest step of all. We had a child.

The process of becoming a father was a wonderful, spiritual experience for me. I soothed my maternal instincts by participating in the pregnancy as much as I could. We did everything we could to share the miracle that was unfolding inside of her, week after week after week. We took natural childbirth classes together. We prepared a nursery. We planned for the future. It was a wonderful time in our lives.

Matt was born in December, 1985. He was 15.9" and weighed 6.2 pounds. His sex, according to the original birth record, was MALE.

I was actually pleased, even relieved, that we had a son. It was just easier for me to be a father to a boy. I knew how boys thought. I knew what boys liked to do. I knew how to do father/son bonding stuff. Plus, I wouldn't be forced to face all of the significant events in a girl's life that I had never been allowed to experience for myself.

Once we got home, we turned our total attention to the miniature new member of our family. We adapted to his routine. We took turns doing feedings, and diaper changes. We took joy in simply watching his innocent little face as he slept, wondering what kinds of life experiences a baby at that age has to dream about. In the process, we found patience we didn't know we had, and new levels of love that we never knew existed.

By 1987, we were on top of the world.

Part Two

In Touch with
My Feminine Side

CHAPTER FIVE

IN SEARCH OF TRUE SELF

"For those who believe, no explanation is necessary. For those who do not, none will suffice...."

— JOSEPH DUNINGER

Like an old war injury that tends to flare up in inclement weather, my *other* side began to throb again in early 1987, shortly after our son turned a year old. Perhaps she was lonely in her exile to the nether regions of my mind. Perhaps she was jealous of all of the success that Dave seemed to be having in his life. Or perhaps she just needed a sense of relief.

Slowly but surely she began to reveal that she was still there, still waiting, and very unhappy with the way things were going. She inserted herself into my thoughts. She beckoned for attention, for temporary release, for some sort of acknowledgment of her very existence. And for the first time in my life, I absolutely refused.

My life had been going so well that I couldn't allow this issue to intrude upon it and screw things up. My life was not as simple as it used to be. My life as an independent person ended the minute I became a husband; my *personal* issue had suddenly grown to become a *family* issue. Now, my wife and son were affected, as was my career, my family, my circle of friends, my promising future...it all suddenly

55

seemed so much more complicated, and the implications were almost too overwhelming to consider.

So I resisted. Perhaps I hoped that if I ignored the gnawing frustration and curiosity that had lay dormant for so long, it would go back to sleep. Perhaps I felt if I were successful in holding the line this time, it would demonstrate to me that I *did* have the strength, the willpower to excise it from my mind. Perhaps it was just that I was scared to death about what might happen if I let her out, so struggling to keep her in was the lesser of two evils.

I think part of the panic that I was beginning to feel was due to my realization that these urges refused to die. I had done every *male* thing that I could do; so why did these needs, feelings and issues continue to plague me?

It wasn't long before my internal struggle bubbled its way to the surface. I found myself becoming irritable. I found myself becoming confused. I found it difficult to concentrate on anything for any length of time. I had difficulty sleeping. I had no appetite. Soon I found myself beginning to withdraw from my wife and son, from the world that I knew, and the world that thought it knew me.

And for the first time, I got scared. I was scared that I wouldn't be able to hold it all together...scared that this unseen force that was driving me would end up dragging me into an abyss of shame and ruin, and swallowing up those whom I loved as well.

I find that attempts to convert complex emotions or feelings into words in order to describe them are ultimately futile. Often, the entire spirit of what we are trying to convey gets lost in the translation from feeling to word. What does love feel like? What does fear feel like? Do those emotions feel the same for each of us? The only way we can describe what they "feel" like is to compare them to something else that, perhaps, we may be able to describe more accurately or that we think others may be able to relate to.

With that in mind, perhaps the best single word I can find to describe this overpowering feeling is "pressure." There is a steady, unrelenting, unyielding force pushing you towards something that you find too frightening to even consider. There are certainly elements of fear, anger, frustration, confusion, and even sadness, but the overriding feeling is one of pressure. The harder one tries to repress and contain it, the more the pressure builds. As the strategies and efforts to control it fail, one after another, panic begins to set in. Eventually, something will need to give way; a valve needs to be opened.

Oscar Wilde once wrote, "The only way to get rid of a temptation is to yield to it. Resist it, and your soul grows sick with longing for the things it has forbidden to itself."

Although such thinking seems to be counter to everything we are taught, there is a certain common-sense ring of truth to it. I was at that point.

In a culture where we value strength, where we expect our men to be able to handle the difficulties that they face, it can be very humbling to finally be forced to throw in the towel and admit that you've lost. Just ask a man who is obviously lost to stop and ask for driving directions and you'll see just how difficult it is for men to ask for help in even the simplest of circumstances. They don't like to do it. Period.

After all of my emotional options had been depleted, I came to the realization that I needed help. I had a lifetime of questions and frustration to unload and I felt I would find no comfort or peace until I had some answers. I needed someone who could tell me, with some sense of authority, whether I really was transsexual, as I felt myself to be, or was I somehow deluding myself and my problem lay elsewhere. I could have accepted either conclusion. At least I would have an answer. It was that need to find something, *anything* concrete after so many years of wondering and thinking that finally provided the impetus to reach out.

One day I barricaded myself in a small meeting room at work, and dialed the gender clinic at Stanford University. As the phone rang, my doubts suddenly gripped me. Was this really the right thing to do? Maybe I should just hang up. Maybe nobody will answer. But suddenly, there was a voice on the other end, and it was time for me to say what I needed to say.

I explained that I was battling some very perplexing gender issues, and needed to speak with someone who might be able to help me find some answers. The voice on the other end was very kind and sympathetic. She told me that the closest professional that specialized in working with transsexuals was Dr. Garret Oppenheim, who lived in New Jersey just outside of New York City. I thanked her, and after hanging up sat alone for a few minutes to decide what to do next.

Life in the late 1980s was very different than it is today. Psychologists specializing in gender issues were few and far between. There was little to no public access to the Internet. General accessibility to Email was still several years in the future. There was the telephone, and there was the U.S. Postal Service.

After some long, difficult deliberation, I decided that I needed to arrange an entire daylong session with him. I contacted him to discuss his rates and services, and started to collect money to fund my visit. I saved a couple of dollars every day, as I knew that small amount would not be missed. Although Elizabeth somehow seemed to know how much money I had in my wallet at any point in time, I could always explain what was missing as lunch money.

After a few months, I had saved enough money to see the doctor.

For right or wrong, I decided that I needed to keep all of this from Elizabeth. This secret life that I harbored had suddenly started to grow in complexity and in scope. Hiding it caused me quite a bit of guilt, but I rationalized it all by telling myself that perhaps there was no need to tell her. Perhaps the doctor would tell me that this was just a phase; that I was a garden-variety transvestite or something, and she need never know about my struggles. Besides, I was convinced that if she had discovered my confusion, she wouldn't look at me the same anymore. She would doubt me, and that doubt would spread to every aspect of our relationship…eventually undermining everything we had built together. I found it easy to convince myself that I loved her too much to tell her until I had something concrete to say. Denial is convenient that way.

One day in early October, 1987, I woke up, showered, and left home for work as I did every other day, leaving my wife and infant son asleep at home, unaware of my clandestine plans. Instead of going to my office, I drove to the airport where I boarded an early morning flight to New Jersey, hopped in a cab, and went to spend a day with Dr. Oppenheim.

Dr. Oppenheim was a small, old, frail man. His thin frame and crooked back left him hunched over and he shuffled when he walked supported by a cane. His office was in his house, and he invited me to sit in a large, comfortable, overstuff chair amid all the various books and papers he had collected. In an odd way, it reminded me of my own dad's office.

He sat facing me, and explained the plan for the day. We had much to accomplish in a relatively short period of time. He said that he had many questions to ask me, and the only way for this process to be valuable was for me to answer honestly and openly. If I did, he felt that he would be able to tell me something that would either confirm or deny my self-diagnosis as being transsexual at the end of our session.

The doctor asked me lots of questions. Gender questions. Sexuality questions. Family questions. He asked me about my hopes and dreams and fears. He asked if I had ever been sexually interested in men. I told him no. He asked if I could imagine being sexually interested in men. I told him it depends. As a man I could not, but as a woman I told him it was possible. I could not understand why he seemed to dwell on sexuality questions for so long.

He asked questions about Elizabeth and Matt. How did I feel she would handle the news that I was transsexual? Could she support herself if I were to leave? Would her family help to raise Matt? How did I feel about the prospect of having that happen? It was almost too painful to even consider, much less try to put into words.

After lunch Dr. Oppenheim asked me if I believed in past life regression. I admitted that it could be possible, although it was not something that I felt strongly about either way. I had always liked to believe in the remarkable, like UFOs, and ghosts, and other paranormal occurrences. Dr. Oppenheim explained that he believed strongly in this phenomenon, and had done much research and writing about it. He believed that a person's life force, or *soul*, gets used over and over, and each of these different lives could be reached through hypnosis. He called this phenomenon "Past Life Recall." He said that, under hypnosis, he had several patients who were able to recall the details of previous lives, even to the point of taking on the personalities of their former selves and speaking in foreign languages. Often, he found that transsexual patients had unresolved previous lives as women.

Being hypnotized was an interesting, intense experience. I lay on the couch, closed my eyes and listened to his quiet, relaxed voice. I felt as though I were resting. He told me that I would feel a comfortable warm sensation start in my toes and work its way up through my knees, and up my legs. And to my surprise, I did. He told me that my right arm would be lighter than air, and raise itself, and I would be unable to put it down, and he was right. I could tell that I was there, with my eyes closed. I was aware of everything around me, and certainly did not feel hypnotized. But apparently I was.

I do not remember specific details of my hypnosis experience. I don't remember the questions he asked, or my answers. I don't remember how long it took.

What I do know is by the end of our day together I was completely spent. I had quickly come to learn that expending emotional energy was every bit as fatiguing as using physical energy. He took some time to collect his ideas before coming to me to discuss his thoughts. He sat down, took a long look at me and said "The first thing I need to tell you is that I believe you to be truly transsexual, and I will do anything in my power to help you."

I was stunned. I couldn't believe it. Those words both thrilled me, and chilled me, to my core. To finally have someone confirm my self-diagnosis was a huge relief for me. But at the same time, it was like having a mysterious lump diagnosed as cancer. It is a relief to finally know what it is, but it is a whole other story to consider what that means and what you plan to do about it.

His words became much more somber. He said, "The next thing you need to do is decide how you are going to handle this. If you continue treatments with me, we will need to set up a regular schedule. You need to be prepared to lose everything and everyone in your life. That is not to say that you WILL lose them, but the risk is there and you need to know that and face that."

After our day was finished, I hopped back into the cab and flew back home. I got home at dinnertime, as if nothing out of the ordinary had happened during my day. My trip out of state went unnoticed, and I had much to consider. At that point, I could not give specifics, but I knew that my life had changed. I just didn't know how.

I spent the next few weeks doing a considerable amount of soul searching. Dr. Oppenheim's words about being ready to lose everything rang in my head, and I tried to determine whether I was ready to risk that. I considered many scenarios of things that could happen. I tried to imagine my life five, ten, twenty years down the road. Gradually, I made some decisions.

First, I concluded that I was *not* ready to lose everything. I enjoyed my life too much to give it up for the unknown. I loved my wife too much to do this to her. I was not ready to leave my one-year-old son fatherless.

But at the same time, I felt incredibly ashamed at having to sneak around like this behind my wife's back. I slowly realized that much of the pressure I was feeling was a direct result of this terrible sense of guilt, and that the only way to do anything about that was to tell her how I was feeling. I decided she deserved to know, and once she knew, perhaps everything else would become a moot point.

I struggled with the "how" of my disclosure to Elizabeth for days. How could I expect to explain something to her that I barely understood myself? How do I put that "feeling" into words? How could I defend myself against her anger? How could I explain that I had not purposefully deceived her? How could I assure her that I continued to love her as much as I ever had, and that it was because I loved her so much that made this so difficult? How could I explain that this was not about her, but it was about me? The more I thought about it, the more agitated and nauseous I became.

Finally, one night after we had gone to bed and turned out the light, I couldn't keep it in any longer. The pain of it all was killing me. "Honey," I said, "I have something that I need to tell you."

She asked, "What?"

I thought for a long second and replied, "I'm not quite sure how to say this or how to put it into words. But it is something that I have felt for my entire life, and I need for you to know."

She was quiet.

I spoke slowly and deliberately. "I have a very strong…" I paused knowing that once this was said it could not be un-said. I took a breath, "I have a very strong female side to my personality." I lay in the dark waiting for a reaction. I could hear the sheets rustle as she turned to face me.

Elizabeth had known that I was somewhat odd when it came to my feminine interests. She had thought that perhaps I was just kinky. One year during college I was working as a waiter at a popular restaurant, and I went to work on Halloween dressed as a ballerina. Another year, when Elizabeth was pregnant with Matt, I dressed as a pregnant woman, but came under a little-too-much scrutiny when one of my co-workers noticed I had even painted my toenails. I had occasionally asked to be able to shave my hairy legs, which she allowed up to my knees. My quirkiness was accepted, and no questions had really been asked up to this point.

After pausing for several seconds, she spoke to me, "Are you telling me that you're gay?" she asked.

"No, of course not. I'm saying that part of my mind is very 'feminine' in its thoughts and needs. I don't know how else to describe it."

She turned back over, said a soft "Oh God," and started to cry quietly. And that was that.

Over the next few days, she avoided me. She indicated that she needed to process what I told her, and I gave her the time and space to do that. Eventually life returned to our normal routine, or at least it *seemed* normal. Everything was the same, but at the same time everything was different. I could tell what was happening, and I let it happen. Our "Don't Ask, Don't Tell" years had begun.

Over the next ten years, Elizabeth did not mention the incident again. However, it was clear to me that it was never too far from her mind.

Any time there was anything in the newspapers about female impersonators, or about cross-dressers, she removed the article before I could read it as if it would suddenly trigger a relapse in me. Anything that she considered feminine was now verboten to me, and any protest to the contrary on my part was sure to cause friction between us. No more shaving the legs, no more going out as a girl on Halloween, no more public expression of Donna. I'm sure she was secretly hoping that the situation would get better on its own, just as I was. But it didn't.

Actually, just the opposite was happening. My intense soul searching helped me to slowly realize that the main source of my distress had not necessarily been my gender issues, so much as my struggle to hold it all back and keep it all in. That was a losing battle, and one I was convinced that I could not win. In order to maintain harmony in my life, I needed to change that tactic. Rather than fear Donna, and what her continued existence could mean to my life, I needed to embrace and accept her as a healthy part of the total person that I was. This was not some disease to be feared and avoided. It was another side to a complex personality that obviously needed freedom and understanding. I needed to find opportunities not only to express this part of me, but also needed to actively explore it as well. Now that I had disclosed my situation, I felt a greater sense of freedom to do this.

I contacted the local chapter of Tri-Ess (a national support group for cross-dressers), and met someone from the group for lunch one day. He brought a recent copy of their newsletter, and we had a very pleasant discussion about transgender support groups and resources in and around Rochester. During our conversation, he told me about Jumelle Cosmetics.

Jumelle is the French word for twins. It was a make-up studio owned and operated by twin sisters. Apparently, others in the support group had been clients there and had raved about them. I called the salon and scheduled an appointment. In my paranoia about somehow getting caught, when they asked my name my mind seemed to freeze for a second, and the name that came out was David Booth. Now I was making up fake identities for myself.

At my first appointment I met Deborah, one of the twins who operated the salon. I had never met anyone quite like her. She was pretty. She was intelligent. She was articulate. And perhaps the most overpowering thing about her was that she was a very spiritual person. At our first appointment, she explained Yin and Yang to me.

Ancient Chinese scholars developed the concept of Yin and Yang to explain the world. It argues that there are two natural, complementary and contradictory forces in our universe. YIN represents the FEMALE; softness, darkness, moisture, nighttime, negative, even numbers and docile aspects of things. YANG represents the MALE; hardness, dryness, positive, brightness, daytime, odd numbers and dominant aspects. Yin and Yang are the male and female forces that control all changes in the universe, exist in everything, and are continually in the state of flux. The key concept is that they are always looking for the balance point. When one moves, the other always responds.

Deborah explained that all people contain different aspects of Yin and Yang, or male and female, and she was honored that I chose to confide in her. She accepted both my male and female selves immediately, and it is through her handiwork, that I got my first true glimpses and tastes of the possibilities down the road.

I found our discussions fascinating. They opened my eyes to an entirely new side of my situation. They helped me to view it not as something abnormal and bad, but as something natural, and ageless, and spiritual. It was a very refreshing perspective.

Of course, the main reason for my visits to Deborah was to learn about make-up. Every couple of months I would call and schedule an appointment with her. I snuck out of work to go to her studio, where she would work her make-up magic on me. I used to sit on the big stool in front of the mirror, and I'd stare in awe at what she could do. Sometimes I went for a lesson, so that I could learn to apply makeup myself. Other times I just let her apply it. I'd sit there, watching as my face was transformed, and I'd feel as though my personality became transformed, too. Sadly, the time to wash it off and return to work came all too quickly. It was as if the make-up allowed Donna a brief sense of self-expression and freedom, but washing it off closed that dungeon door again until the next time.

At one point, we bought a wig. We spent a session cutting it and styling it. And when she applied the make-up to go with the wig, I sat transfixed at what I saw. The reflection staring back at me was closer to who I really felt myself to be than anything I had ever seen before.

This simple outlet for my feminine self kept things on a very even keel for many years, and I owe Deborah my most heartfelt thanks. I cannot imagine what life is like for others, who do not find a sympathetic "Deborah" in their lives, especially at the beginning.

Chapter Six

Donna Emerges

*It is amazing to think that all these things that we dream
about for so long are actually within reach...*

— Journal Entry

Elizabeth and I had hoped, no...we *expected*, to be able to live the
good life. The thought of being financially stable to the point of being
able to retire early, and enjoy a life of relaxation and travel appealed to
both of us. It was a very realistic goal, as we were already on the fast
track to realizing that lifestyle.

Each winter we fled the chill of upstate New York, escaping to
sunny, warm destinations that we thought might eventually be good
retirement communities for us. One year we visited North Carolina.
Another year we visited the Gulf Coast of Florida. Another year we
visited Southern California.

In December of 1994, we visited Scottsdale, Arizona. We immediately fell in love with it. The weather was the perfect compliment to
the deep blue skies. Warm, inviting and relaxing during the day, and
cool and invigorating at night.

We had expected to find Scottsdale to be the colorless desert that
one would expect for an area that routinely hits 110 degrees for weeks

at a time during the summer. We were amazed to find the Valley of the Sun to be more akin to the Garden of Eden.

Less than 18 months later, we had completely relocated our lives and ourselves to the Valley of the Sun. We had purchased a house there, sold our old one, packed the things we wanted to keep, and moved across country. Neither of us seemed to feel any regret in leaving 15 years of memories, and scores of friends and family behind. In fact, I think we were just ready for a change, and we dove into our new life headfirst.

Moving across country was very exciting; it was almost like a new beginning for us. We spent time looking for new furniture and household items. Although we didn't know a single soul there, we felt very much at home. We spent our days exploring all there was to see and do. We spent our nights sitting in the back by the pool, looking up at the incredible vista of stars and talking about the future. We often strolled through the amazing beauty of the Sonoran Desert and luxuriated in the incredible panorama of the Arizona sunsets. It was a very good time.

This was the apex of Dave's life. We had money, and we were on the fast track. Elizabeth and I were happy. Matt was doing well. We were enjoying our new home, and our new life. Life truly was good.

As in the Garden of Eden, the joy of the moment was not to last.

Towards the end of 1996, and into 1997, the need to express Donna began to well up inside of me again. She seemed to have the worst timing, like an intrusive salesperson, or a boss who walks in unexpectedly and catches you goofing off.

Instead of sneaking up on me like the gently but steadily rising tide of previous encounters, this onslaught hit me like a tidal wave. It swamped me, and left me floundering. It wasn't long before things came to a head.

Elizabeth's parents had come to visit, and the entire group of us went to spend an afternoon at the mall. I was edgy and anxious. I did not want to be there.

As we strolled, Matt said something insignificant that made me angry. I grabbed his shoulder. Matt was twelve years old and chock-full of attitude. He did not like to be provoked. He turned, and with a defiant leave-me-alone look on his face, he brusquely pushed me away. It was all the provocation that I needed.

It took less than a second for me to wheel around, and land a punch directly to his chest, knocking him flying, and to the ground. Elizabeth and her folks stood there for a second, their jaws wide open at what had just occurred. Matt was not really hurt, but as he picked himself off the ground there in the middle of the mall, he was stunned by what I had just done. As was I.

Nobody could understand what had gotten into me. I just didn't seem like myself. I was like a stranger. Less than a year after having moved to Arizona, the intensity of my internal struggle matched the crisis ten years earlier that had caused me to reach out for help.

Who can say what triggers the things that happen inside of us? Sometimes, reasons seem so obvious, so clear and unmistakable. Other times, reasons can only be deduced after time has passed, and things can be viewed in context. I sometimes wonder why my pressure grew to be so overwhelmingly intense, so quickly, once we moved to Arizona.

The easiest and most convenient answer that I can offer is that I was facing a unique sort of mid-life crisis. I was about to turn thirty-nine years old and was staring at the prospect of a second puberty that was even more debilitating to my body and my psyche than my first one. My hair was thinning. I was faced the prospect of experiencing middle age as a man. My opportunities to fix nature's mistake were dwindling, and I felt that my delay in acting on it could mean the difference between opportunities either for a fulfilling, successful transition, or a life of missed opportunity. Perhaps I had a feeling that the time was now or never. The inevitable tick, tick, tick that marked the passing of time grew louder and louder in my head.

Elizabeth had noticed that my birthday always caused a sort of depression in me. I could not explain why, but her observation was very astute. And every year, as I blew out the candles on my birthday cake, my wish was the same: that this would be the last birthday I would spend as Dave.

Unraveling ourselves from our old lives is one of the most daunting difficulties for anyone facing a mid-life transition. This is as true for marriage transitions, career transitions, or *any* type of mid-life transition, as it is for gender transitions. We have spent a lifetime building friendships, careers, and families. We are husbands and wives, mothers and fathers, sons and daughters, and friends. We have often grown comfortable in the world we have built for ourselves. We have carefully crafted how we want others to perceive us, and how we expect others to treat us. Each role has any number of tentacles representing responsibilities, expectations, and obligations that wrap us and hold us in their tight, desperate grip.

By the time middle age arrives, we are often so suffocated by all of the tentacles wrapped around our lives that we can barely breathe. Eventually, we realize that we can't define who we are and what we want anymore because the complex network of tentacles we have built for ourselves obscures the answer. We suddenly realize that we have become prisoners of our own lives! Escape seems impossible.

I had unwittingly overcome this hurdle by moving to Arizona. Suddenly, my circle of friends and relatives was 1,500 miles away. The tightly wound cocoon of expectations and obligations that I had created over the past 15 years of living in upstate New York, suddenly seemed much looser and more manageable, and the playing field appeared to be much more open. Perhaps I was beginning to realize that I really *could* escape!

Regardless of the reason, this crisis that was quickly building in my mind was real and overwhelming. It came out in anger, frustration, and irritation with everyone and everything. I did not like the person I had become, but I felt powerless to do anything to change it. With very little prodding, I came to the conclusion that this was not something I could, or moreover, should, handle alone. It was another milestone event in my life and I realized that I needed help. Again.

Perhaps the major difference between the crisis I had experienced some ten years earlier and this one was the blossoming availability of transsexual information on the Internet. All at once, successful and inspiring real life stories were plentiful and available, published in cyberland for all to see. These stories filled me with hope, courage and empowerment. Of course, my newfound strength quickly evaporated by the time I got home and was faced with the grim, heartbreaking reality of my situation.

In early 1997, it was time. Using the Internet, it was not difficult to find a list of psychologists who worked with transsexuals. There were three or four of them in the Phoenix area.

I decided to call Dr. Sheila (pronounced Shy-la) Dickson, not because of reputation or personal recommendation, but due to the fact that her offices were the closest to Scottsdale. As I dialed, I realized that I had no idea how to even begin a conversation with her, but when she answered, I somehow mumbled something coherent. I told her that I had found her name as a gender specialist on AOL, and was hoping to be able to talk with her. She knew exactly why I was calling, and she could obviously sense my apprehension and anxiety. She spoke in a very calming, caring tone, and immediately took the initiative to ask me a few questions.

She asked me if I had a "femme" name. I told her that I did, and that my name was Donna. From that point on, she used that name exclusively. She was the first person to refer to me as Donna.

During the course of our brief conversation, I made an appointment to meet with her.

As I hung up, I felt numb. I couldn't believe it. I realized, or at least I thought I did, that I was opening a Pandora's Box by doing this. Suddenly, brand new possibilities appeared on my horizon. I had no idea where they might lead.

As I considered all of this over course of the next week, I made what I considered to be a major decision: I made a vow to take things slow. Although I did feel time was an imperative, I knew that I could not afford to make a mistake, for my own sake as well as for the sake of my wife and son. I did not want to go into this process like a firefighter through a burning building, or a horse with blinders on. I wanted to make sure I was fully aware of what was happening, what I was doing, and why. Later this proved to be a wise plan.

My first appointment with Dr. Dickson was at 10:00 a.m. on March 4, 1997. I drove to her office from work, as I was to do many times over the next couple of years. I did not know how to prepare or what to expect, anticipating that all I needed to do was show up and she would know what to do. I prayed that I would be able to express and articulate the battle that was raging inside of me, although I had no idea how to find the right words.

She shared her office with a couple of other psychologists, and there was a common waiting area outside. When I got there, I made myself comfortable, and waited to see her. I wondered what she would think when she saw this buff man who claimed to be a transsexual, and who came to discuss issues he had never dared to share with anyone before.

Right at ten o'clock, her door opened, and a tall, elegant woman stepped to greet me.

"Donna?" she asked as she smiled and extended her hand to greet me.

"Y-y-yes," I stammered. I stepped into her office.

As we sat down, I studied her. She looked to be in her late 40s, had a gentle, kind face, a friendly smile, and a very soothing demeanor. She was tall and thin, had boyishly short hair, and put on a pair of round John-Lennonish reading glasses as we were about to begin our session.

At the very beginning, I was self-conscious of *everything*: how I moved, how I talked, what I said. I almost felt torn between two roles, and wasn't sure which one was supposed to be in control at that point.

Sheila seemed to know just how I was feeling. She seemed to be able to empathize with all of the inner turmoil I had endured over the years. Gradually, her gentle manner and patient compassion soothed and comforted my very scared, confused soul.

71

At the end of our initial meeting, Sheila had two suggestions. The first was to buy and read a book titled *True Selves* by Dr. Mildred Brown and Chloe Rounsley. We could discuss it at our next meeting. The second was to make arrangements to take the MMP-IV psychological profile test. She said that the scores on the test would provide some insight into my personality that would prove useful as we moved forward. In the following weeks, I did both of those things.

Reading *True Selves* was an emotional experience for me. It finally provided the sensitive, comprehensive, down-to-earth, real-person perspective that I had hoped to find during my library searches so many years before. It demonstrated just how diverse a group we really were. As I read, I thought, "Yeah! I have felt that way too!" It was a very empowering, sensitive book, and to this day there are several copies on the bookshelves of various family and friends.

At the beginning, I met with Sheila every couple of weeks. We reviewed the results of MMP-IV, which she said fell well within the typical female range. We discussed *True Selves*. But mainly, I talked. I allowed my thoughts, and my frustrations flow. And Sheila listened.

This was to mark our entire history together. I would arrive, and take my customary seat on the couch. Once there, I'd talk for an hour or more and she would take notes. Occasionally, she would make a comment, or ask a perfectly timed, thought provoking question. However, most of our session time consisted of me doing a "verbal dump" on whatever topics came to mind. My family. My life. My wife. My job. My fears. How I was feeling. What I was thinking. I was never at a loss for things to talk about, and our sessions often spilled into more than my allotted hour.

Sheila never challenged me to prove anything. She never rushed me to do things before I felt ready. She never suggested that I come to our sessions "en femme," as she knew that I wasn't ready for that, and it just wasn't possible at that time. She was perfect, and I looked forward to my bi-weekly visits to see her.

Of course, I hadn't shared any of this with Elizabeth. I had decided it best not to tell her about it until I had come to some sort of understanding, and had something to actually tell her. As a result, I found myself embarking upon another life of secrecy that was to grow over the next months and years. In retrospect, it is not something of which I am proud, but at the time it was my only way to deal with my issues, so it was easy for me to rationalize.

Chapter Seven

Sugar and Spice and Everything Nice...

I won't say that I have no idea what the answer is because I do. And I am willing to risk everything I have and everything I am to find out.

— Journal Entry

The Harry Benjamin International Gender Dysphoria Association is the governing body that defines standards of treatment that caregivers should provide to transsexual patients around the world. Named after a pioneer in the field of transsexual care, this group has developed an internationally accepted protocol; a series of steps, rules, and guidelines, that are known as the Standards of Care (SOC).

The first step in the treatment protocol is to work with and be evaluated by a licensed psychologist for at least three months. During this time, the psychologist does his or her best to determine whether a person's self-diagnosis seems accurate, or if there are additional, underlying issues that may be causing the patient's distress. They evaluate a person's physical and emotional readiness to face the difficulties of a gender transition. And perhaps most importantly, they gauge whether a gender transition is likely to improve a patient's quality of life based on all of the factors that are involved.

Based on the results of this evaluation, a psychologist can recommend that a patient move to the next treatment level by writing a referral letter. The next step is to allow a patient to begin hormone replacement therapy (HRT) appropriate for the patient's self-identified gender.

Beginning HRT is an important step for several reasons. First, it brings a medical doctor into the treatment process. They manage the hormone regimen. They monitor their patient's health and blood periodically to ensure that all is going well, and that no adverse conditions (such as liver issues) are happening. They can offer additional support and advice above and beyond what a psychologist can provide.

Second, up to that point most of the things I tried were only temporary. It is easy to put on some makeup, and then wash it off to make sure nobody else is aware of what is happening. Once the hormones kick in, though, permanent things start to happen. Bumps start to grow. Curves start to form. Permanent sterility lies on the horizon. For transsexuals, these are all welcome things. For those who aren't at a critical decision point it lays on the not-too-distant horizon.

Third, the effects of the hormones are *amazing*. Although the physical changes are certainly significant and oh-so-welcome, the mental and emotional changes dwarf them in comparison. A sense of well-being and contentment somehow seems to take hold. A flood of new emotions and sensations is suddenly unleashed. For someone not used to it, looking at the world through an estrogen-filled lens is a very intense experience.

During one of our appointments at the end of June, Sheila began to discuss the fact that I would soon be eligible to begin HRT. She said that she planned to write a referral letter for me when the time came. She recommended a doctor who she worked with, and who had an active transsexual program, so he understood the unique needs and challenges that are involved. His name was Dr. Ken Fisher.

I had been looking forward to this day. I had wondered if I would show any hesitation, any reluctance to take this next step. I made the decision right then and there that this was something I needed to do, and I felt I was ready.

My first impression of Dr. Fisher was that he was a very no-non-sense, all-business, just-the-facts ma'am type of doctor. He looked to be in his late 30s or early 40s, was very tall, and had a very command-ing presence. At first, I found him to be intimidating, but as time passed and we got to know each other better I began to see his softer side, so he didn't seem quite so scary to me.

The goal of HRT is to introduce female hormones into the system, while at the same time reducing the amount of male hormones that are produced. The overall effect is to feminize the body, and the psyche. Different doctors have different hormone regimens to accomplish this. Most include estrogen in one form or another given orally, by injection, or via a transdermal patch. They often prescribe a testosterone blocker, such as Spironolactone[tm], to prevent the testicles from producing male hormones. Some doctors also prescribe progesterone, which may provide additional feminine secondary sex characteristic development.

The result of this regimen on a TS patient is that she will begin to go through a sort of second puberty, facing the same physical and emo-tional challenges that teenage girls must face, on top of all the other issues that she must battle.

The physical affects of this treatment on the male to female trans-sexual are many:

- ◆ It causes breast development. The level of breast development that a patient can expect is dictated by the specifics of the regi-men, the age of the patient (the younger the patient, the better the chance for significant development), and genetics.

- ◆ It causes a reduction, or end to male pattern hair loss.

- ◆ It causes the skin to feel softer and more supple.

- ◆ It causes a redistribution of fat to around the hips and butt.

- ◆ It causes the testicles to cease the production of sperm, and after an extended period, the patient is rendered sterile.

- ◆ It affects a patient's emotional state.

There are several things that an estrogen regimen does not do. It does not affect a person's voice. And, it does not stop male facial hair growth.

Dr. Fisher explained that his regimen included significant doses of oral estrogen, a testosterone blocker, and progesterone. Plus, I would need to visit his office for bi-weekly estrogen injections in my butt. I started the regimen immediately.

Who can say how big is big? In a brand new life that measured itself in firsts, this was a huge first. As I sat on the examination table, watching the doctor fill the syringe with the oily yellowish-brown estradiol, I could only begin to imagine where this would lead. It's like a child taking the time to contemplate her first steps before actually making them. The significance is that big. It's not as though the child wonders, "Should I really do this?" before attempting to balance on her feet while slowly but clumsily putting one foot in front of the other. It's more a matter of knowing that you're ready, and just doing it.

As I stood there, my pants down and the upper portion of my buttocks exposed, I looked around the room. There was a big picture of Liza Minelli, a huge smile on her happy lips, almost as if she knew what was about to happen. I hated shots, and did my best to keep my mind off the long intramuscular needle that would soon be buried in my muscular butt.

The sting of the needle as it went into the fleshy portion of my upper buttocks took me by surprise, but before I knew it…it was over. Or maybe, it had only just begun.

In those early days the effects of the estrogen shots were quite intense. By the time I paid my $45 and got to my car, I swore that I could feel it making me a little light-headed. By the time I got to work I was convinced that I could feel my breasts getting puffier and more tender. Whether they were or not wasn't really all that important; the affect of the shots was amazing.

The anticipation of my bi-monthly visits was tempered by my anxiety/anticipation that visible changes would soon begin to happen, and I still did not know how I planned to deal with it all, especially given the fact that my wife did not know what was happening. I tried to put the thoughts out of my mind as best I could, and decided to deal with them when I had to.

Being a transsexual is an expensive proposition. At that time, my hormone regimen cost me nearly $200 a month. My monthly visits with Sheila cost $100 each. Electrolysis, when that started, would cost over $100/session. These kinds of expenses are difficult to hide for any period of time, and finding a way to fund all of this without being caught added to my already heightened sense of anxiety. But I found a way. Or so I thought.

In order to create a *slush fund* that I could use for my transition expenses, I wrote myself a check against a brokerage account that we had. Elizabeth had little interest in the account, and I felt confident it would not be missed. Little did I know that the cancelled check would be returned to us for our records. It arrived at the house one fateful Saturday in mid-July, while Matt and I were out shopping.

When we returned home, Elizabeth was waiting.

The first words out of her mouth sounded ominous. "You've got some explaining to do, mister!"

I froze.

"Just what is the idea of writing a check to yourself for $3,000?" she asked. "What did you spend it on? What's going on?"

She didn't sound angry. Yet.

The room suddenly got hot. My face turned pale. My mouth was dry. My mind raced. In a split second, I had decided what I had to do.

"I'm spending it on therapy," I replied, trying to compose myself for the battle that I knew was coming.

"Therapy?! What kind of therapy?" she asked.

The time had come.

"You know that problem that I told you about ten years ago? The gender problem? It has gotten bad again, so I've been talking about it to a therapist who specializes in gender issues."

Elizabeth was getting angry now. I could see it in her face. She waited for a second, and asked a fateful question.

"You're getting therapy for it? You've got to be kidding! Therapy to fight it, or to give in to it?"

I didn't answer. I didn't know what to say. It wasn't one of those questions that I could answer in ten words or less.

My hesitation told Elizabeth what she wanted to know.

"God damn you!" she hissed, and then stormed off to the bedroom, slamming the door behind her.

I had thought about this moment for years. I had thought about all the things I wanted to say in my defense, all of the things I wanted to say to help her understand what I had been going through. I had even dared to hope that she would understand and that when the secret was out, perhaps we would be able to reach new levels of intimacy and love. Hah! Here I was, standing in the kitchen, all alone, and there hadn't been time to do any of it. It had all happened so quickly; lasting just long enough for my life to be turned upside down. I was numb.

I wish I could say the episode ended there, but it didn't. She came out to confront me shortly afterwards.

"If you're having therapy to help you become a woman, we might as well get divorced now," she challenged.

I tried to explain that I had no real agenda. At this point I was just trying to understand these needs and deal with them. "She is not helping me to *fight* them, but at the same time she isn't pushing me to do anything I don't want to do, either."

"Why the hell do you need to talk to some shrink who doesn't even know you? You're married to me, and you don't try to share these things with me."

This was the opening I needed.

"You have shown no interest in even trying to understand. When I told you about my gender situation ten years ago, I opened my soul to you. What did you do? Did you show compassion? Did you show any interest in 'sharing' way back then? NO! You told me that it had no place in our marriage, and you shut the door right back in my face! You expected that it would go away by itself, but it didn't. So I've dealt with it. Alone! And it's gotten to the point in my life where my strength to fight it has run out, and I have no choice but to figure this thing out, wherever it leads!"

I didn't realize it, but by the time I had finished my little tirade I was almost yelling. Now it was me who was getting angry.

Matt came into the kitchen to investigate all the commotion, putting an end to the brewing storm. Neither of us wanted to fight in front of him. We could not say the things that needed to be said with his innocent eyes and ears there. We both withdrew, knowing that this discussion was not over.

Life became very "chilly" in our house after that. I moved out of our bedroom into the spare bedroom. Elizabeth became distant and angry. But little else really changed. I was relieved that things were somewhat out in the open, but also a bit disappointed that I had not told her everything while I had the chance. I had not told her about the hormones. I had not told her about the long-term plan.

Over the next several weeks, I think the more that Elizabeth thought about what had happened, the madder she got. She felt deceived and betrayed. She felt used. It was as if news of my gender situation had totally and completely undermined our entire relationship. She seemed to feel that if her love for me was based on a lie, then our entire marriage had been based on a lie as well.

I certainly couldn't blame her for the way she felt. I suppose I was fooling myself if I thought that there could have been any other possible outcome. Although I secretly hoped that time would soften her feelings, the realist in me told me I was nuts, and if anything things were bound to get worse. At an ever-quickening pace, Elizabeth and I drifted farther and farther apart as our lives headed in different directions.

I had not cried in 30 years. The fact that I seemed unable to cry actually concerned me. I felt as though I was emotionally constipated; some kind of emotional cripple. All those years of *not* crying caused me to wonder if I actually *could* cry. In a physical sense, I'm sure everyone can cry. It is an innate response we all share as infants. However, part of actually crying as an adult is *letting* yourself cry; it's a matter of relinquishing control and allowing the tears to start flowing. *That* was something I feared I could not do.

Women in our society see no need to prevent themselves from crying. They cry when they're happy and cry when they're sad. They cry at home, at work, with family and with friends. Crying is just another form of emotional expression that women in our society are allowed to display.

Men are not. Men are taught *not* to cry. Babies cry. Girls cry. Boys don't cry. Boys are expected to be tough and strong, and in that world crying is considered to be the epitome of weakness. From the time boys are young, they actually resist crying for fear of being called a crybaby, or a sissy. Instead of letting it happen as a healthy form of emotional expression, boys build defenses to prevent it.

There had been times in my life when I wanted to cry, when I *needed* to cry, but couldn't. I remember taking our German Shepard, Murphy, to be put down. She had been a member of our family for 12 years until her deteriorating hips made each step a living torture for her. Eventually, she couldn't even get up off the ground, she couldn't control her bowels, she lost her appetite, and she just gave up. We knew what we had to do.

When I got returned home from the vet my wife and son were both sobbing uncontrollably. We huddled together on the couch to comfort each other in our grief. And as much as I *wanted* to cry, and felt that I *should* cry, nothing came out.

One night, several weeks after the incident with Elizabeth, and several months after beginning my estrogen program, that all changed.

81

I had gone to the movies alone. Elizabeth had very little interest in going to movies with me, especially at that point, so I had the choice to either go by myself or stay home. This particular movie was *Alien Resurrection*. In the movie, Ripley kills the queen alien, and all of her baby aliens. It was not considered a sad movie. In fact, I'm sure that nobody else in that theater cried.

After the movie was over, I left the theater and walked to my car. It had been the last show of the day, so it was late and the parking lot was almost deserted as I got into the car and started the 15-mile drive north into the Sonoran desert night towards my house.

About half way home, an intense wave of sorrow came over me. It was like a tidal wave of grief that seemed to well up out of nowhere. It was uncontrollable. It was incredible. I think it was the culmination of all the anger, frustration, fear, and sorrow that had been welling up inside of me, finally finding its way out. I started to cry. Tears were rolling down my face. My nose was stuffy and I couldn't breathe. I could barely see where I was going.

I pulled off to the side of the road, as years of tears suddenly found their way out of me. I was sobbing uncontrollably; for me, for Elizabeth, and for Matt. I glimpsed at the reflection of my contorted face in the rear view mirror, feeling almost as if I were watching someone else's tears of grief, and that I should look away out of respect for their sorrow.

I don't know how much time passed before the storm blew over and I started to calm down. It could have been ten minutes. It could have been an hour. I had long since run out of tissue, and had been blowing my nose into anything that wasn't already goopy. As I peeked back into the mirror before pulling back into traffic, I saw a stuffy-nosed, puffy-eyed, red-faced mess staring back at me.

The rest of the drive was calm and serene. I felt at peace. I felt comforted to learn that I actually could cry. And I sensed that the estrogen in my system was working its magic. Learning to handle the flood of emotion that lay just around the corner would prove to be a profound learning experience for me.

The range of emotion between happy and sad is much greater for women than it is for men. Women can get incredibly, exhilaratingly happy, and devastatingly, excruciatingly sad. Men, however, tend to be on a much more restricted wavelength, and don't seem to be able to achieve many of these same extremes. I used to joke that men live their lives forced to wear an emotional condom that reduces sensitivity and response but achieves maximum safety.

Women often feel an emotional reaction to things that they see, or that happen in their lives. They can easily empathize with others, and they react emotionally as though they, themselves, are actually involved. I began to understand why women cried while watching greeting card commercials, or when watching someone else cry. It's because they "feel."

Besides being more emotional, women, I discovered, are far more sensual than men. As the estrogen began to affect my brain chemistry, I noticed that every single sense was becoming heightened. Colors seemed brighter and more intense. My sense of smell became much more acute. My sense of taste was brimming with new flavors. Even though I was to learn that this was just the tip of the sensuality iceberg, it was as though I was experiencing a brand new world.

It did not take long for me to start noticing subtle, and then not-so-subtle, physical changes as well. Although I was anticipating some of them, other things began to happen that nobody had prepared me for.

For example, one night I lay down on the bed to rest for a few minutes after dinner. The next thing I knew, without any provocation or prompting whatsoever, I felt cum welling up inside of my penis, and then gushing out all over the place. Rather than the usual consistency, this was a liquid, more like soap water than like semen. It scared me to death. What if this happened while I was at work? Or sleeping? How could I explain it? Was this normal?

And then my boobs started to grow. In the weeks following my first estrogen injection, they started to become extremely sensitive. I didn't notice any real visible difference, but they felt different, so I knew that something was going on. My doctor said that I was growing breast buds, similar to a teenage girl, and he checked them during each of my visits. All I knew was that they hurt to touch, or to sleep on.

I couldn't keep my hands off of them. Everywhere I went I peeked at the reflection of myself to see if I could notice them. Each morning I stood in front of the mirror and cupped each one in my hand, gauging whether or not they felt different or more substantial than they had the day before.

A couple of months after I started my hormone regimen, I was getting dressed in the bathroom. As I put on my T-shirt, I noticed the unmistakable outline of little titties poking out. A chill ran through me as I stared at them to see if maybe I was just cold or something. They didn't go away. I poked them. They popped right back out, like a pair of turkey timers. I knew titties when I saw them, and these were the real deal.

The reality of what was happening started to sink in. It's one thing to hear about or read about, or even fantasize about, all the changes that estrogen induces. It's a totally different ballgame to see them happening and experience them first-hand. If you're not ready for it, and even if you are, the impact of it all can be overwhelming.

It was time to buckle the seatbelt, because I had a feeling this ride was about to get very bumpy.

Chapter Eight

No Place Left to Hide

"I'm more than willing to tell you about things if you'll only look at me through your 'love' eyes, and not your 'disgust' eyes. If you can continue to love me knowing the full truth, we will be okay. If not, it will be you who falls out of love...."

— DISCLOSURE LETTER TO MY WIFE

In mid January, my in-laws arrived to spend a month with us. I had to move back into the master bedroom during their visit. The atmosphere between Elizabeth and me was not pleasant. Our public façade indicated that we were the same close, loving couple that we had always been. When alone, however, we rarely talked.

It was obvious that Elizabeth was deeply troubled and affected by my disclosure to her. We had seemed to resume the "don't ask, don't tell" policy that had kept the surface waters smooth throughout our marriage. I tried to bring it up a few times, but it was obvious that this was not to be discussed.

In early February, she was to learn more. A second revelation would come to light, and this was one from which our marriage would not recover. Elizabeth learned that I was on estrogen.

I had wanted to tell her for a long time, but we were barely on speaking terms. I suppose I used that as my excuse *not* to tell her. Hiding the physical changes that were happening was starting to get difficult. The fact that we seemed to live in different parts of the same house certainly made things easier, but our day-to-day interaction held many challenges. I wore only baggy shirts; nothing tight or clingy. I couldn't risk going swimming in our pool. I often wore a sports bra under my shirt to flatten everything out. Keeping this secret had become an elaborate pretense that I needed to reveal, but I had no idea how to even bring it up. On February 9, I was relieved of that obligation.

During the entire eight months that I had been on estrogen, I visited Dr. Fisher's office every two weeks for my shot. I usually went there just before work, or during lunch. I made it a point to pay cash for each visit, and the total always came to forty-five dollars. At some point in January I went to the payment desk after my injection, and after ringing everything up the cashier told me that my total for the visit would be forty dollars. I figured that perhaps the price had gone down, or maybe she was giving me a discount, but I certainly wasn't going to complain. I paid my forty dollars, and I left.

Well, on that fateful day in February, a bill arrived at my house. It was from my physician, for an estrogen shot. The balance due was five dollars.

I was at work that afternoon, listening to a jazz guitar CD. I can picture it perfectly. Elizabeth called me on the phone. I could tell from the sound of her voice that she was upset and that something had happened, although I had no idea what. She asked me one question.

"Are you taking estrogen injections? We just received a bill for estrogen injections!!"

I felt like I had been hit in the head by a sledgehammer. I didn't know what to say. My mind was racing. How could I possibly explain this? The pause seemed to last forever. I think she already knew the answer. All that was left was for me to say it.

"Yes," I answered in a surprisingly firm voice.

"GOD DAMN IT!" she yelled, and she hung up the phone.

My world would never be the same.

There was so much I wanted to tell her. There was so much that I needed to explain. I knew she wouldn't give me a chance to tell her in person, as the emotion of it all was far too overwhelming for both of us.

I had started a note to explain it all weeks before, perhaps secretly hoping that I'd never have to use it. Now was the time to finish it, and to give it to her.

The next day, I left it for her to find while I was at work.

Hon:

I'm so sorry that you had to find out about this in this way. I wanted to talk with you about it directly, but was planning on waiting until all of our guests had finished their stays so we could do it in private. I even started this letter several weeks ago in an effort to work on it. But now that things are out in the open, in a way I'm very relieved.

Here's what you need to know. I told you in July when we talked about this stuff that I had seen a psychologist who specializes in these issues. The initial stages of getting to the bottom of my situation requires talking about it, as well as taking some written psychological testing stuff. After a couple of months, a diagnosis is made. In this case, as I told you, I was diagnosed as having Gender Dysphoria.

This is a medical condition, not a mental one. It is not a form of mental illness, or anything like that. One of the specialists on the Internet describes it like this:

> Of all the afflictions humankind must endure, Gender Dysphoria must certainly be one of the most unusual and distressing, and not because it produces great morbidity or mortality, but because the accompanying emotional conflicts can engender much unhappiness for the patient and his/her family with possible later problems involving social activities and associations with colleagues at work.
>
> The etiology of this condition is obscure but we are quite certain that the problem occurs in utero and is therefore Congenital in nature and not Genetic, that is, it is not something that is passed

from generation to generation. Management and treatment are difficult since the mind's gender is immutable. We cannot change a person's gender no matter what we do; historically we know of no case where a mind changed spontaneously from Male to Female or vice versa. Compounding the problem are the varying degrees of severity which, from a practical point of view, simply means that Sex Reassignment Surgery is not for everyone.

— "A Source of Happiness" by Dr. Eugene Schrang

The important points here are that (a) it occurs in-utero and is not something learned, (b) management of it is very difficult and (c) it varies in severity from person to person.

What you need to understand, and I have tried to tell you time and again, is that my personality is made up of two very separate and distinct sides. One is male. It is the one who naturally has charge, because my body is male. But I also have a feminine side, and this part of me is usually kept in the dark, submerged and isolated because of all the shame and embarrassment it can cause. But the struggle to keep this part of the personality down is a very difficult one....you can't even imagine. It even drives some people to suicide.

Another thing you need to understand is that this has nothing to do with sexual orientation. The very first time I told you about this, 10 years ago, the first question that you asked is whether or not I was gay. The answer is no. I love only one thing in this life, and that's you and Matt.

The most important thing to remember, though, is that this is a MEDICAL problem. It is not a mental one. So, once the psychologist has made a prognosis of Gender Dysphoria, the next step is to get in touch with a doctor who specializes in this stuff. You can't see the doctor without first being recommended by the psychologist. That is how I got in touch with the doctor.

The first thing the doctor does is to check to see if there is an obvious medical reason for the situation. I told you that they did a blood test, which I fainted at. They check to make sure nothing is out of whack, and there wasn't. The next thing to do is to ease the problems that the conflict is causing in your mind. This is done with estrogen. It's like gender dysphoria is the illness, and estrogen is the cure. It's as simple as that. They have found that doses of estrogen helps the mind of gender dysphoric people feel more comfortable with itself, and eases the conflict within. I have certainly found it to be true.

One of the main sources of conflict comes from the fact that the body does not match the mind. It's almost as simple as that. That's why some people go all the way and have sex reassignment surgery....to make their body match their mind. Another source of conflict is the shame that goes along with this whole thing.

I can show you many, many examples of people who have been through this. Doctors, lawyers, all kinds of people. They all come to terms with their problem in one way or another. Some deal with it from time to time when it causes a problem. Others go all the way to sex reassignment surgery. As it says, there are varying degrees of this condition, so finding where you fit on the spectrum and becoming comfortable with yourself is very important.

I can also show you many examples of couples who have learned to deal with it together. But I can show you just as many who could not, and it caused their relationship to crumble.

The things I do to help myself are minor in comparison. So what if I want to pick a few stray eyebrow hairs? So what if I don't like hair on my legs? In the big scheme of things, what's the harm? I'm still a loving husband, a good father, and a generally good person. Those are the important things in life, and no matter what happens after this, they will still be true.

I needed to try this to see how it would work. It does not work for everyone. I didn't want to tell you that I was taking estrogen, have you freak out, and then find that it didn't help me after all. As far as I was concerned, I was in a lose-lose situation. Frankly, it has helped me more than anything I have ever done, and (until today) has made me happier inside than I've been in a long, long time.

I don't expect you to understand or sympathize. I can't speak for you, but I know I can speak for myself. My love for you is unconditional. Pure and simple. I love the person that you are, not what you're not. I love the life we've built, and the life I hope we'll build in the future. If you were to come to me with ANY problem......I might not understand...I might not be able to see why it was important....but my love for you would allow me to see past any prejudices or preconceived notions and I'd do whatever I could to help you out. I'd never insult you, or ridicule you, for anything you could ever do. If you told me that you always felt you were a hamster, and sometimes needed time to crawl around and chew on sawdust, I'd find a way to accept that. Period.

As for my driving you away from me, that was never my intention. You indicated early on that you felt that this situation was only in my head, and that I needed to deal with it myself. You have indicated many times that anything I do to deal with it in my own way (the eyebrows are a good example) will open me up to being insulted and ridiculed. How the heck am I supposed to react to that? I'm trying to work out a problem that is ripping me up inside.... all by myself.... and all I get from you is insults. This whole thing makes me very defensive, and the way you treat me sometimes makes me even more so.

I also never intended to keep anything from you. But several things were evident to me. First, I have a problem that I cannot deal with alone. Second, you are disgusted and revolted by any mention of what I feel. I would have thought that you would have gone and done some research on it after we talked about it before. You did when they said that Matt had whatever the disease was with the coffee spots. But not about this. So my only recourse was to do it on my own. I knew a day would come when we would talk about it....but until I gauged how things were working I was willing to handle it by myself.

I'm more than willing to tell you about things if you'll only look at me through your love eyes, not your disgust eyes. If you can learn to do that, I think our relationship can be stronger than ever. If you can't, then I don't know what we're gonna do. I don't want this thrown into my face every time we ever have an argument in the future just because you know it will hurt me.

So here we are. Almost 40 years old. With a 12-year-old child. Two people with the best marriage of any couple that I know. Two people who share the load in the family, and are perfect examples that opposites attract. Things that you're good at, I'm not. And things that I'm good at, you're not. We've built a great life and love each other very much. I still have the letter that you wrote in July when this whole thing happened then, and you said you needed time to sort things out for yourself. You said that you loved me and hoped that we could get through it without any harm to the great relationship that we otherwise had. I agree with you that our relationship IS great...in all the important places.

What happens next? I think it's up to you. If you can continue to love me knowing the full truth, we will be okay. If not, it will be you who falls out of love. But don't give up on us. It's easy to make rash decisions when we're mad or frustrated or confused. But you need to keep focused on what's really important in our lives. At this time I think we both need support, and I only hope our love is strong enough to be there for us when we really need it. I know mine is.

You'll never, ever find anyone who loves you like I do. Don't forget that. I may not be perfect, but no one else is, either. At this time I think we both need support, and I only hope our love is strong enough to be there for us when we really need it. I know mine is.

> luvyerhun,
>
> Dave
>
> — Explanation Letter

I wanted to talk about this. I wanted to discuss it. No, I *needed* to. But talking to Elizabeth was like talking to a stone wall. She had closed her mind and her heart. She had been hurt terribly, and her natural reaction was to pull away.

One of the effects of having everything in the open now was that it made me feel freer to work towards a possible transition and I began to take the steps that I felt needed to be made. I started to do things that I had wanted to do for a long time, but had felt nervous about doing for fear of angering Elizabeth. I started to take steps to free Donna from her exile.

On my 39th birthday I shaved my legs. They have been shaved ever since. By then my breasts had grown to a point where I could no longer wear t-shirts without displaying myself. I needed to wear baggy shirts to camouflage the pointed breasts that were growing. I started to wear an athletic bra under my clothes, which opened a whole new group of concerns. What if someone could see it through my shirt? What if one of the straps was showing? What if someone touches my back and realizes I am wearing it? These things all added to my stress level, but certainly did not stop me from doing what I felt I needed to do.

Elizabeth, on the other hand, had started to shun me. Worse than that, she began to ridicule and insult me. She told me I walked like a "fag," and that I was a "freak." She told me I made her sick to her stomach. I'm sure that the thought of what was happening to me was indeed repulsive to her, and she lashed out the only way she knew how.

It was no fun for me to be around her, so I avoided her as much as possible. And thankfully, she avoided me. When I went into a room, she left it. If I stayed home, she went out. Weekends, when we both had things to do around the house, were the worst. I dreaded them.

Easter arrived early in April. We had developed an Easter tradition of going to a late brunch as a family, and despite all of the ill winds that were blowing in our marriage we tried to keep things as normal as we could for Matt, so this year was to be no different.

On Easter morning I was getting ready to go. Despite the fact that it made me so uncomfortable, I was wearing a suit and tie. Elizabeth had just showered in the master bathroom, and I expected her to be ready soon, as we were crunched for time and needed to get going. As I finished up, I called to Elizabeth.

"Elizabeth, are you almost ready? We need to get going."

She didn't answer.

"Are you almost ready?" I asked again, this time a little louder.

She answered. "I'm not going. Go without me." She was crying.

I became alarmed.

"Not going?" I asked. "Why? What's wrong?"

I went into the master bathroom to make sure she was okay. Matt was right behind me. As I came around the corner, I saw that she had taken a shower, but had gotten back into her pajamas.

"What's going on? I thought we were going to brunch," I said.

She exploded at me. She told me that she couldn't go to brunch with me; that it was just too painful to see all the happy families there and know what I was doing to ours. She told me that I was fucked up, and my entire family was fucked up. She said that I had lied to her before we got married, and that our entire relationship was a lie... that I was never the person she thought I was and that I would go to hell for doing this to her and Matt. She told me the only thing for her to do was to get a divorce. She told me to take Matt and go to brunch without her. She was yelling. She was crying. By the time she was finished, she was almost hysterical.

I suppose I had expected something like this. I knew all too well what happens when a person tries to keep something in, and the pressures build to dangerous levels. Eventually, something is going to blow, so that didn't really surprise me. What did surprise me was the hate in her voice. And the fact that Matt was standing right there, and witnessed it all.

Even at 12, the stifling tension and discomfort in our house must certainly have been obvious to him, although none of us really ever said anything about it. Now, it was all out in the open. He had seen something that I think shocked him. It worried him. It affected him. And, it filled him with questions.

Matt and I did go to Easter brunch alone. What did mom mean? Why was she crying? How did I lie to her? Why did she want a divorce? Who would he stay with? I did everything I could to deflect his questions, as I was still too stunned myself to think straight. But at the same time, I needed to reassure him that we both loved him no matter what happened, and that everything would be alright. Unfortunately, I no longer believed that myself.

JOURNAL ENTRY

I can't believe this is really finally happening. After all the times I've thought about it, and worried about it, and wondered when and if the pieces would all fall apart, I think it's happening. And the weird thing is, I don't know whether to be glad or sad. Inside, I feel like crying, but I also look forward with anticipation (and some fear) to what the future will bring.

As I think back over 18 years with Elizabeth, it really tugs on my heartstrings. And to think that the bond that held us together so tightly has come so completely unwound so fast is really mind-boggling to me. But it seems as though Elizabeth has decided that our whole marriage has been a lie and a sham. That I was never the person that she though I was, or who I seemed to be. And because of that, all that we've done and been through doesn't really matter. But I also think she's afraid as to where that leaves her. Here she is, almost 40 years old with a house and a very impressionable 12-year-old and two dogs and no source of income for herself...where does she go from here? The thought that I ruined her life, which she has accused me of doing more than once so far, really hurts, but I can see why she thinks that.

I feel like such an outsider. It's like when you travel to a strange city, and there are people and semi-familiar things everywhere, but it still all feels so foreign. When it's your own city, you feel so at home, so comfortable and familiar. I don't have that feeling anymore. Things that I felt sure were forever, and perhaps took for granted, are now nothing. I cannot see past today, much less than into the future. I fully expect to get a call from a lawyer that Elizabeth is beginning divorce proceedings or go home to an empty house with a short good-bye note.

The hard part is, even if I wanted us to stay together, I don't think that it's possible anymore. The trust is gone. The feelings are gone. The familiarity is gone. In its place are two strangers who thought they knew each other, but really didn't know anything at all. And there's hurt....hurt at being deceived, at ruining a life, at "choosing" this course for my life rather than all we hoped and planned for, at leaving her in a mid-life lifeboat without an anchor or a paddle, or any sign of land.

But the sad thing is, I knew this day was coming. No matter how much I denied it to myself, or tried to pretend that it wouldn't be like this, I think deep inside I knew. Every time I went to the doctor's for my shots, I knew that it was the kiss of death for my marriage if and when she ever found out....and finding out was only a matter of time. So as I weighed what I was doing, I obviously chose the shot and the feeling of moving to my new life, over the marriage. And even if she were to give me an ultimatum that I must stop the shots and all that goes along with them to save the marriage, I know deep inside that I couldn't do that. And with that thought in mind, it's clear that my priorities, however screwed up they may be, lie in the direction of my new life, and not my old one.

As I said, I feel like an outsider. And I think it's going to get worse long before it gets any better.

In the days that followed, Elizabeth and I could barely speak to each other as we drifted ever farther apart. Despite the fact that we weren't talking, we still had so many things that we needed from each other. We started a chain of very emotional emails as I did my best to try to explain/ defend/express myself, and she tried to vent her anger/frustration/fear. Unfortunately, there was no way for me to appeal to her sense of logic and reason, as the entire situation had become completely emotional, and in that context there could be no acceptable defense.

Email to Elizabeth

There's a big difference between telling a lie, and not telling something at all. And quite frankly, I didn't feel there was anything to tell in the first place. At that time, this was a mere molecule in my soul, a drop in the ocean that was Dave. It was something that cropped up from time to time, like a migraine, and I dealt with it and eventually it went away again. That did not make me a bad person. You seem to have the impression that it's something that I consciously hid from you before we got married, which is not the case at all. It never even crossed my mind that it would become such a big problem, so there was no reason to even consider revealing it.

I dealt with it as best I could, without exposing you to it, because as it grew I KNEW it would only cause pain and unhappiness. I kept it to myself to PREVENT causing you pain. But in the end, I was damned no matter what I did. They say the road to hell is paved with good intentions, and in this case it looks like that's true...

And to be honest, I would have gone without telling you for the rest of our lives if I could have because eventually I knew that it was nothing but heartache. But guilt is a terrible thing. I knew there was this deep, dark secret and it really made me unhappy to keep it all in, so I eventually told you about it. That was 10 years ago. It was the hardest thing that I ever had to do in my life. I fully expected you to dump me back then, and was prepared for that. But life went on, and it faded into the background and we went on to be happy again. You certainly didn't accuse me of living a lie back then. You made it abundantly clear that no expression whatsoever was going to be tolerated, so I did my best to honor that. I tried to keep it all in...for all our sakes.

But as time goes by, that gets harder and harder to do. Maybe it has something to do with the change of life...I don't know. It's like a balloon that's getting bigger and bigger. Eventually it's going to pop. And on top of that, frustration builds with the anxiety and makes a very nasty combination. Especially when you feel like you can't share it with anyone (which is how you feel now). And I know you'll take this the wrong way, but I couldn't share it with you even if I wanted to...I was much too ashamed. So, I looked for someone who had experience with these kinds of things who could give me some advice...that's the psychologist I talked with last summer. And getting some of this stuff off my chest was such a relief...I can't tell you. I didn't do it to hurt you, even though I knew that if you found out it would...I did it to help myself cope. And I know you're going to say that's very selfish of me, but it's something that I HAD to do just to keep my sanity.

I guess the bottom line of all of this is that you can't be honest with others until you're honest with yourself, first. And here I am, stripped bare and trying to be honest, and I'm ready to face whatever the world brings. Although I'm certainly not proud of some of the things I've done, they're things I did to cope as best I could. I'm only human, and I'm sure I made mistakes along the way. And as I try to be honest with myself, I'm learning to be able to accept myself as well, rather than be ashamed of myself. That's a big step.

I guess the "roommates" strategy works for now. It really hurts to love someone and have them reject you and make you feel like scum...not being able to eat together or even be in the same room together. Do you really think it's going to get any better? Do you think you'll ever be able to kiss me like we used to kiss again? You keep saying it's up to me, but in a large sense it's up to YOU. Well, let's try to see where things go... . If you need even more space, let me know and like I said, I'll find somewhere to go until this thing works itself through.

Although I'm sure you'll disagree with me (again), I don't see anyone to blame here. I only see victims.

Chapter Nine

Resourceful

Necessity is the mother of invention...
— Alfred North Whitehead

According to the SOC, the next step in the treatment protocol is for a patient to successfully live as female for a full year before she can be considered for sex reassignment surgery (SRS). This time is known as transition, or Real Life Test (RLT), and it provides an opportunity to learn and adjust and adapt to the day-to-day pressures of life in our new role before the permanent physical changes are made.

RLT is a difficult, dangerous, proposition. Very few who start it actually finish it. Many find that the quality of life they experience in their new role does not meet their expectations, so they have a serious *life direction* decision to make. Some cannot continue for health reasons. Some turn back because of the intense psychological pressures involved, or because they get unbearably lonely. Some simply get stuck, unable to more forward or back, because of finances or sometimes because they just lose their way.

It was daunting to realize that I had already started down the path to live my life as a woman, but I had not spent even a single hour as Donna outside the safe confines of my house or my bedroom. I had absolutely no experience at all in the simple life skills I would need to know to spend an afternoon as a woman at the mall, much less live successfully as a woman in society.

As I seriously considered my own transition, it became apparent to me that I needed to find some help. I knew that relying solely on my own observation skills, and trying to mimic what I saw, would only scratch the surface on everything I needed to learn. Just as Deborah had helped me learn about makeup, I knew that I needed to find others who could, and more importantly would, help me with some of the other skills that I would need.

In our culture, there are gender-specific behaviors and ways of doing things that our society defines as typically masculine or feminine. How a person walks, or runs. How they fold their arms, or cross their legs. How they stand. How they move and gesture. How they bend down to pick something up. How they talk. All of these behaviors are different for men than they are for women.

If someone hasn't participated in the natural socialization process, as girls do throughout their entire lives, how does somebody learn to do these things in a feminine way? Perhaps even more difficult, how does somebody un-learn all of the male mannerisms they'd already learned, which had become second nature? I keep visualizing the scene from the movie *The Bird Cage*, where Nathan Lane's ultra-effeminate gay character is trying to learn to walk like a straight man, and uses John Wayne for his role model. The resulting gender-bending mixture is hilarious, but I had serious concerns that I would encounter similar problems that would not be so funny.

I needed help. Lots of help. In fact, I needed a coach. So, I found one.

I met Sandra in early 1998. She owned a small modeling agency that held classes in poise and modeling. I had done a little research in the phone book, and decided that I had nothing to lose by calling in hopes that she would be able help me. I had no idea how to explain my situation without sounding like a complete lunatic. So I lied to her.

Sandra was a few years younger than I was, and had more energy than any three people I know. Her short black hair was a perfect compliment to her red, full lips and broad white smile. I could tell right away that I would enjoy working with her, if only I could find a way to avoid frightening her away.

At our first meeting I nervously explained that I was a journalist, and I was preparing to write an article on what it was like to live as a woman, from a man's perspective. I told her I needed her help in training me for this assignment, as I had no clue as to where to start. She had no reason not to believe me. In fact, she seemed intrigued by the possibilities, and jumped into my little project head first, saying that this would probably even be fun!

She gave me a shopping list of things I would need to get started: a pair of pumps, a dress, and some nylons. I felt like I was some kind of criminal as I bought it all. I couldn't try any of it on so I just bought things that looked as though they should fit. I hastily tossed them into my shopping cart and pretended to talk on my cell phone as I paid the cashier to avoid actually having to explain. Sandra had specific ideas about hairstyles she thought would look good on me, so she helped me purchase a wig. She even started to shape my eyebrows, which caused me no small sense of alarm, but seemed to go unnoticed by everyone else.

I met with her every week or two, driving to her studio during my lunch hour with my small bag full of all Donna's worldly belongings. Sandra would often videotape our sessions, and we would watch them together as she critiqued my work. The vision on the screen was an odd one. Here was Dave, a strapping guy with short hair, wearing high heels, walking down the runway with his hand cocked in a feminine way, posing clumsily at the end of the stage, turning and walking back. Thinking back on it now, it must have seemed ludicrous to Sandra. But she never let me see that. She took our sessions very seriously, and really seemed to want to help.

Practice, practice, practice. I used to wake up early, before anybody else in the house, go out into the garage, slip on my heels, and walk back and forth, back and forth for a half hour before taking my shower. I had to concentrate. One foot directly in front of the other. Small steps. Move the hips. Move the shoulders and upper body correctly. Gliding, no bouncing. Sandra had even shown me how to turn at the end of the runway, like a model does, so I practiced that too. The mechanics of it all are actually pretty sophisticated. But as time passed, it got easier and more natural.

After a couple of months, Sandra felt I was ready to begin practicing in public. She decided we should spend a couple of hours shopping together. I did not share her confidence level, and the prospect of taking my act from the privacy and safety of her studio to the shark-infested waters of the shopping mall scared the bejeezes out of me. She did her best to assure me that things would go fine, but that couldn't chase terrifying visions of little kids pointing and yelling, "Look, mommy! Look at the man in the dress!" from my mind.

I was so scared that I remember very little of our shopping adventure. I remember looking straight ahead to avoid having to look directly at anyone, sure that the surveillance cameras had identified me as someone suspicious and that store security would be stopping me at any moment. My mind was flooded with questions: Is it really this hot in here, or am I having hot flashes? Do women really sweat like this? Do you think anyone would notice if I started sobbing right here in the purse department?

I was stumbling in my shoes, trying to walk as we had practiced all those times while at the same time making sure I didn't get more than two feet away from Sandra for fear of losing her amongst the clothes racks. It is a terror that only those who have done it can appreciate.

To think that our trip provided any sense of pleasure, or of satisfaction, or even of happiness for me would be wrong. As with my early cross-dressing efforts, I was thrilled at some level with actually getting ready to go, but once out I couldn't wait to get back to the relative safety of being Dave.

Shortly after our mall excursion, I told Sandra the real reason why I had originally contacted her. I told her that I was a transsexual, and was preparing for an eventual transition. I explained my difficult family situation to her. She seemed to be okay with it all at first, and we even made plans for a big shopping spree in order to begin my feminine wardrobe. But it did not take long before she would not return my phone calls, and one day her assistant called to say that she felt as though she was in a difficult spot and was sorry, but she couldn't help me any more.

After Sandra I realized that my need for a coach was as great as it ever was. I needed to find someone else to help me. I hoped to be able to find someone who really felt passionate about what I was planning to do, and not just someone who was willing to endure how odd this all sounded for the sake of getting paid. My confidence in finding that *someone* was not high.

One day I was at work reading a local woman's magazine and a photograph caught my eye. It was of a pretty blonde woman, posing with two dogs, and one of the dogs was wearing a pair of sunglasses. I started to read the article about a woman named Julie, who ran an image-consulting agency. In the article, she said all of the right things to perk my interest. She described how she worked with people to un-cover and express each person's unique individuality, and how fulfilling it was to be able to make a difference in another person's life. From the way she expressed herself, I thought that perhaps she might be able to understand what I was trying to do, and would actually *want* to help.

I decided to call her right then and there. I had learned from my experience with Sandra that it was best to be honest from the begin-ning and see what happened. I dialed. When she answered the phone, I realized that I didn't really know what to say, so I fumbled for words for a few seconds.

I told her that I had read her article in the magazine, and that I hoped she would be able to help me. I told her that I realized that I wasn't her target demographic, but had a very real and pressing need for someone like her. I took a deep breath, and just blurted out that I felt awkward about asking, but that I was a transsexual preparing to transition and had no idea about how to learn or do the things I was supposed to know in my new life.

She didn't drop the phone, or immediately hang up, so I was encouraged. In fact, if she was flustered at all she hid it very well. She said that she didn't really know much about the topic, so she would have to do a little research on it and suggested a face-to-face meeting later that week. It was more than I could have hoped for.

We met for coffee a few days later. She looked even more spectacular in person than she did in the photograph of her and her dogs. She was very pretty and, like Sandra, she had a very bubbly and friendly charm. She had a compassionate way about her, and it was apparent early on that her article really did reflect her true goals of helping others.

Julie had done quite a bit of research since our initial conversation. She had several pages of notes, and asked intelligent, articulate questions about my plans. I was very impressed, and as our chat ended it was apparent that we both felt comfortable with each other. In the end, she said she would be glad to work with me. I was ecstatic.

There is a plastic surgeon who is a legend among transsexuals. He is known affectionately as Dr. O. He reshapes faces.

Dr. O has performed detailed studies on the typical features and characteristics of male and female faces. He can tell you the typical distance between the eye and the hairline for a female, or the perfect ratio between eyes, nose and chin. As a result, he has developed surgeries that are very effective at feminizing transsexual faces. He is the only one in the world who can perform much of the bone structure work that he has invented. His work is the ultimate. And as such, it is expensive. Ungodly expensive, but incredibly effective.

I once read a quote by someone who stated that once you have surgery by Dr. O, you will never be mistaken for a man again. Whereas most plastic surgeons work with tissue, Dr. O specializes in working with bone. He has developed surgical procedures to reduce or eliminate typical male bony facial features, such as the brow bossing (the jutting bone above the eyes), or jaw structures typical of men. He replaces existing masculine features with much more feminine looking ones: a smaller turned-up feminine looking nose, a shortened space between the lip and the nostrils or between the eyebrows and the hairline, and a significantly reduced or eliminated male-looking trachea. His magic on my face was key to my transition plans, so I arranged to visit his offices in San Francisco at the beginning of July for a consultation.

Dr. O is a very caring man. He has a calming effect about him, and he immediately put me at ease despite my heightened state of frenzy. I'm sure he has done the same consultation hundreds of times before, but the way he performs it makes it seem like he's just doing it for *you* and you alone. We chatted for a while, getting to know each other a little bit. He took out several instruments and took my measurements, studied the set of elaborate skull x-rays that I brought with me, and jotted down different numbers and ratios.

His most impressive sales tool is the book he shows of previous clients. It was filled with incredible before and after photographs that caused my heart to leap. On the left side of the page there would be a picture of a profoundly masculine face. On the right, there was a picture of a very pretty, soft feminine woman. Page after page. Face after face. The realization that these were actually the same people, and that the incredible transformation was do to Dr. O's handiwork, made me realize just how amazing his work was. Perhaps even more importantly, I saw for myself that there was hope for masculine faces like mine. I had seen proof. All it would take was money and opportunity, as I already had the motive.

After the examination, Dr. O explained what he thought he could realistically do for me, what he couldn't do, and why. He gave his specific recommendations to feminize my face. I sat, listening intently as he described each procedure. He suggested scalp advancement to reduce the distance between the hairline and the eyes. He wanted to remove the typical male skull brow bossing that jutted out above my eyes. He said he'd need to redo my Rhinoplasty to reshape my nose into a more feminine shape that would fit better with the rest of the new face. He urged a procedure that would reshape and reduce my chin to reduce the strong, square male characteristics, and would reduce the angle of my jaw line to a more feminine contour. Finally, he suggested a tracheal shave to remove any hint of my typical male Adam's Apple. It was a substantial laundry list of procedures.

Once he was done, and we totaled it all up, the price tag for the complete package would be in excess of $30,000! I had prepared myself for the sticker-shock, so at that point all I could do was chuckle.

To me, the facial work that Dr. O recommended was more important to my gender transition than even the genital surgery. Nobody sees what you have, or don't have, in your pants. They do, however, see your face. I cannot overemphasize the importance that I put on finally seeing another face staring back at me when I looked at myself in the mirror. Some people seem to think that those of us who go to Dr. O do it out of some sense of vanity, and perhaps in the beginning that is at least partly true. However, when we are used to seeing the same old face in the mirror it doesn't matter how much make-up you apply or how you style your hair...we still tend to see the same manly face that we always saw. Dr. O's work changes that. It helps us to see ourselves differently. It helps to give us a sense of self-confidence. It helps us to see a new person on the outside to match the person we know we are on the inside.

Of course, none of Dr. O's work would be covered by insurance, so the financial demands alone are enough to scare away all except the most dedicated (and affluent) of souls. I had no idea where I would find that kind of money, but I vowed that someday, somehow, I would make this happen.

At the end of July Elizabeth and I celebrated our seventeenth wedding anniversary. It was a bittersweet event. If our marriage had been a hospital patient, it would have been on life support with doctors pounding on its chest in a frantic effort to somehow revive it.

We really had been so perfect for each other in so many ways. My sister had recently sent an email to us saying that she felt we were as close to the "perfect couple" as anyone she knew. Boy, was *she* in for a shock!

The in-between time of transition is very difficult. That's when a person looks not quite male, but not quite female, either. There are unmistakable characteristics of both, which tends to be very confusing and awkward. For example, my breasts had grown to be at least an A cup by the time my one year hormone anniversary came around. Hiding them from the outside world was a full-time activity. I did the best I could to hide them by wearing only baggy shirts, with a sports bra underneath to keep things flat, though my fears of being discovered were constant companions.

My fitness regimen was as strenuous as any I had ever followed. I worked out every day during lunch at the fitness center across the street, running three or four miles on the treadmill and doing hundreds of sit-ups. Although I didn't do any upper body work at all, I must say that I was probably in the best overall physical shape of my entire life. Changing clothes and showering at the club was quite an ordeal. I would need to take all my workout clothes into one of the bathroom stalls to change into my sports bra and my t-shirt and my sweatshirt. That was not difficult. It was getting *out* of the bra, and taking a shower in a man's locker room that was a challenge.

I had begun to grow my hair out, slicking it back with gel. Elizabeth hated it. She thought I looked sickly. She said I looked like I had AIDS. When a neighborhood friend told Elizabeth that she had seen me running alongside the road, and had thought I was a woman until she passed me and noticed who it was, Elizabeth lashed out at me.

"What are you doing to yourself? What are you doing to *us*?"

I had no reassuring words for her in reply.

In October, I had the opportunity to take a full-time job at a company where I had originally been a consultant when I had first arrived in Scottsdale. I knew many of the managers there. In fact, the director of the division was a good friend, and had personally called me about an open position on his team. I went in for some interviews, and was offered the job. It seemed to be a good fit.

I had a free week at the end of September before beginning my new job. I decided to fly back to Rochester to spend that week with my dad, who was suffering from the ravages of diabetes. Every time we visited Rochester as a family we had so many people to see and things to do, I never got the chance to spend as much time with him as I wanted. His kidneys had failed and he was on dialysis. His circulation was not good, and he had difficulty getting around. He lived in an assisted living apartment, and just hated being so dependent. He was only in his early 60s, but his body seemed to be that of an eighty-year-old man.

Dad and I had a very good week together. We sat around his apartment listening to classical music, or watching the Food Channel, or just talking and reminiscing. We looked at old photographs. We went out for dinners. We did some shopping.

At the end of the week, I said goodbye to my dad and headed home to start my new job. I was very happy to have spent that week with him. Little did I know it, but that would be the last time I would see my dad alive.

CHAPTER TEN

No Looking Back

Life is made up mostly of small steps. The only way we can see our progress sometimes is by setting and reaching milestones. Friday was a milestone; both in terms of my transition process, and in my own coming to terms with my situation. To tell a stranger, who has control of our livelihood in the palm of their hands, about something as deeply personal as this was a very frightening experience. It's not frightening in the sense that you are worried if it's the right thing to do or not. If that's the case, don't do it. But it's frightening in the sense that you no longer have total control. Oddly enough, having the strength to relinquish that sense of power is a very empowering act. I am very proud of handling things the way I did, of being able to do what I did.

— Journal Entry

I started my new job at the beginning of October. As I sat through the seemingly endless drone of new-hire orientation, I kept my radar up for hints or clues about the company's feelings on diversity and tolerance. I was well enough acquainted with corporate tongues to realize that many companies put on their diversity face because it had become the vogue thing to do.

Near the end of the long day, the Human Resources Manager of the company came to talk to us. He spoke at length about all of the core values of the company. Integrity. Honesty. The usual rhetoric. He shared a utopian vision of acceptance and brotherhood, where everyone got along and everyone was productive and everyone was happy. I must admit; it was very inspiring. The more I listened, the more comfortable I became that perhaps this would be a good place for me. I took notes, just in case I needed to use them later as a reminder of what was said, if push ever came to shove. As I started my new job I was optimistic that perhaps, just perhaps, I could transition here.

The company was fairly large, around 2,000 employees. I worked at our corporate headquarters; a beautiful campus in Scottsdale only about 15 miles from my house. The main business of the company was to manage prescriptions, and at that time we took pride in being the largest PBM (Pharmacy Benefits Management) company in the world.

My official job title was Consulting Analyst, which was a fancy name for computer programmer/analyst. I provided project management expertise, wrote complex computer programs, mentored some of the junior team members, and generally took an active leadership role in the projects of my group. After being a consultant for so many years it was a role and an environment that fit me well, and I easily made friends and earned respect during my first couple of months on the job. I made particular efforts to get to know our Human Resources representative, Lin, as I knew she would play a pivotal role should I decide to announce my transition. In fact, I almost felt sorry for her.

Halloween arrived shortly after I began my new job. I knew from past work that I had done with the company that Halloween was a big deal there. They had elaborate costume and cube decorating contests, and it seemed like almost everyone participated in one capacity or another. Early that late October morning, I was sitting in my cube when I heard some of the guys in the group talking about a third person that was walking up the aisle.

"OH MY GOD!" one of them said.

"Look at you! I can't believe you!" said the other.

I poked my head up out of my cube to see what the ruckus was about, and there, right by my cube, stood a very professional-looking, attractive brunette. It took me a few seconds to realize that this was one of the programmers from the other side of the building. It was a guy!

He was dressed very stylishly. His makeup was perfect. His medium length wig was elegantly styled. He was a vision of femininity. More and more people began to notice him, and stop over.

"Who did your makeup?" someone asked.

"My wife got up early this morning and did it," he explained.

"Oh my gosh. You even shaved your legs!" someone else exclaimed.

It caused quite the commotion.

As he left the little group that had gathered, heading down the aisle towards his desk on the other side of the building, some of the guys lingered and talked among themselves.

"I don't know about you," someone said, "but that gives me the *creeps*."

"Yeah. That was a llliiiiitttttle too realistic for my tastes."

"His wife did that to him? I dunno about that. You wouldn't catch me sitting still if my wife tried to do that to *me*!"

"I think I'm going to keep my distance from that…*thing*," said a fourth.

I smiled as I listened to their reactions. I had two thoughts. First, I figured that this person obviously had his own gender issues, as guys don't dress up that realistically just for the fun of it. And second, I couldn't help but feel that this might be a glimpse of the reaction I would get if I started there full-time as Donna.

After just a couple of months there, I had come to the conclusion that this was the perfect place and time to take that next step. I got along well with everyone in the group. My boss was a good friend. My HR Rep seemed very capable, and very nice. The company seemed as though it would be accepting. Everything appeared to be as right as it would ever be to reveal my situation and begin making real plans for a full-time transition. My dad once told me that timing is everything, or nothing, and all of my planets seemed to have become aligned to help me do this.

So, at the beginning of December 1998, I wrote an email to Lin, my HR Rep, indicating that we needed to get together to talk about an important issue. I realized then that I was about to tell her things about myself that could never be un-said, but I felt that I was ready to move to the next plateau. Our meeting was scheduled for December 11th, at 8:30 in the morning.

In preparation for the meeting with Lin, I drafted a letter that outlined everything that I wanted to say. I worked on it for a couple of weeks; rereading it, fine-tuning it, trying to get it just right. The more I read it, the more I tweaked it. Thankfully, the morning of our meeting came, and I felt that it was a good as it was going to get.

On that morning, I walked over to Lin's office, well aware of the magnitude of what I was about to do. It was a wonderfully sunny, cool, Phoenix winter morning, and I remember taking time to notice the warmth of the sun on my face, the songs of the desert birds as they went about their morning chores, and the people who calmly went about their own lives unaware of what was about to happen in mine. I was calm. I was ready. I was hopeful.

Once in her office, we chatted for a few minutes about work and our families. The time to hatch had arrived.

I gave her the letter. I asked her to read it slowly and carefully.

Hi:

I have worked here for almost three months now. Prior to that time, I worked here on contract for almost 2 years. I have enjoyed working with the people here, and find the work that I am doing to be both challenging and exciting. I look forward to being here and contributing to the success here for a long, long time.

However, I do have a very personal issue that I need to discuss. It deals with a subject that is the basis for many prejudices and misconceptions. It has caused me many years of anxiety, guilt, and confusion. But the time for hiding from myself has passed. I have finally reached a point where I can be honest with myself, and can now finally be honest with others, whatever the consequences may be.

The issue of which I speak is gender. A person's gender identity can be divided into two parts…physical gender and mental gender. A person's physical gender is determined by chromosomes, and there are no questions in that regard. However, their mental gender is assigned based on a complex series chemical processes that react on the developing fetus' brain. People assume that your physical gender naturally matches your mental gender, as it does in most people. But there are people who have the mental identification with one, but the obvious physical characteristics of the other. This affliction causes a lifelong struggle, beginning as soon as a child realizes there is something wrong with the way the world looks at them and the way they perceive themselves and how they fit in. They do their best to cope in a world in which they feel uncomfortable and alone. The term given to people who suffer from this situation is Transgendered. I am one of these people.

Unfortunately, people who suffer from this affliction are often stereotyped. They are often depicted as mentally ill, homosexual, or as having some type of deviant fetish. I am certainly none of these things. I have been married for almost 18 years to a woman that I love very much, and we are trying very hard to work our way through this. I am a very devoted father to a 13-year old son. I have had a very successful career, and will continue to do so in the future. Being transgendered has nothing to do with sex or with illness, it has to do with self-identity, and the two are worlds apart. It is an affliction that I certainly did not choose, but one that has affected me for my entire life, and one that I am working to correct right now.

The pressures on a transgendered person are tremendous. They must live their lives in a role they feel they were not born to play. They must create a persona that is acceptable to the outside world, but may or may not represent their true selves. They must internalize their struggle for self-acceptance, which forces them to live a very uncomfortable existence. All these things lead to a tremendous amount of stress and strain on the transgendered person, and at some point in their lives they reach a point where they cannot keep it in any longer, and must work to correct their situation.

There is an internationally accepted protocol of treatment for people who are clinically diagnosed as being transgendered. Since it has been proven that a person's gender identity cannot be changed, this treatment deals with a person's physical world, which can be changed. It is designed to make the transgendered person feel more comfortable within the confines of their own skin by making their body more closely match their mental gender, and often leads a person to complete gender reassignment surgery.

I am planning to begin my RLT in February or March of 1999. I will be taking a couple of weeks off to prepare for my transition prior to that time. I will be legally changing my name to reflect my new gender role, and as a result of my hormone regimen I am currently eligible to be declared a legal female in the state of Arizona by the Superior Court. I will be living and dressing totally as female.

Needless to say, a change of this magnitude needs to be coordinated with many people. I know of many instances where work place transitions have gone very smoothly and without incident. This is typically the result of much planning, forethought and sensitivity for all parties involved. That is why I am coming to you at this early stage.

I ask for your patience and your tolerance during this very difficult time. Besides these very difficult issues here at work, I am going through a very painful time with my wife, family and friends as they struggle to accept my situation. I am feeling every emotion that you can imagine.... excitement, fear, nervousness, wonder...you name it, I'm feeling it. I feel confidence, because I know what I am doing is the right thing for me to do. I feel pride at finally having the courage to confront issues that have perplexed me for my entire life. But most of all, I am feeling relief in the sense that my years of hiding from myself are almost over. Anything you could do to make this process easier would be greatly appreciated.

I was hired here because of my background and my track record for proven hard work and results. It was deemed to be up to very high standards by which the company judges its applicants for positions of this level. In the short time that I have been here, I feel that my work has lived up to this and am very proud of what I have accomplished. Although some things about me will certainly change, the things that make me a hard working, dedicated, loyal employee will not. In fact, I believe that without the extra mental baggage that I have carried for these many years, these qualities will be enhanced.

During my New-Hire Orientation here, a gentleman spoke with us late in the afternoon. He was talking about the values that the company promotes and expects from its employees. One of the words we discussed was "Integrity." We discussed that it meant being honest with yourself and others, and with taking pride and ownership in everything you do. It is a word that has tremendous meaning to me, and in my eyes this is a good opportunity for the company to demonstrate that it is more than fancy rhetoric. It is a value that is appreciated and expected in each and every employee, regardless of their unique individual situations. I believe that this is a company that accepts people for who and what they are, across the entire spectrum of humanity.

I thank you for your time.

— HUMAN RESOURCE DISCLOSURE LETTER

Waiting for her to read it seemed like an eternity. I looked down at my legal pad, pretending to write something to keep myself busy as she read. I studied her out of the corner of my eye, looking for a reaction. I didn't see anything.

Finally, she was finished. She took a deep breath, and looked up at me. Her eyes were wide as though she didn't know quite what to say.

"I can't begin to imagine how difficult it was to write this letter," she said. "I'm stunned."

"It was hard. It took me a long time, but I think it conveys everything I need to say. It was even harder to wait while you read it."

She stared at me sympathetically, almost as if feeling sorry for my anguish, and the difficulties I would be facing in the future. I didn't know what else to say.

"I'm sure it will surprise a lot of people," I offered, trying to keep things light.

"THAT'S for sure," she agreed.

Lin told me she did not know whether the company had a specific policy regarding this type of situation, so she would need to do some research and get back to me at some point in January, after the Holidays.

All things must come to an end: the Fall of the Roman Empire, the end of the Renaissance, the end of the Age of Innocence. The last weeks of 1998 marked the end of a golden era in my own life.

It was to be the last Holiday Season that my wife, my son, and I would spend together as a family. It was to mark the end of my efforts to hide Donna from the prying eyes of the outside world. It was to mark the beginning of my real efforts to help Donna emerge and grow. And a very profound event would rock me to my core, would cause me to reevaluate everything in my life, and would provide the strength of purpose and of conviction that I would need to proceed through my transition.

On December 29, my mom called to tell me that my father had died in his sleep.

Chapter Eleven

Life Itself

I've always wondered how I would handle the passing of a parent, and it's a very difficult thing. Especially right now. It leaves an emptiness like I've never felt before. As we grow up we feel that our parents are always there for us if we need them, and now to realize that that isn't true anymore is hard. But I'm learning a lot about myself, and I'm coping as best I can...

— Journal Entry

My dad was only sixty-four when he died. As sons or daughters, I don't know if anything can prepare us for this kind of news, so I reacted with the first emotion that hit me. I cried for days.

Losing a parent can be a traumatic event for those of us who remain behind. It can affect us in ways we can't even begin to imagine or understand. Losing my father happened at a crucial time in my life. It changed me.

Many people ask me whether my father's death was the cause of my seemingly sudden mid-life awakening. As has already been described, my "awakening" was far from sudden. As strong winds do not start a forest fire, they cause it to grow in size and intensity, so my father's death was the wind that fanned the spark that had been ignited. It fanned the smoldering embers of my need for self-discovery, giving my fire strength, definition and purpose.

I take some comfort in knowing that death was not unwelcome for my dad. He felt, as I do, that quality of life is far more important than longevity. He lost much of what gave him joy in life to the ravages of diabetes. He spent four hours a day, three times a week attached to a dialysis machine that filtered his blood. He had lost much of the feeling in his hands and feet, to the point that if he cut himself or stubbed a toe, he would not realize it until someone noticed the blood path from his wound. He could not walk unaided and the fancy wide-wheeled walker that my sister and I bought him was a constant companion. Despite all that, my dad's spirit was never broken. He seemed to maintain his sense of humor, and I never saw him seem defeated, or morose. Towards the end, though, I think he was ready to go. And it provided small solace to feel that he left the world the way he lived his life, on his own terms.

In the days following Dad's death I struggled to find a single word that could describe my dad. After thinking about it for days, I found it. The word was *passion*. Dad had more brainpower than anyone I have ever met, and his passion for discovery and learning was unquenchable. However, those of us that knew him well understood that he had a passion for the sensuality of life, as well. He loved the vistas of snow-covered mountains. He reveled in an opera, a piano concerto, or fugue. He appreciated a good meal, a bottle of fine wine, a snifter of cognac and a good cigar. I sincerely hope that others will be able to use that one word to eulogize me after my own passing. To me passion is the key to living.

My dad had big plans. He loved the outdoors, and hoped to be able to travel, hike and enjoy the good life once he retired, although many of us wondered if he would *ever* truly retire. During our annual summer cross-country drives, he would travel 200 miles out of the way just to stop for a few hours at a National Park. He did his best to instill in his children the same joy he felt for the grandeur and majesty of

117

nature. I think we disappointed him tremendously during these trips because the only question we had when we arrived at our destination was when we could swim in the motel pool. To his credit, though, he never stopped trying.

Unfortunately, Dad never got to realize his plans. His dreams of traveling the world and enjoying the awesome tapestry of nature never materialized for him; his disease ate him up. In the end he died alone in his bed, betrayed by a defeated body that could not keep up with his still razor sharp mind.

I think about that a lot. I wonder what he thought about as he lay there in the dark, about to die. I wonder if his life story flashed through his mind, and if he took his last living moment to consider it all. Was it a happy life? Was he true to himself? Did he have regrets? I often recall him telling me, "It's not the things we do in life that we regret, it's the things we don't do." For a long time I wondered how I would answer those same questions on my own deathbed.

Journal Entry

> I have to go back home [to Rochester] next week for his memorial service. I'm the executor of his will, so I'm preparing myself for the responsibilities and headaches that such a duty entails. Everyone in our family has always looked up to me as the oldest and the strongest. It's a facade that I have cultivated very carefully, which is why my "coming-out" will be so surprising when that finally happens. I need to get myself together before going home, as it's an image that I'm not ready to shed just yet.

Elizabeth chose not to accompany me, so I went to Rochester alone. Our explanation was that bringing her and along would just make things more difficult for me, but the honest truth was that she didn't want to face my family during this crisis, knowing that our own future lay in doubt. It was just as well. I did not need that added pressure and stress in the face of the emotional turmoil I was already feeling. It was my chance to bond again with my family, suddenly missing its patriarch.

Dad would not have wanted a morose wake followed by a symbolic burial. Of all of his children, my sister is most like my dad, and she felt he would have wanted a party to celebrate his life, rather than an event to lament his passing. So that's what she arranged. It was an inspired idea, and a very special evening.

Many family friends attended the event. It was absolutely beautiful. Outside, a terrible lake-effect winter storm raged, and temperatures hovered near zero. But friends from all over the country braved the chill to spend that evening with us and celebrate my dad. We had tables scattered with photo albums, and my dad's books, and some of his paintings, and various things he had enjoyed during his life. People sat around in small groups, eating hors d'oeuvres and sipping drinks, talking about Dad and the things that they had done with him. It was a very nice evening.

Ironically, this event to celebrate my dad's life was to be the last time Dave would wear a suit, or a tie. In some ways, it was a fitting end to that life, as well.

CHAPTER TWELVE

HELPING HANDS

Until recently, I never, ever knew or even imagined how important support is in getting through difficult times. I always felt that looking for support was an admission of weakness myself, and I was unable to bring myself to do that. But tough, tough times are impossible to get through by ourselves. We sometimes need help and support. It took me a long time to be able to admit that, and to look for it, and to accept it, but it has made the difference through some very tough times for me. And it will continue to help me as I work through this.

— JOURNAL ENTRY

As the new year dawned I struggled to find a sense of normalcy and balance in a world that had suddenly been tossed on its ear. After struggling with all that was happening at an increasingly fast pace, I decided to identify my father's death as a milestone on my journey. I needed to find my bearings. I needed to regain my focus. I needed to gauge just where I was, and where I was headed for fear of spinning out of control. I knew that Dad's passing would change things.

I learned early in my adult life that it is often unwise to measure a trip or a task based on how far there still seems to go. Doing so is like trying to gauge the distance to some destination that lays shimmering and shining off on the horizon, such as a heat mirage across miles and miles of endless scorching desert. These efforts all to often end in frustration and disappointment.

Instead, I took that opportunity to measure progress in my transition based on what I had already accomplished; on ground already covered, not just in my transition plan, but in my entire life as a whole. I decided to define some serious milestones, based on significant accomplishments, major events, and on firsts that I was experiencing in my life, to make navigation easier.

Serious contemplation of life and death can lead to some profound observations and insights for those who are patient enough to look deeply and keenly. I took a good, hard look at all of the changes I had seen in just those past few months, and I already saw things accelerating. Towards what? That was still to be determined.

JOURNAL ENTRY

Why do things always have to be so hard? My dad lived his whole life, struggling with the terrible affects of diabetes and what it did to his body, and once he died, it really hit home. All that suffering and struggling to stay alive and live a quality life, and all that's left is a box full of ashes and alot of paperwork. And I am overwhelmed by the question..."Why?"

Now that things have gotten sticky here at home, I struggle to balance my own needs with those of my wife and son. In a real sense, there is no intersection. There is no common ground. There's no place where my need to be Donna intersects with my wife's need for a husband. And for me to have expected anything else is foolish on my part.

My wife and I have avoided each other like the plague all weekend. I go into a room, and she leaves it. We no longer even feel comfortable around each other. It's just so sad. I'm a very strong person. I will survive. But she is not. And this is

121

just killing her. And that's why my heart hurts. But it is tempered with the knowledge that I cannot go back. I cannot let my sorrow cloud the knowledge of what I need to do. And I am hopeful that time will prove to be a salve to soothe wounds and prove that life goes on.

I believe that a person's spiritual sense very often mirrors their conscious one. In the weeks after my dad's death I began to notice that my dreams took on clarity and a definition that they had never had before. Perhaps it was triggered by the recent emotional upheavals in my life, fueled by the heightened sensory effects of the estrogen. Whatever the reason, they suddenly seemed to become so much more vivid and intense, to the point that they sometimes even seemed to be in color. In late January I had the first dream that I could remember in which I was female. *Really* female. In the past I had been a guy dressing as female, afraid that others would detect me. I couldn't wait to get back together with my psychologist to tell her! She listened to me with a smile on her face, genuinely happy for me.

In early January, I finally realized that I needed to meet more people like myself. To my knowledge, I had never met another transsexual face to face. I considered myself to be a loner and had originally resigned myself to doing battle with my demons alone, as I had always done in the past.

I had come to the realization that there was quite a bit that I needed to learn, and the only way to get that information was to meet and talk with other transsexuals. How does one go about doing a name change? How does one get a new driver's license? How have other workplace transitions gone? What other details do I need to know? I suddenly felt a need to find more of my own *kind*. I learned that a local support group met once a month, and I started to attend.

I often told Elizabeth that I had to work in the evening, so getting a little time on my own was not a problem. I had no place to change into my Donna outfit, so after some investigation I identified a private, women's bathroom in a secluded area at work as a possibility. It would later become the bathroom that I would use throughout my transition. I knew it was a little risky, but I didn't expect anybody would be there at that time on Saturday night, so felt I would be able to change undisturbed.

Donna's still puny wardrobe at that time was very basic. I usually wore a blue sweater and a pair of size ten blue jeans. I attached my clip-on earrings, my necklace, and my ladies watch. I carefully applied my makeup and styled my way-too-puffy, shoulder-length, brown wig before standing back and looking at the finished product in the mirror. As I looked at myself in the mirror, making a final inspection just before heading out to my car, it almost felt as though I was looking at someone else in that reflection. It could not possible be me, but I knew that it was and that Donna was ready to face the world.

In the early days it was almost surreal to be going out in public *en femme*. Actually, it's not like I was *really* going out in public, since it was dark outside and I did not expect to have to deal with *regular* people. Of course, there was always the chance that I would be stopped by a cop, or would be involved in an accident, or would have a flat tire or something, but I dismissed those thoughts as being too traumatic to even think about.

The hardest part of the ordeal was often making my way from my car to the meeting center. It was located in a downtown strip mall that was often packed with people on a Saturday night. There was usually a crowd loitering outside a bar there. My strategy was to look straight ahead and make a bee-line for the door, not running, but not going too slowly either. Some nights, just getting in the door felt like a major accomplishment.

Over the next few weeks and months I would meet many more transsexuals, both in person and over the Internet. I would find many that had similar stories to my own, and many others who had completely different histories and perspectives. Many were trying to come to grips with their own private hell, so finding a kindred soul was often a Godsend. We found ourselves bound by our shared unique

123

struggle, and many times our emotional conversations or email exchanges proved to be valuable opportunities to share, to counsel and to console.

Workplace transitions are a big deal. No matter how you slice it, there is nothing else like it. Anywhere. I can think of no other situation where Human Resources will call all of your co-workers into a room, and expose your deepest, darkest secret to them. How terrifying a prospect is that? The balancing act, between an employee's right to transition and other employees' right to be uncomfortable about it, is a difficult one that all too often gets lost in the emotion of the issue.

I doubt that there is such a thing as an *easy* workplace transition. I have heard of workplace transitions that passed without incident, but I am sure that they were far from easy. I have heard about others that are so difficult and painful that I can only imagine how it all ended. Somebody once told me that any workplace transition where nobody gets killed is a successful one, and the realization that things could actually get to that point is a harsh reminder of all the pressures and emotions that are involved.

I think the level of success depends on several factors. First and foremost, it depends on the person involved. Part depends on the type of job he or she holds. Part depends on the culture and level of support of the company. Part depends on good planning. And, part depends on luck.

In late January, Lin and I met again to review the things that she had learned, based on our first meeting.

We sat and chit-chatted for a few minutes, munching on bagels that she had brought for the event. I eyed her carefully for any sign that she now somehow felt uncomfortable around me, and to gain a sense of what she was about to relay to me. I could sense nothing.

Eventually it was time to get down to business. She started at the top of her list.

"First, I just want to reassure you that your job is not in jeopardy because of your revelation."

It never occurred to me that it *would* be in jeopardy. My last performance review had been stellar, and it never crossed my mind that a personal issue like this could potentially be grounds for dismissal from my job. Although we like to think that there are discrimination laws to protect us in this country, I learned to my horror and disappointment that they often do not cover transgender situations, and I could indeed have been terminated.

She continued, "Next, we've spoken with your health care provider and they have agreed to continue your coverage for as long as you are an employee, and your family coverage for as long as you are married."

It had never occurred to me that my health care was in jeopardy because of this, either! Apparently, in my case, ignorance was bliss. They would have been well within their legal rights to terminate my coverage right then and there.

She went on to affirm that the company did not have a problem with my situation, and would do anything they could to help in any way I felt best. They considered this to be more a *personal* matter than anything. She felt it was their job to simply let people know what was going on... and towards that end, she asked me how I wanted to handle that.

I thought about it for a second.

"I do not want to get up in front of a room full of people and tell them. That would be way too traumatic for me," I said, my insides twisting up at the mere thought of it.

I thought about it for another second. "I can give you something to read, but I really don't want to be around for that part."

She agreed with that approach. "How would you like to handle telling the management team?" she asked.

I had already given this a little thought. "Brian is a good friend, and I'd like to tell him. I'd rather that you tell everyone else."

She agreed to that, too.

She asked if I would be comfortable making myself available to people if they had any questions once I began my transition, and I told her that would be fine.

My cube was right on the main walkway, and she asked if I would be more comfortable being moved to someplace with less traffic, and I told her no. I thought it was best that we downplay the situation; that the bigger a fuss we made about it, the bigger a deal everyone else would make of it as well.

We both felt that the first week or two would be difficult, because everyone would be curious and would come around to take a *look-see*. However, it would eventually become old and the work routine would return to normal.

"If you ever feel discriminated against or harassed in any way, please make a bee-line over to my office, as the group will be given strict guidelines for acceptable behavior. This is a zero tolerance issue." Her statement reinforced the severity of what we were discussing.

I assured her that I would, but that I hoped none of that would be necessary.

We went down her list, item by item, making plans and agreeing on almost everything. Until we got to using the bathrooms.

Of all the issues that must be resolved in order to begin a workplace transition, bathroom arrangements are often the stickiest. Men do not want you in their bathroom and you don't want to be in there, either. However, many women still consider you a male and don't want you in the ladies room either. This situation can become so contentious that I have heard of situations where the company has had to provide a private bathroom to support the transitioning individual. I expected at the outset that there would need to be some education and negotiation on this point.

When she got to the bathroom issue, Lin said, "And of course you'll continue to use the men's bathrooms until you have your surgery."

I stopped her right there. "No. I can't do that."

She seemed surprised.

"Can you imagine how awkward that would be?" I asked.

"But before you have your surgery you'll still be a man," she reasoned.

"No. By the time I start here as Donna I will have had my name legally changed. I will have changed my name on all my official documents, including credit cards, passport, school records, and even my social security card. I will have a new driver's license with my new name, and with the sex designation "F" for *female*. All this will be done based on letters of recommendation from my doctor and psychologist. At that point, I will be living totally and completely as female. I suspect that if you tried to force me to use the men's room, you'd have a riot on your hands," I argued.

"I didn't realize that you would be doing all that, and it certainly makes a difference. I'll have to do a little more research to see what we can do."

I had done my own research, and I told her that there was a small women's washroom in the next building that had a lock on the door, and I thought very few people had access to it. I told her that I thought it would work out very well, and she made a note of it and she told me she would investigate that possibility.

Just before we were finished, I asked her if she had any questions for me.

"Yes," she answered. I do have one.

For some reason I braced myself for a difficult question.

"What is your new name going to be?" she asked.

"Donna," I said, relieved that she seemed genuinely interested.

"That's pretty," she said. "Next time we get together we can review all the paperwork you'll need to fill out to change our records here at work."

As I left her office she said all that's left is for me to set a date, and she'd take care of the rest. I told her I would tell Brian sometime in the next couple of weeks, and would send him to her if he had any questions.

Brian was more than my boss. He was a friend...he was a *good* friend.

I met Brian a couple of years earlier and we had quickly bonded. He was in his mid 30s, although his boyish enthusiasm and boundless energy made him seem much younger.

Brian had a motivated, corporate go-getter veneer tightly wound around a West Coast free-thinker's core. He would wear a corporate monkey suit and tie, complimented by sandals and *socks*. He was a jack-of-all-trades, specializing in managing, marketing, coding… you name it and he did it. He not only did it, but he did it well… and with style.

Being around Brian was often very amusing for me. He loved women, all women. Whenever we were out together, his head would swivel as he'd watch all the women go by, simply admiring them as much as lusting after them. He'd think out loud about how they looked, or what they were wearing, or what they might be like if he actually got to know them. He'd verbalize all sorts of unique, funny and creative ways to introduce himself to them, although I soon learned that his bark was much worse than his bite. I found his one-tracked mind humorous, and harmless, as I often couldn't help but wonder, "Are all men really like that?"

At his core, though, Brian had a heart of gold. He really cared about people. In the wilds of the cold corporate jungle, he tried to maintain his aloof tough-guy image. But I knew he was really just an emotional, sometimes insecure, softy. He was a very real person, flaws and insecurities and all, and *that* was the heart of our friendship.

A week after my meeting with HR, I was working late, and Brian stopped by my cubicle to chat, as he often did. Although Brian *loved* women, he couldn't begin to understand them, so he enjoyed getting my perspective to help him with his own girlfriend.

He sat down, and we chatted for a few minutes. Although I hadn't planned to do this so soon, I sensed that this was my opportunity. I suddenly realized that this was the perfect time to tell him, so as I sat nodding and not really listening to what he was saying I could feel my courage building. I briefly considered *not* doing it, and waiting for another opportunity, but something just told me that the time was right. I just hoped I was ready for the fallout that would soon come raining down upon me.

As long as our gender issues remained confined to our own heads, we alone are our own worst enemies, and our own best friends. Once they are unleashed upon the workplace, though, who can even begin to imagine where they will go, or how much damage they can do? As we unleash our deeply personal issue into the workplace it suddenly becomes free to mutate into all sorts of cancerous demons in the minds of people who may not be sympathetic to our plight. One moment, we are a trusted friend and peer, and the next we are seen as something sick, dangerous, and evil. One moment we are secure, and the next we are indefensibly vulnerable as our jobs, our careers, even our very livelihood, are suddenly jeopardized by something that has absolutely nothing to do with our work performance.

Was I ready for this? Was I really, truly ready? I told myself that it wasn't too late to back out. I could always wait for another day to tell him. Another opportunity. But even if I did, would I ever be any more ready than I was right now? No. This was my time, so I spoke calmly and slowly. "Brian, I need to tell you something. Something big. Something huge."

I had his attention.

"I consider you to be a wonderful friend, and a very capable manager, and what I have to say to you affects you in both of those roles. But no matter how it affects you, it affects me more than you can even imagine. It affects everything in my life."

He was immediately genuinely concerned. "Are you okay?" he asked.

"Yes, yes. I'm fine. It's really not health related, but there are very few things that could affect me more than what I am about to tell you. It puts everything I am, everything I have, and everything I love at risk: my wife, my son, my house, my career, everything."

He said he couldn't imagine anything having that great an impact.

"Brian, once I tell you this, you'll never look at me the same way again. The way you perceive me will forever be changed. It's that big!"

"Oh my God! What is it? You're killing me!" He was genuinely worried now.

"It's so difficult for me that I have a hard time putting it into words." I paused.

"It is something that has been plaguing me for my entire life, and I am just now finding the strength to face it. Rather than have to explain it to you, I wrote it all out on paper." I took the paper out of my desk.

"I've already talked to Lin in HR about all of this, so none of this is news to them. In fact, telling you was one of the tasks I need to do based on our last meeting." I held out the paper.

"Please take this, and read it slowly. Make sure you understand what I am telling you, because I'm already rreeaaalllyy nervous about this."

I looked him straight in the eye, so he would understand the seriousness of what I was saying. I gave him the paper to read.

After a couple of minutes, he was finished. It was done. He looked at me.

"Oh…My…God," he said, pausing between each word. He was flabbergasted.

He had no idea how to react, which I suppose is natural. He searched for words.

He joked that I was his best friend in Arizona, and how he wasn't about to let a little thing like a sex change come between us (humor is always a good tactic). To his credit, he seemed to handle it well, and he expressed concern not only for me, but for Elizabeth and as well.

Before I left to drive home, he walked me down to my car. He asked if there was anything he could do for me.

I thought for a moment.

"Yes," I answered. "There is something. Please watch my back. Please don't let me be surprised or blindsided."

I was afraid that somehow the political machinery of the company would mobilize against me, and I would have to defend myself against a sneak attack. I'm only partly sure that such thinking is paranoid, but at the time, knowing that Brian would do that for me helped me rest easier.

CHAPTER THIRTEEN

THE BREAKING POINT

For a very, very long time I have lived a life of fear. It is a life that no one should be forced to endure. It is a life of self-imposed exile, where refusing to accept what I know to be true in hopes of continuing my façade of a life has always been the top priority. You tell me that I'm trying too hard to be what I'm not, and you're absolutely correct. But our ideas about who and what I am are most certainly not the same.

— LETTER TO MY WIFE

By the middle of February my consultant, Julie, felt I was ready to make my feminine public debut. She felt that I needed to start spending time in real-life situations, so she made plans for us to spend an entire day together at a local mall.

My only point of reference at that point was the terror I had felt during the hour or so I spent with Sandra several months earlier and I didn't feel any more ready now than I did then. I could think of hundreds of different *bad* scenarios, most of which were alarming enough to get my stomach so knotted that it felt as if someone were squeezing it at both ends. The only *good* scenario I could envision was that no bad scenarios happened. I was scared to death.

I took the day off from work, and drove to her house to dress and prepare.

As we drove to the mall, a car pulled next to us on the highway. There were a couple of guys in it, and I noticed them both craning their necks to get a look at us. One had a lecherous leer on his face, saw that I had noticed him, and puckered up to mimic a kiss. Oh brother.

Although I was absolutely terrified, I managed to get from the car to the mall without encountering a major incident. Once inside, we strolled (actually, she strolled, while I stumbled) around for about an hour to gain a sense of confidence before we got to the real meat of the day: buying the basics of my new wardrobe.

I had already perfected the art of looking straight ahead and avoiding eye contact with anyone. I could somehow sense when Julie was getting too far away, as panic bells would go off in my head and I'd rush to catch back up with her.

Once we started shopping, I relaxed a bit. I asked lots of questions. "What's the difference between Junior and Petite sizes?" "What were good brand names I should look for?" She explained different kinds of fabrics, necklines, sleeve styles, color considerations, sizing, and prices. It all seemed so much more complicated than shopping as a guy, when all I needed was a pair of 31/30 jeans and a shirt, and I was all set.

Eventually, I was led to the safety and relative comfort of the changing rooms. I was amazed that women had such large, posh changing accommodations in their stores. Men's changing rooms weren't that nice! Julie would bring back outfits for me to try on, one after another after another, as we attempted to define my style. At some point, I stopped being nervous, and actually started to enjoy myself!

Mid-way through the morning, I had to pee. I held it as long as I could, but right around lunchtime I really needed to go. I told Julie, and she grabbed my hand, saying, "C'mon." I followed her as she led me to my first visit to a Ladies washroom.

Peeing for women can be much more involved than peeing for men. There are just so many layers: pull up the dress, unroll the nylons, pull down the panties, and then putting it all back into place again. It can be quite the complicated ordeal. Now I understood why there always seemed to be lines of women waiting to get into the ladies bathrooms. It took so long to get everything free, and then put back together again, that a traffic jam was inevitable.

As we ate lunch, we took time to review our purchases, our impressions of the morning, and our plans for the afternoon. Julie wanted to make me actually have to talk to the salespeople, as she had done most of the talking in the morning. I was having enough difficulty trying to look right...sounding right added a whole new level of complexity to things. I told her I'd do my best.

By the middle of the afternoon I started to realize, to my utter amazement, that no one seemed to notice me. No one seemed to be craning their neck or snickering or staring. We had been going in and out of stores for five whole hours, and not a single incident had occurred. Everyone was coming and going, and minding their own business, and I guess nobody really looked closely enough to notice anything out of the ordinary. It was extraordinary. Julie said that I looked beautiful, so to just relax and enjoy it, and by the end of the day I was doing just that.

To top the day off, I learned that women actually take the time to compliment other women. At that point, the only necklace I owned was a gold heart with a pretty dove on the front, with the Serenity Prayer inscribed on the back. One saleswoman said, in a sincere tone, "That's a beautiful necklace!" I didn't know what to say. I was tongue-tied. I think I considered several possible replies, before a weak "Thank you" actually found its way out. Men don't do that! Men would rather be hog-tied than compliment another guy. Being a guy was like being in a competition. Being a girl seemed more like being on a team.

By late afternoon my feet had had as much as they could handle. I carried all my purchases out to Julie's truck to go home and get washed up. For the first time in my life, I was not in a hurry to get back to being Dave. I wasn't ashamed. I wasn't afraid. I was happy, and I was comfortable, and I was relieved.

Of course, it would fade by the time I got home to face Elizabeth, whom I knew would be full of questions about where I had been all day. Indeed, when I got home, I found a note on the table saying that she was fed up and couldn't take much more, and that perhaps I should just move out and let them get on with their lives. I was very sorely tempted to pack a bag and do just that, but frankly I didn't want to face that trauma on my fortieth birthday weekend. Besides, I was far too pleased with the way that the day had gone to ruin it at that point.

My Donna-day gave me renewed enthusiasm for progressing in my transition. The glow of that experience was to last for several weeks. The first thing that I did was contact Lin in HR with a specific date. We had discussed dates in early April, and I chose April 19th.

On February 22, 1999, I turned forty. Forty years. Four decades. It was a major life milestone.

Elizabeth and I had spent years discussing and planning all the big events we hoped to do to celebrate our 40th birthdays. Perhaps a cruise. Maybe a trip to Europe. Instead, it was the evening before my birthday and Elizabeth still hadn't given any indication that she even planned to give me a birthday card, much less actually celebrate *anything*. A week before some friends had called to inquire whether we had any major plans to mark the occasion and Elizabeth just burst into tears and had to hang up.

I decided to take myself to the movies, knowing full well this that might be the extent of my celebration. I went to see *Shakespeare In Love*, which was a mistake. I ended up crying all the way home; partly from sadness from the movie and partly from feeling sorry for myself.

When I got home, everyone was in bed and the house was dark. There was, a note on my bed wishing me a happy birthday, and saying that we could meet for dinner after work to celebrate. That made me happy.

We met at a nice steak restaurant for dinner. Halfway through the meal Elizabeth stood up and said she just couldn't do this anymore, and hurriedly gathered her things and left. I sat watching, with nothing to say, wondering how I would explain this to Matt who had almost gotten used to such sudden situations. After she left, he and I stayed and finished our dinner, eventually sharing the free birthday dessert. As I blew out the candle I wished for the thing that I wished for *every* year…that this would be my last birthday as a boy. The only difference was that this time, I actually believed that it might come true.

At home, Elizabeth and I continued to fight and argue as the death spiral of our marriage continued downwards.

One evening, as we both watched TV in separate rooms, the door opened and she poked her head in to say, "I can't even stand to look at what you're becoming. You're not even a man anymore! You're some kind of freakish creature." And with that, she headed off to bed. I was actually starting to believe that she hated me.

These incidents proved to be the impetus I needed to *finally* tell Elizabeth everything. I could not go on hiding any longer. It wasn't fair to any of us.

At that point, we had known each other for just under 20 years, and we had been married for 18 of them. It had been just over 11 years since I first told her about my feminine side. I had been seeing my therapist for almost two years. I had been on hormones for 18 months. She had learned things little by little since that time.

I had tried to talk to her, but she wouldn't listen. I had tried to get her to come to talk to Sheila with me, but she wouldn't go. Whether she wanted to hear it or not, it was time to get it all out into the open.

There was so much I wanted to say…so much I wanted to tell her. But how? I doubted that a face-to-face confrontation would be effective, as the discussion would last only as long as it took for her to turn on her heels and slam the door in my face. Even if I could get her to sit and listen to me, the combination of nerves and stress would likely wipe my mind clear of most of what I wanted to say. So, I decided to write it down and give it to her.

I spent days writing and editing a letter. As time went on it got longer and longer as the words just seemed to pour out onto the page. The end result was an emotional outpouring of frustration and resignation, a plea for compassion, and a heart-wrenching confessional all rolled into one.

One morning about a week after my birthday I printed the letter and left it for her to find, propped on my pillow in my bedroom.

I almost went home a half dozen times throughout the morning to take it back before she could find it, but somehow I found the strength to hold myself back with the knowledge that she *needed* to read it. I felt like the pilots of the Enola Gay, having dropped the first atomic bomb, just waiting for the flash of light and the mushroom cloud to confirm that it had landed.

Shortly before lunch, we hit ground zero.

Hon:

You are my everything. I have told you that since day one, and that has not changed through all that has happened, through all the years. It remains as true today as it ever did. And I will love you until the day that I die.

Life is sometimes unfair and cruel, and I think our current "situation" is a perfect example of that. We both know that we were made for each other that we are better as a team than as individuals…that our love has been strong enough to survive even the biggest bumps. The vows we made about our love…"in good times and in bad, in sickness and in health, until death do us part"…really do mean something in our lives. But life has given me a very difficult condition for me to deal with, and perhaps because I loved you too much, my problem has become your problem. Although I certainly apologize from the bottom of my heart for the pain I have inflicted upon you, I too feel very much a victim.

I do know one thing. We cannot go on living like this. We cannot continue to fight, and live different lives. We are drifting apart, and we keep hurting each other. It's not fair to either of us, and especially to Matt, and it's time to make some decisions.

My family has always been good at hiding from things. At putting things off and making small talk. But my situation is one from which I cannot hide. It is one that consumes me totally. I cannot continue to live the lie that is my life. I need to be who and what I really am, or face a fate worse than death in a vain attempt to hold it back. I need answers to questions that have plagued me for my entire life, and I need to find those answers for myself. And although at this point I do not know what the answers will be, I know that I cannot and will not continue to live my life without finding out.

For a very, very long time I have lived a life of fear. It is a life that no one should be forced to endure. It is a life of self-imposed exile, where refusing to accept what I know to be true in hopes of continuing my façade of a life has always been the top priority. You tell me that I'm trying too hard to be what I'm not, and you're absolutely correct. But our ideas about who and what I am are most certainly not the same.

I have done a lot of thinking lately, especially since my dad died. I have been thinking about life…particularly the quality of life. The saying "life's too short" has never held more meaning for me. If I died right now, at this moment, I would die with the regret that I never got to live the life I feel I was born to live. I would die knowing that I allowed the pressure of others to dictate how I lived my entire life. In short, I would die knowing that I was given one shot at life, and instead of living it, I let it slip away.

I look down the path of our lives to see what lies ahead. We have built hopes and dreams, and made plans for our future together. I would never want any of that to change. But I also see a life that cannot continue in its present condition. I see my situation eating away at us both, and never, ever relenting or retreating. I see it causing a lifetime of unhappiness and hurt for us both, when we both deserve so much more. I see that fear is driving our decisions, and as long as that happens we will both continue to struggle and fight and drift apart. These issues need to be addressed with honesty and courage and conviction rather than fear and shame in order to come to some sort of closure so we can all move on with our lives and live them as we were meant to.

My life is made up of many roles. There is Dave-the-Husband, and Dave-the-father, and Dave-the-employee. And underlying all of that is

137

Dave-the-person. If Dave-the-person can't function, then he sure can't do any of the other roles. And that's not fair to you, or Matt, or me. In this case, Dave-the-person is going to change. But that doesn't mean that any of the other roles will be lost in the shuffle. That all depends on you.

My father was a very brave man. He faced his situation with courage and dignity and a smile on his face. He had his shortcomings, as we all do, but he did the best he could to live a good life. I am very proud to have had him as my father. I find the decisions that I have made, and am about to make, to be amongst the most important and difficult in my life. They require a bravery that I did not feel I could ever muster, but have somehow found. And although my emotions are very much in flutter, my soul is at peace with what I have decided to do.

You know about my situation. I do not need to detail it for you here. I truly feel that I have been mis-cast in this life....mis-packaged if you will. The causes of this situation are immaterial now. Whether it is all in my mind, as you feel, or is of biological origin, as I feel, it is a condition that has plagued me for my entire life, and one that continues to eat at me and gnaw at me from the inside each and every hour of every day. Fighting this has taken an unbelievable amount of energy and willpower on my part, but the time for fighting is over. The time to face it and deal with it is here, and I will do so with the same courage and strength that my father did until his last day on this earth. I refuse to be its victim any longer.

So here's what I have decided to do.

I am going to begin a transition to see if my feelings are true, or somehow misguided and confused. I am going to assume a female role in life for an extended period of time. I am going to learn for myself if I have truly been born in the wrong skin, or if things I have believed about myself for my entire life have been misguided. Towards this end, I have already made several arrangements.

I've already talked with Human Resources at work about my situation. We have had 3 long meetings. They know all about me, and we've met several times to develop a plan to implement my transition there at work. They are very supportive and sympathetic and accepting, and have actually made me feel more comfortable than I am when I'm around you. They have assured me of several things. My job is certainly not in jeopardy, as they are very happy with my performance to date. No matter what happens, as long as you and I are married none of our benefits will change. They vow to protect me from any harassment or discrimination of any kind. The bottom line is that they value diversity in people, and they see this as a personal situation, and they have offered to do anything they can to help.

I've already had a long discussion with Brian (my boss) about it. Needless to say, he was very surprised. But he knows the type of person that I am, and he can see how much pain I am in, and he told me that he'll always be here for me if I need him. He says that true friends are people who are there when things are hardest, not just when they're easiest, and he has proven to be a true friend. He has offered to protect and support me in any way he can, and has earned my gratitude and trust with the gracious way that he has handled things.

They are in the process of disclosing the situation to the rest of the management team. We have picked a target date of Monday, April 19 for me to begin work there as a female. I will take the prior week off, and HR will disclose it and explain it to the rest of the group. In the meantime, there are legal things that I need to do. For example, I will legally be changing my name, and all documents and accounts where it appears.

You will need to decide how you are going to handle this. It's one thing for you to know about it, and you have tried very hard to keep it in the closet. It will not remain in the closet for very much longer. You need to be very careful in what you do now, and not let your emotions make you do something that we'll all regret. Do not react out of fear or anger or hurt, as there has been more than enough of that around us lately.

If you want me to leave, I will do that. For a week, a month…whatever you tell me. I will find someplace to go. That's totally up to you.

I have no idea how it will all work out. I may find out that it is the life I should have led all along, and that would make me very happy. I may fall flat on my face and find that I can't live that life, and will revert to the old Dave. But at least I'll know that I tried my best and had the courage to face it, and I can live with that. I'm not afraid to admit that I was wrong, especially in a situation as deadly serious as this.

You have threatened me in the past, saying that if this becomes public knowledge I will lose everyone and everything that means anything to me. I am working to prove that you are 100% wrong. As long as I try to live a lie, I risk losing everything, as living this life has very little meaning. I need to be honest and strong and brave, not deceitful and weak and fearful. I have determined that I will handle a bad situation as best I can, and others will have to decide for themselves how they want to deal with it. I have told several people over the past weeks, and every, single one has reacted with care and compassion. It has truly touched my heart, and given me renewed strength to do what must be done.

Not too long ago you told me that Matt had become the number one priority in your life. You have vowed that he never know. In that case, you had better pack him up and move away as fast as you can, and never let us speak again, because otherwise, he WILL know. I think you're being unrealistic and unfair to all of us with that attitude. He needs BOTH of us, and can adapt to pretty much anything. I think it's your own fear and embarrassment that is the problem here. As with most things, the feared result is usually much worse than the actual result. By taking him away, you automatically deny him any say in the matter, and you yourself are the problem...not me. We need to work together to help him adjust and understand, and he'll be just fine.

You have said a few things to me over the past year that really stick in my mind. Once, you told me that you rather that I had cancer than this. You said I was better off dead than in this situation. You told me that you could NEVER accept it. I cannot make you accept it, and after comments like that I doubt you will. I just hope you give it time. Time is a great healer, and you may find that it's not as bad as you fear. At least give me a chance. If you want some time apart, that's one thing. But to end the marriage now, without giving me time to work out my situation, would show me that our love is not nearly as strong as I had thought it was.

But I am not going to sugar coat things. I am going to give this test 100%. I will not allow you, or anyone, to make me feel as though I am some sort of deviate or criminal. If you want to be with me and continue to share our lives, that's one thing. If you want to help me, I think our relationship could be stronger than ever. Underneath, I'm the same person that you have always loved. But if you can't see past the exterior, and can only accept me as the old Dave, then it's best we be apart. If you continue to harass me or call me names, I will leave. I'd rather be alone than live with you like that.

I'm planning to do several things in the next couple of months. I'm going to have some cosmetic surgery on my nose (and probably my chin) to make it less conspicuous. I'll use some of the money that I got from my dad if I have to, or I'll get a loan, but I will do it. I'm going to buy a complete new wardrobe, and will live full-time as female. I'm going to be the type of person that I want to be, not who anyone tells me to be. These things are not open for discussion.

I have told you before that the main reason that I have fought this so hard and for so long is for you and Matt. That has been the ONLY reason. My refusal to fight it any longer is in no way saying that you and have become less important in my life. You remain the things that I value most. But there are some things that a person needs to do to continue living, and this is one of those things. My dad's death demonstrated just how important the people we love are. We need each other for love and support, especially when we are hurt and weak and vulnerable, and I have never needed you more. You can turn your back and walk away or you can stay and see what happens. It's up to you. I deserve your sensitivity and caring and love, not your hate and spite.

I have prayed and prayed, asking Him what to do. And the answer comes back loud and clear. He tells me to follow my heart. And my heart tells me that this is a time of healing and inner peace, and this is what I need to do. And I feel very comfortable with that.

There is some time before these things happen, so there's no need to do anything right now, unless you decide you want to. The next step is yours. I'm being open and honest with you, and expect you to be the same with me. Either this will end up bringing us closer together in a loving, caring, sharing relationship, or it will break us apart. I suppose only time will tell.

I love you.

Dave

— LETTER TO MY WIFE

141

She called me shortly before lunch. I could barely understand what she was saying through her sobs. She sounded like a wounded animal, and my heart sank and my soul heaved as I listened to her. It was awful.

JOURNAL ENTRY

My wife just called. She's a mess. She told me she needs answers, because she can't live like this. I told her I'd give her answers if I could, but I don't have them right now. That's what this is all about...finding answers to questions that have plagued me for my entire life.

That's not good enough. She's sure that I'm in the grip of some evil force that is making me do these things. She thinks my psych and my doctor are pushing me into doing this, and that I can't break out of their grip. She thinks I should be seeing a psych to help me FIGHT this evil force, not give in to it. And she thinks that if I choose to continue on my current path, it is basically saying that following this "compulsion" is more important than my wife and family. She says she needs me to be strong because she needs the old "me" back. She accused me of bringing her out here to Arizona on purpose so she would be far away from all her family and friends and would be alone.

She said that she absolutely does not want it as a part of her life. If I come to work like that, she says there's no way I'm dressing there and that I better clean up before I come home. I told her I will not agree to that. I will get dressed in the morning just like everyone else does. Then, she said, I had better make arrangements to leave because it will screw Matt up for the rest of his life. She said she'll tell I took a job out of state or something, but she absolutely refuses to let it touch his life. I told her that she was acting out of confusion and anger, and THAT'S what would hurt Matt and not necessarily what I was doing, which made her even angrier. I said that I will not be one person at work, and another at home, so if that's the way she feels, then I'll find someplace else to live while I work this out.

It's so hard to be here, knowing what I'm putting her through. There is absolutely nothing I can say or do to make it better, short of backing out completely, which I cannot do. In some ways I feel guilty for looking forward to my new life, while my wife looks forward and dreads hers. I feel, in a very real sense, that I am shedding many of the roles and responsibilities that I have carried for these many years, and she will take it upon herself to pick up that burden. Why does life have to be so difficult?

As I made the preparations for beginning life as Donna, I called Dr. O to schedule my facial feminization surgery. My dad had left me some money in his will, so the facial surgery that once seemed so unattainable was now very much within my reach.

I was extremely disappointed to learn that the doctor's schedule was full for at least four months, meaning his earliest opening was late May or early June. Little did I know that this seemingly insignificant delay would prompt me to make a series of bad decisions that nearly had tragic consequences.

CHAPTER FOURTEEN

THE WRONG STUFF

> *Whatever you do, you need courage. Whatever course you decide upon, there is always someone to tell you that you are wrong. There are always difficulties arising that tempt you to believe your critics are right. To map out a course of action and follow it to an end requires some of the same courage that a soldier needs. Peace has its victories, but it takes brave men and women to win them.*
>
> — RALPH WALDO EMERSON

During our initial meetings I had offered to have my psychologist come to speak to my peers at work to announce and explain my transition but HR turned that idea down. Although the company agreed that they needed help and guidance through these uncharted waters, they preferred to engage someone who would be perceived as being impartial to the situation. The sense I got was that they were getting a little nervous about the psychological and legal implications of what was about to happen, especially when I got an email from Lin saying she was having a meeting with our corporate legal counsel to discuss my transition.

A few weeks before my transition date, I received an email from Lin saying she we needed to chat again.

Some of what we discussed were little details. She reviewed some of what would need to happen to change my badge and employment information to match my new name. She was working on a plan to meet with all of the managers, and then all of the employees, in my department, to announce what was happening.

They had approved my recommendation to use that secluded women's washroom, and gave me a key. It was all the way on the other side of the campus in an adjoining building. In one sense, I was relieved that the bathroom issue seemed to have been resolved to everyone's satisfaction. But the thought of having to actually walk a quarter mile through potentially *hostile* territory, each time I needed to go to the bathroom didn't thrill me.

Perhaps the biggest bombshell was that the company had apparently contacted our mental health care provider in San Francisco, and had engaged the services of someone who specialized in facilitating gender transitions. They were looking to her to help make this process go as smoothly as possible. As time went on, I began to refer to this person as "the Specialist."

Lin indicated that the Specialist had participated in several other corporate transitions, and found that a "Big-Bang" type of approach generally caused the least distraction and difficulty for everyone involved. Using such an approach, the scenario for my transition from Dave to Donna at work would be a sudden one: they would announce my situation to my entire group of co-workers on a Friday, and I would show up for work that following Monday as Donna.

This type of approach wasn't what I originally had in mind. I had expected a much more gradual transition that would allow me to ease into my new role. However, I assumed that the Specialist knew what she was talking about, and felt that it was important to be intelligent about choosing my battles, and this didn't seem worth fighting about at the time. How wrong I was.

I quickly became frustrated and impatient with having to wait four whole months to go to San Francisco for facial feminization surgery. I had convinced myself that there was no way I could pass successfully as a woman with my existing male face. To me, I felt that my features were far too masculine, and that a failure to do something about that would doom any attempted transition to failure.

I could not stand the thought of living out my life being considered to be a freak; not male but not female, either. The prospect of being considered to be "a man in a dress," and the subject of snickers and ridicule every time I stepped outside my front door was too difficult and painful to consider. I truly believed that death would be a far more acceptable alternative.

However, the more I thought about it, the more I convinced myself that *any* competent plastic surgeon could shape a nose. People have nose jobs all the time, don't they? Scottsdale seemed to be a hub of plastic surgery, and I began to consider some options that might speed up the process. I reasoned that I could find a surgeon and my have rhinoplasty *before* my transition at work, let it heal, and then go and see Dr. O in June for the other procedures.

I discussed my idea with Julie, who knew several local plastic surgeons. Little by little, a plan started to come together. It was not a good plan, mind you, but it was certainly a plan.

At some point in our discussions, she suggested the possibility of having breast augmentation surgery at the same time. By that time my breasts were an A cup, almost a B. But I wanted more. I wanted full, round, feminine looking breasts.

The amount of breast development that a transsexual achieves is determined by age, by genetic predisposition, and by the specifics of the hormone regimen they are following. Often, these factors prevent our actual breast development from living up to our voluptuous ideals and expectations. This inadequacy is sometimes magnified by the fact that we often have larger frames and shoulders, so our breasts just don't seem proportional to everything else.

Of course, this issue can be easily fixed in the same way that it is for many genetic women who are unsatisfied with their breast development. Many TS gals have breast augmentation at the same time that they have SRS. The more I thought about it, the more I saw this as an opportunity to have mine early.

All it took was for the seed of an idea to be planted in my head, and it quickly grew into a full-blown plan. The mere thought of having a full set of breasts during my transition almost took my breath away. Logic and reason sometimes reared their ugly heads warning that breast augmentation was probably a bad idea for someone who hadn't even spent a single day as a woman yet. But I shoved those thoughts aside like a rude guest at a dinner party.

I had crossed the great divide. When it came to my body I was now thinking emotionally, and not logically. No amount of reason could change my stubborn mind, or wake me from my estrogen-induced stupor to the danger of my folly. In rapid succession I met with a plastic surgeon, discussed my intentions, provided letters of support from my psychologist and doctor, and scheduled surgery for both my nose and my breasts. The surgery date was scheduled to be March 24, which was less than six weeks away.

The surgeon was an older doctor, just nearing retirement. I'm sure had had seen many things during his career, but I'm confident that he had never seen anything quite like me before. At our pre-op meeting he discussed everything he planned to do.

He explained that my nose was already very significant, and although he could certainly reduce it there were limits on what I could expect. I told him to do what he could.

When he started to discuss my breasts, he said he would enlarge them so that they would be proportional to my shoulders. That sounded fine to me, although I didn't know what his idea of *proportional* really meant. I didn't want huge, attention grabbing breasts, but I certainly wanted something more significant than what I had grown on my own.

In order to show me what he had in mind he gave me a bra to put on, and grabbed a couple of pre-filled breast implants. He stuffed one of the implants inside one of the cups of the bra, fiddled with it for a few seconds to get it straight, and stood back to take a look. I stared in disbelief at how big it appeared. I had assumed he would put the other implant into the other bra to gauge how things would look. Instead, he put it inside the same cup! He put the two of them together on the same side! He said that the implants he expected to use would be roughly the same size as the two of the ones he was using as an example. Oh my God!

I think the doctor noticed that my eyes had grown to the size of small saucers as I stared at this huge breast hanging from my chest. He assured me that, once they were in, they wouldn't look quite so large, and that part of my initial shock was simply the fact that I just wasn't used to them yet. He also assured me that this size would be proportional to my shoulders and to the rest of my body. I chuckled to myself that it really didn't matter what plastic surgery I did or didn't have on my face, as once I had a chest like that nobody would be looking above my chest.

As I prepared for these permanent changes, I started to give serious thought about how I would share the news of my situation with my family. Although it was still very awkward and uncomfortable for me to discuss, my disclosures to a few close friends had seemed to go well. But, telling my family presented more of a challenge for me. I knew that I wanted to tell my sister first, expecting that she'd be the most accepting and supportive, but the how's and when's of it all hadn't been worked out in my mind yet.

Fate has a funny way of intervening in our lives sometimes, and all my planning and worrying became a moot point as I returned home from work one day in early March. I was at work, and my sister had called the house to inquire about something having to do with my dad's estate, unaware of the emotional tumult that had engulfed our household.

Jude and Elizabeth were talking on the telephone when suddenly Elizabeth couldn't hold it together anymore and started crying. My sister had no clue what was going on, and tried to talk with her, but the more Elizabeth tried to explain the more upset she got.

That's when I got home. As I came through the front door, I could hear Elizabeth in the kitchen, crying loudly. I immediately became concerned that something was wrong with her parents, or that something had happened to Matt.

As I rounded the corner and approached her to see what was wrong, she handed the telephone to me without a word and went running for the bedroom, sobbing harder with every step.

I put the phone to my ear to see who was on the other end. "Hello?" I inquired.

"Dave?" came the familiar voice on the other end. It was my sister.

"Hi. Yes. It's me," I replied.

"What the HELL is going on there?" she asked in a very concerned voice.

Although I did not know the specifics of what had been discussed, I at least knew that Elizabeth had not told my sister what was happening.

"Way too much to go into now," I told her, wanting to end the conversation so that I could go and check on Elizabeth who whose muffled sobs could be heard through the locked bedroom door.

"Are you okay?"

"Yes. I'm fine. I have a lot to talk to you about, but now is not a good time. I need to go and check on Elizabeth," I told her.

"When, then?" she persisted.

"When, what?" I asked

"When are you going to call me? I'm very concerned for you now," she replied.

"Tomorrow. I'll call you tomorrow and we can talk about it."

"Okay. As long as you're doing okay."

"I'm fine," I lied.

I didn't have the chance to call Jude the next day. She called me. Apparently, her mind had been racing all night, trying to guess what possibly could be happening to incite such an emotional outburst from Elizabeth.

I didn't know how to actually tell her, so she started to question me, listing all of the possibilities that she had considered based on hints that Elizabeth had given before becoming completely overwhelmed by emotion.

"Are you gay?" she asked.

"No," I replied, amused that she would ask.

"Are you an alcoholic?"

"Nope."

"Are you cheating on Elizabeth?"

"Of course not!"

"Is it sexual?"

"No, not really."

"Porn?"

"NO!."

"Is it health related?"

"No. I'm fine. Really!"

"You'll *never* guess," I told her. "It's something I have been dealing with for my entire life, and I'm just now actually facing with it. It's crushing Elizabeth."

She continued to guess, and I continued to deny. Until she got too close to home.

"Are you a transvestite?" she eventually asked.

After a second, I responded. "No. But you're getting close now."

And with that, I explained it all to her.

Once I had finished, she said that she was happy that I was healthy, that she loved me, and that she was there for me if I needed to talk. She said she was ready to help me tell the rest of the family whenever I felt I was ready.

After we hung up, I somehow felt as though something major had just happened. I had just *come out* to someone in my family, and my world hadn't imploded. My fears of having to explain, and facing rejection and shame, had not materialized, yet.

If my sister was uncomfortable or was stunned by our conversation, and I assumed she was, she seemed to take it all in stride and hid any discomfort well. She shared my revelation with her husband and her daughters almost immediately, not able to absorb it all by herself. It seemed to create universal shock and disbelief, but also universal acceptance, and that's more than I could have ever hoped for. But most importantly, I had a confidante and supporter inside the family!

EMAIL FROM MY SISTER

I'm worried about you. You've chosen such a hard road for yourself! It's going to have so many difficult moments. Moments at work, with your family, with friends... I have to admire your guts and determination to put yourself through it just to straighten out something you feel got hopelessly tangled up so long ago

If you want my help with Mom or anything else, I'm here for you. I can't say how she's going to react to all this. I haven't a clue. But eventually, even if she reacts badly at first, I think she'll come around. I'll work on her if need be.

During one of our early discussions, while we were still actually talking *to* one another and not *at* each other, Elizabeth made it clear that a decision would need to be made. She continued in her steadfast belief that Donna had no part in *our* life, so that if there was anything I needed to figure out that included Donna, I'd need to leave my home and family to do that. She told me that I needed to decide whether to stay at home and be the husband and father that she and Matt expected me to be, and that I had vowed to be, or else leave to do whatever I needed to do. As far as she was concerned, the choice was mine. The line in the sand had been drawn.

In my naivety, I still clung to hopes of being able to live at home with my wife and son, and transitioning as Donna until such point as I decided that this life path was really not for me, or that I needed to pursue it to its logical conclusion. Elizabeth said it sounded as though

I wanted to "have my cake and eat it too," and I suppose that's exactly what I wanted. I didn't see why that wasn't possible. Elizabeth would have none of it.

She seemed to be fixated on the clothes aspect of the transition, as if all of this fuss was just about clothes. As she began to realize that I might actually follow through with my plans, she offered what, to her, was a major concession. "You can live in the house as long as you changed into Donna's clothes at work, and change back into Dave before you come home," she offered.

I explained that a gender transition, like any profound journey of self-discovery, is a full-time commitment, and that there would be no disguising it. It would affect every aspect of my life. I absolutely could not compromise it to the point where the end result would prove nothing; that wouldn't be fair to any of us. She expected and deserved someone who could be the husband and father that I had been, but I couldn't be that now. Although I realized that the thought of having any association with it was a tremendously embarrassing to her, a gender transition is a very public process. That's the whole point.

In my own mind there was no choice to be made. I had tried to fight this for my entire life, and that's what got me into this mess in the first place. That strategy had failed. As tough as I was, and as much as I loved Elizabeth, I could not hold back the overwhelming need to explore myself and find answers. Real answers. And if Elizabeth felt that I had to leave our home and our family to do that, as much as the prospect of it all hurt and scared me, I would honor and respect that. I would leave.

In preparation for leaving home and living full-time as Donna, I rented a one-bedroom apartment not far from our house. I told Elizabeth what I had done, and she seemed stunned that I actually seemed to be following through on my plans. I tried to get her to understand the urgency of my need, but there could be no compromise.

During the evenings I escaped the stifling tension at home by driving to the apartment as soon as Matt went to bed. I assembled the sparse furniture that I had bought, and got everything ready for what seemed like ever more imminent occupancy.

Our weekends around here just get worse and worse. Last night in particular was very difficult. My wife basically told me that she had wasted the last 20 years of her life, and that I was to blame.

I can't wait to leave. In fact, tonight may be my last night here. I doubt that she'll even say goodbye at this point.

Anticipation of what lay just on the horizon left me feeling physically and mentally drained. I was not sleeping well, often getting only three or four hours of uneasy rest. My stomach was churning, and my insides were all knotted up, all the time. I would wake up at two or three in the morning and would wander towards the den in hopes of falling asleep on the couch in front of the television. The morning sunrise would find me still awake, taking a cold shower in hopes of making it through another day. It would have been difficult to handle under the best of circumstances, but the fact that I got no sleep and felt like my insides were going to explode made things immeasurably worse.

To be honest, the thought that was most often in my mind wasn't my upcoming surgery, or my transition, or even my wife. It was my son. Elizabeth had told me that if I ever told Matt about *any* of this, she would take him and I would never see him again. Although I certainly doubted that she could or would do this, for some reason I felt the need to spare him from what was about to happen until I had made some decisions of my own. At least that's what I told myself. Perhaps it was because I was afraid to tell him. Perhaps it was because I enjoyed being the person that I think he thought I was, and I didn't want to threaten that. Perhaps it was because I had no clue what I would say.

Rather than tell him I was moving out because I was about to venture across the gender line, I told him that I would be going to Dallas for work for a few weeks. He accepted that without question. It was a ludicrous charade that we went to ridiculous lengths to maintain.

153

As the last few days before my plastic surgery ticked away Brian seemed very concerned. The plan, as far as he knew it, was a relatively simple one. I would have my facial surgery. I would take two weeks off to heal and spend time getting comfortable living as Donna. They had made arrangements to fly in the Specialist from San Francisco to handle the announcement at work beginning on Thursday afternoon. And that following Monday, I would start at work as Donna. What could be simpler?

Things would not go nearly that smoothly. The fact that I hadn't mentioned my impending breast augmentation to them was to become a big deal.

Chapter Fifteen

All Alone On My Own

The tragedy of our situation is the feeling that we can never allow anyone near us. We need love and compassion and companionship more than anyone could know, but we're trapped with secrets of a second life that will haunt us until we die. We are condemned to a lonely life, and it really makes me sad. It all seems so useless sometimes.

— Journal Entry

My marriage was almost dead. Any sense of trust had long since been lost. Any sense of intimacy had been drained. I sometimes wondered if we kept it alive in the hope it would somehow miraculously be revived and would regain its strength to live a long, happy life, or because we were afraid to admit defeat and let it go. Sure, we still loved each other. Neither of us doubted that, or we would have abandoned each other long ago. But the question we both asked ourselves: is love enough?

All Elizabeth wanted was to keep things the same as they were. I don't think that was really asking too much. Of course, far too much had happened to think that all the damage that had been done could be undone. In a perfect world, true love offers itself unconditionally. In our feeble human world, though, I had become jaded to the point where I had lost my faith in that kind of love. I was learning that there are *always* conditions.

Things had been so perfect for us. Too perfect! It was no wonder that Elizabeth didn't want them to change. She resisted it with every fiber in her being, with every tactic she could muster, and I certainly couldn't blame her. I probably would have, too. She fought with the strength of a scorned wife to keep her husband, and with the sense of purpose of a threatened mother to maintain her family. I felt it ironic that the other *woman* in this scenario was Donna. The discomfort I felt in playing the two adversarial roles of both husband and temptress in this unique triangle ensured, that no matter how this ended, I would end up as both villain and victim.

Such had been the torture of our marriage, and of our relationship, over the previous 18 months. It was the evening of March 23, 1999, and Elizabeth and I had been married for seventeen years, seven months, and five days. She was the first and only woman I had ever loved, and continued to love. And I was about to put a dagger deep into her heart.

Elizabeth and had gone out for the evening, and it was with a mixture of sadness and relief that I wrote a short note. I told her I was leaving to move into my apartment and take the next step on my journey of self-discovery. I apologized for all that had happened, and for all that was about to happen. I told her to take care of Matt, and to kiss him goodnight for me. I told her that I loved her, and that I still clung to hopes of a life together. I cried as I finished the note, struggling to maintain my composure, and to control the grief that I was afraid would overpower me as I left.

With a mixture of growing sadness, fear, and excitement, I said goodbye to the dogs, collected a few personal items, took one last look around the world that had already come to feel cold and foreign, and drove away to face my future. My sadness was for myself...wondering why this force inside me forced me to do this. My sadness was for my wife, and the terrible sense of guilt and responsibility that I felt at leaving her alone at the time when she needed me most. And my sadness was for my son, who faced a possible future without a father and whose only wish was to be part of a loving family. It all seemed so hopeless. But there was no turning back now.

The next morning, my good friend, Karen, stopped by my apartment to pick me up and take me to the hospital. I was dressed in a sweater and a skirt, well aware that this was the first time that any of Dave's friends would actually meet Donna face to face. Considering everything else that was on my mind, however, I really wasn't very nervous about it.

I had promised myself to avoid worrying about what was happening at home…about how Elizabeth might have reacted upon finding and reading my note. I needed to maintain my focus. I needed to maintain composure. I needed to have faith that she would have the strength to get through this, and so would I.

Karen was very supportive all day. She told me how good she thought I looked. She was surprised how feminine my body really was, freed from the protective tent of baggy clothes that had camouflaged me for the last six months. She kept me calm as I filled out the admission paperwork and chatted with the nurses at the surgery center. And it was with a mixture of thanks and sadness that I said good-bye to her as the anesthesiologist inserted an IV and prepared me for my surgery.

JOURNAL ENTRY

I was unusually calm and relaxed as they wheeled me into the operating room, which made me feel very good. I got onto the operating table, and they covered me with warm blankets. They made sure the back of my gown was undone so they could get at it. The anesthesiologist began playing with my left arm, saying I'd feel a sting and a brief warm feeling, and I did. He started the drugs, and said I should be getting very relaxed, and that was that…

I don't remember all that much about waking up. That whole evening is a blur. I remember that they had put a big, hard thing around the breasts to keep everything in place, and it was HUGE. My nose throbbed a bit, but my face had all kinds of splints and things taped on it. I didn't feel nauseous or anything.

I had to pee so bad I thought I'd explode, so the nurse helped me over to the washroom. It was quite a struggle, as I was very wobbly, and still attached to the IV. But I felt so much better after peeing. My mouth had this terrible case of cottonmouth…there was gunk all over the place in there and I just couldn't get it moist. It was pretty nasty. The nurse eventually brought me some ice chips, which was a Godsend.

That night was one I thought would never end. I couldn't sleep, but I was so tired. I didn't hurt too badly, but had to go to pee every half hour or so. At one point, the IV ripped me and I started bleeding pretty badly. I couldn't find a nurse, so wandered down the hall with my IV, bleeding all over the place, until I found the nurse station. They fixed me up.

I was running a fever for most of the night, and couldn't get comfortable. I couldn't turn on either side or on to my stomach, so I tossed and turned, going from hot to cold, all night long. I finally started dozing off near morning. The doctor showed up about a half hour later. He cut off the big bandages holding the boobs in place, and had me put on a vest that zips up the front. I asked him how much fluid he used to fill the implants, and he said 450 cc's. Wow. He said they look great, but I haven't had a chance to look at them yet. They feel like two big water balloons in my chest. He gave me instructions on what to do over these next few days…no shower, no getting face stuff wet, lots of rest, ice on face….

Karen thought I looked like Darth Vader, as my face was all covered in bandages and my eyes were swollen and a bit purple. She drove me home, and I went straight to bed. I was so tired. Throughout the entire day I couldn't stay asleep for much more than an hour, so I slept for an hour, and got up for an hour. My eyes continue to turn a deep, deep shade of purple and to swell, and at the moment they look far worse than they feel.

My first few days after surgery consisted of sleeping with a bag of frozen vegetables on my face, watching television, eating, and more sleeping. My nose throbbed horribly under the cast that was taped over the middle of my face, keeping everything in place. Every few hours I needed to change the piece of gauze that was taped under my nostrils, as the blood and goop that was draining out of it was pretty steady and unpleasant.

My breasts seemed ungodly huge, and caused me quite a bit of discomfort and distress. I couldn't sleep on my stomach; they were far too big and tender for that. I wore a vest that kept them strapped in place, although my arm and chest muscles were sore for those first few days.

A couple of days after surgery, Brian stopped over to the apartment to see how I was doing. I opened the door, and he immediately saw more than he had bargained for. His smile faded, and his eyes grew big and wide as he saw my proud new breasts protruding from under my sweatshirt.

After some brief, awkward small talk about how things were going and what was happening at work, Brian asked if HR had been aware of my plans for breast augmentation. I told him that I hadn't shared that information with anyone, as I really didn't know that it was anyone's business. He looked concerned. No, he looked angry!

"This isn't funny," he said. "This is gonna make things a hell of a lot more complicated."

He told me to avoid stopping by work, or even talking with anyone from work, until he had cleared it with HR and determined what to do. I told him that I would comply.

He called me later that night to tell me that he had talked with Lin from HR, and that if I failed to follow his order to stay away from work it would be grounds for termination.

I found that the hardest part of healing from the Rhinoplasty was getting used to breathing through my mouth. The nasal canal was packed tightly with gauze, and although that in and of itself wasn't really uncomfortable, having a completely plugged nose for a week, day and night, was not pleasant. I was counting the days until I could have my face back.

A week or so after the surgery, the nasal packing and splint was removed from my nose. Although it didn't really hurt, the feeling of the packing being removed was very odd. The nurse held my hand as the doctor pried them loose, and tears streamed down my face as he pulled them out. It felt like the bandages were endless, going almost up into my brain! Once it was over, it was a huge relief to be able to breathe again. As I studied my profile in the mirror, it really didn't seem all that different to me! Certainly, it was a little smaller. But it did not provide the dramatic difference that I had hoped for.

In contrast, my breasts were *huge*. They were 38D monsters! For the first few days they sloshed and gurgled, and I hoped the massive size was due to swelling. As they healed, though, I concluded that their size was due to the fact that they were just big.

For someone who has never experienced their own pair of breasts, this was like going from kindergarten to college grad, from training wheels to Lhamborghini, from bunny slope to Matterhorn, all in one drastic step. I never imagined, in my wildest dreams, the emotional and physical impact that they would have.

JOURNAL ENTRY

I decided to go for a run on the treadmill. It has been a few weeks, so I put on the sports bra and a t-shirt and a sweatshirt, and up the hair went into a ponytail, and I went for a jog. HOW THE HECK DO YOU HANDLE THESE BOOBS DURING A RUN???? It was a lost cause. Rather than running my usual pace, I ran real, real slow. I figure I'll have to work my way back, but learning how to handle the "bounce" will be difficult....

Now that I had my days to myself for a little while, one of the things that required immediate attention was my facial hair.

At the time I was transitioning, the only proven method for permanent hair removal was electrolysis, which involves killing the hair follicles one at a time. A typical male face contains upwards of 65,000 pores, so permanently clearing it is often a long, painful, expensive process.

Electrolysis is the bane of our existence for many transsexuals. I did not realize it at this point, but over the next 12 months I was to spend over 200 painful hours lying on a table as an electrologist peered at my pores through a large magnifying glass. She skillfully inserted a needle into each follicle…one at a time. She applied a current of electricity for several seconds to kill the follicle before pulling out the dead hair, by the root, with a pair of tweezers. The long-term result would, hopefully, be a smooth, hairless face. The short-term result, however, was a face that looked and felt like hamburger; swollen, red, scabby and raw.

Transsexuals are *strongly* urged to begin electrolysis as early as possible in their transition process. It is a time consuming, expensive, uncomfortable effort. If not, she will find herself in a very awkward position. On one hand she needs to shave her face closely to avoid growing a telltale beard, which would be a definite no-no in her new gender role. On the other she will need to grow her beard out in order to give the electrologist enough hair to work with.

As far as I was concerned a totally smooth, clear face before going full-time was non-negotiable. Unfortunately, there had been no room in Dave's life for the effort that would be needed to see this through. Little did I realize that my delay would mean that my life would soon become almost totally consumed by it: lying on a table with needles in my face for hours and days on end.

There would be a time a little later in my transition when a typical day often consisted of waking up at 3:45 a.m., driving halfway across Phoenix for my 3-hour 5:00 a.m. electrolysis appointment, putting in a full day at work, then driving back to the electrolysis clinic by 6:00 p.m. for another three hour appointment. By the time I got home, had dinner, and spent a little time recovering from the day, it was usually after eleven o'clock. Then I'd get up at 3:45 a.m. and do it all again. I'd often spend six or eight or more hours there on weekends. It was a very difficult schedule to maintain day after day, week after week.

Electrolysis hurts! Different parts of the face hurt more than others. I found that the closer the area was to the lips, the more sensitive the skin. The entire upper lip area was pure torture. I must admit that I ended up in tears several times…unable to finish my treatment.

Often, transsexuals use a topical anesthetic such as Emla cream to reduce the pain. Others even have a dentist inject an area with Novocain. Personally, I found it all to be more of a bother than it was worth. After a couple of sessions I decided that I could mentally manage the pain. Perhaps that's part the wrestler mentality in me.

Maria was an electrologist in Phoenix who had worked with the TS community there for over 15 years. She advertised her services in the TS support group newsletter, so one day during my convalescence from surgery I called her to get information. I asked questions about rates, types of treatments, etc. She asked me straight away if I was a transsexual, which took me a little by surprise, and I told her I was.

She asked if I had a date for going full-time. I told her it was to be in mid-April, only a few short weeks away. She explained that we'd have to get very busy very fast if we had any chance of be getting my face anywhere near being cleared by then. She emptied her schedule for me and booked up each and every day, for the following two weeks, with day-long sessions.

Maria's office was a half-hour from my apartment. The first time I met her, I remember that she did not fit the mental image I had formed in my head after talking to her on the phone. She was in her early 30s (although she seems to be much younger), a little over five feet tall, and had reams and reams of jet black, curly hair. She had glowing olive skin, very pretty, sympathetic eyes, and a warm, friendly, infectious smile. She always seemed to move in fast motion, whether it was walking, working, or talking. Her energy level seemed to be endless.

Maria is perhaps the single most important person who I met during my transition. She has an uncommon understanding and empathy of what it is that we, as transsexuals, face and endure. She has worked with many TS clients through the years, and readily offers valuable advice and feedback. During the countless hours that I lay on her table we talked and talked; about my past life; about my family situation; about my hopes and fears; about my transition. Besides having the hair on my face removed, our sessions turned out to be a very effective form of therapy for me. She eventually became an informal therapist, den-mother, advocate, advisor, and dear friend.

Maria really cares about transsexuals and what we endure to be ourselves. She was married, had three kids, worked at her husband's restaurant, had a house to run, but was somehow still able to meet me at 5:00 a.m. for my sunrise sessions, and sometimes all day on Saturdays or Sundays.

Sometimes, she sang to me as she worked. Other times, she'd turn on the early morning news in the background. Sometimes we talked. And sometimes, I dozed. Whisker after whisker. Pore after pore. Hour after hour.

Maria introduced me to other TS gals, who were to become my unofficial support group. All in all, Maria saved my life more than once. I cannot imagine anyone surviving a transition without at least one "Maria."

Although I struggled with the physical pain caused by my surgeries, and my anxiety over the upcoming transition at work, not to mention the intense electrolysis schedule, by far the most difficult issue I faced was being alone. My sudden separation from my entire previous life filled me with an incredible and indescribable emptiness.

For the previous 20 years I had been part of a family. I had been part of a *team*. I had been loved. There was always a reason to go home at the end of the day. There was always someone with whom I could share my happiness, or my sadness. All of that was suddenly gone, as though I had been whisked away to some parallel universe and placed on the outside of my old life, looking in.

I missed Elizabeth and Matt terribly. I knew that they were only a few miles away, but it may as well have been a few thousand miles, and that hurt deeply. I wondered what they were doing. I wondered how Elizabeth was holding up, wishing I could be there to hold her and comfort her. I wished for a miracle that would help her to understand the pressures that had launched me on this journey, and that she would somehow become an ally, instead of my most-loved adversary.

I did everything I could to keep my mind off my emptiness. I tried to be upbeat about my transition. I tried to keep myself as busy as I could. But my solitary confinement did not allow me to escape myself, and I often ended up in tears.

I wasn't eating, and lost ten pounds in the two weeks after my surgery. I wasn't sleeping well. The time I had planned to use to prepare to live as Donna was spent on Maria's table with needles in my face. As the days passed, the initial excitement and optimism for my transition faded, and I started to become very worried for myself.

Easter Sunday had always been a significant holiday for our family. Perhaps not so much because we were particularly religious, or that we were celebrating the religious significance of the day, as for the spiritual *rebirth* that it represented.

My favorite picture of Elizabeth as a young girl was taken on Easter. She was maybe five or six years old at the time. She was posed before church in a pretty light purple dress, with a matching purple hat, white gloves, and patent leather shoes. She held a little white purse in front of her, looking so grown up and adorable, as her pretty, soulful eyes seemed to reach out of the picture to grab me.

When Matt was young, we'd spend the night before Easter hiding candy and eggs around the house. Once he woke up we'd follow him around the house, sharing in his excitement as he searched high and low for the candy and small presents that the Easter Bunny had carelessly hidden so he could easily find them.

It had been just one Easter ago when Elizabeth exploded at me in front of Matt, which marked a huge turning point in our relationship and my struggle.

This year, it was Easter, and I was alone. It was dreary and cold outside… so cold, in fact, that some areas around Scottsdale actually saw snow. I was mentally and physically in pain. I was lonely; I was confused; and I spent the morning crying…feeling sorry for myself in my self-inflicted predicament.

Around noontime, Brian called. "Hey, whatchya doing?" he asked.

"Surviving," I replied, trying to sound as cheery as possible.

"You don't sound so good. Are you doing okay?"

"To tell you the truth, it has been a rough morning. But I think the worst is over and I'm feeling a little better."

"Do you have any plans for Easter dinner?" he asked.

"Nope. Just whatever I have in the fridge."

He paused for a moment. "Hey. How about if I pick up some barbecued chicken, salad and desert, and head over there for Easter lunch. I have plans later for Easter dinner, but I'd love to stop by for a little while if you want."

It only took a second to think about it. "Yes," I replied. "I think I'd like that."

He was at my apartment, bearing food and beer before the hour was over.

Over the previous few weeks, as I prepared for going full-time, Brian had done his best to understand. We had had some deep conversations, but in the end I'm not sure he was any closer to comprehending the power of the forces that were driving me. Despite my best attempts to help him understand, I still think he thought it was about the clothes.

That afternoon, as we snacked on chicken and drank beer, we had an in-depth, emotional chat. I did my best to verbalize my fears and my discomfort. I explained my loneliness, and my despair. I explained how difficult it was to go from a role in which I felt so secure and natural, but empty, to one in which I felt so insecure, vulnerable, clumsy and unprepared. For the first time, he seemed to *get it*, at least some of it. Perhaps it was because I looked and felt so pathetic. Perhaps he had had a sudden moment of clarity. I don't know. What I do know is that I will never forget the kindness that Brian showed to me that day, as his efforts rescued me from one of the lowest points in my life.

I had very little time to recover from my Easter doldrums. I knew that I needed to go out and spend some time getting comfortable as Donna, *alone*. I had planned to spend these entire two weeks doing this, but between recuperation and electrolysis, it was something I still hadn't been able to fit into my schedule. I felt it was critical to overcome this hurdle, both for my shaken confidence and my maturity. I understood that a bad experience could have a negative, potentially devastating effect, but I tried not to let my mind dwell on what could go wrong.

One morning I decided I wanted to spend a few hours walking through the mall. I took the day off from electrolysis so that my face would not be so chopped up for this important excursion. It may sound trivial, but I challenge any man reading this to dress up as a woman, and go to the mall to see the reaction. Be prepared to be taunted. Be prepared to have people point, look and stare. Be prepared to be the target of ridicule, and perhaps even outright hostility.

I planned it out. I carefully got ready, trying to look as plain as possible in desperate hopes of blending in. This seemed improbable, however, as I continued to grapple with my large breasts and the feeling that they automatically drew attention wherever I went. I planned to arrive at the mall shortly before it opened. I thought that this was the time when the fewest people would be there, so I had the least chance of getting harassed.

I got to the mall and parked near the door. I gathered my things together to go in for a short walk. I got ready to go in....

I couldn't do it. I could not get out of my car. I could not get my mind off of what could happen. I promised myself that I'd count to four, like a swimmer preparing to jump into icy water, and then just go. But when I got to four, there was no going.

After what seemed like an eternity, but was actually probably only ten minutes, I knew it was over. I knew I had been defeated by my fears. As I sat there, contemplating my defeat, I started shaking and crying. All the fear and frustration and disappointment welled up in me, and my crying became sobbing.

I started the car and drove home, absolutely devastated with my inability to do something so seemingly simple and harmless as walk through the mall. How could I ever hope to exist in the world as my true self if I couldn't do something so basic as show my face in public? I refused to consider a life hiding at home, shopping late at night to avoid the crowds, ordering pizza for fear of going to a restaurant. Such a life would be trading one prison for another, and neither was worth living for.

That evening, Karen and her husband Kevin wanted to take me out for something to eat in hopes of helping to shake my ever-growing feelings of despondence and despair. I accepted, more out of not wanting to be alone than for the opportunity to go out. At that point I had lost nearly fifteen pounds since the surgery, and my face was gaunt, gray and hollow.

Although nothing *bad* happened at dinner, my overall discomfort and inability to find solace is all that I remember. I begged them to meet me in the parking lot, as I didn't want to go into the restaurant alone. As we stood in the bar, waiting for a table, I was absolutely positive that everyone in the place was mocking me. All through dinner, I tried to express my feelings of hopelessness that I would ever be able to live the kind of life that I felt was my destiny. Somehow, death almost seemed to be a better alternative than the living hell I had crafted for myself.

The devastation of the day sent me into a tailspin from which I could not recover.

I sit here tonight more confused than I have ever been before. I've had a weekend which has made me question everything in my entire life, and nothing seems real right now.

The bottom line is that I probably LOOKED okay, but I felt more uncomfortable than ever. And I don't know if I'll EVER be comfortable....It really has me perplexed.

I talked to Elizabeth tonight. Her birthday is on Tuesday, and I wrote her a card and a poem. I miss her so much. And Matt. And the fear and pressure and doubt is pressing at me harder than ever before. Elizabeth wants me back. Only as Dave (of course). And in some ways I want to go back. We had a good cry together. I feel like calling up a surgeon, having the boobs taken out, and running home. But I'm not ready to do that. Yet.

We'll see if tomorrow brings a new frame of mind. Tonight I am a wreck, and can't wait to take a pill and get some sleep....

Be careful what you ask for because it might come true....

There is no way that anyone who has not endured an impending "transition" can begin to comprehend the pressures involved for those who are not mentally, physically, emotionally, and spiritually prepared. As I considered my sorry situation, it was obvious that I was not.

The pressures that I had placed on myself were incredible. They were suffocating. They had sapped every ounce of energy and hope and enthusiasm that I once had.

I had originally intended on a gradual transition to a new life as Donna, but the recommendation of the Specialist from San Francisco had been that the "big bang" approach is more effective for everyone involved. I was doing my best to accept and accommodate that. It was becoming obvious that I couldn't.

To top it all off, Brian had started feeling the pressures of my impending debut, as well. He began to feel the conflict between his obligations towards me as my friend, and his responsibilities to the other 30 people in our group as their manager. He suddenly realized that publicly supporting me could be guilt by association, and that his power, his influence and his position could be undermined. His support for me started to waver.

I don't know if it's that I hadn't planned well, or that my expectations were unrealistic. Maybe I had simply overwhelmed myself. What I do know is that it was a very dangerous time for me. My days were spent in pain, fear, frustration and loneliness. Each day the feelings got stronger and stronger. My emotional state was fragile at a time when it needed to be strong. I was scared at a time when I needed to be confident. Rather than looking forward to my upcoming transition, the though of it filled me with terror. By midweek, I was only a day away from the Specialist from San Francisco arriving to announce my situation to the world, and I was ready to die.

As the clock ticked down to the point of no return, and the week spiraled out of control, I did the only thing I could do to survive.

I pulled the plug.

Chapter Sixteen

I Caved.....

*"The greatest test of courage on earth is to bear defeat
without losing heart."*
— Robert Green Ingersoll

At the time, it really wasn't a difficult decision, just as needing to
finally address my gender issues was not all that difficult. Both were
life-sustaining imperatives, natural instincts of self-preservation. Once
I had made it, I didn't hesitate in making it actually happen. I got
busy making phone calls. It was all over in just a few minutes.

First, I called Brian at work. I told him that I needed him to call
everything off; that I was done. He sounded only mildly surprised and
asked if I was absolutely sure I knew what I was doing. I'm sure he had
sensed my desperation. I told him I that I had gotten to the end of my
rope and was sorry that I couldn't follow through on his "Once committed, stay committed," philosophy. He said he would call HR to
make the appropriate arrangements.

Physically. Mentally. Emotionally. Spiritually. I needed to become a boy again. I needed to pick up the pieces of the life I had left
behind, assuming there was any life there to go back to. I needed to
undo some extensive and expensive work that had brought me to
the brink of my transition.

I called the surgeon to see if he could take out the breast implants. He sounded relieved with my change of heart, said he could fit me in at the end of the week, and that he would not charge me for the procedure. He warned that I would be pretty sore and tender for a few days, but that I should be healed enough to go back to work on Monday.

I called my beauty salon to arrange for the hair extensions to be removed, my hair cut, and my acrylic nails soaked off.

Once all the details had been arranged, I called home to tell Elizabeth.

As usual, she didn't answer. She was screening her calls. I asked her to pick up the phone because I wanted to come home. She picked up the receiver.

I told her it was over. I told her that I couldn't continue. All I wanted right then was to hold her and hug her and cry with her over all the pain we had both endured over the past few days and weeks and months. I told her I wanted to come home. She sounded thrilled, but was also cautious.

"Are you *sure* you're doing this for the right reasons?" she asked. "I don't want you to have *any* doubt. I don't want you or me or Matt to have to face this mess again, so if you need more time take it."

I assured her I had figured out that I could not envision a life without her and Matt in it, no matter what my gender. And I assured her I had completed my self-discovery.

JOURNAL ENTRY

I caved. I put a stop to everything. I called Brian and told him to cancel all the meetings for Thursday. I suggested they cancel the lady from San Fran. I went and had all the extensions taken out of the hair, and had it colored back to near its original color. I have the nails taken off today, and the boobs come out tomorrow (no fee). I just can't do it. I'm done.

The pressure and the awkwardness and the discomfort and the unhappiness are not things that I will deal with for the rest of my life. I have learned alot about myself in these past two weeks, and am just glad I had some time and space (and money) to be able to do some serious soul searching. I'm not regretting any of this for a single minute...

I have the de-boobendectomy tomorrow. Elizabeth is driving me to surgery. The surgeon is doing it for free. I think I'll be back in my house by the weekend, but we'll see how things go. No hurry.

I'm comfortable with myself and my decisions. I think jumping in feet first into deep waters and trying to swim has shown me things I could not have learned any other way, and I'm glad to get out of the pool before drowning.

She didn't know whether to laugh with joy, or cry from relief. I felt the same way. She invited me back with open arms.

email from: Elizabeth
Subject: *THERE IS A GOD! (in response to my phone call saying I am coming home)*

Honners,

I have been carrying the weight of the world on my shoulders for what seems like forever, and after our talk tonight, I feel like that weight has been removed. I sure hope you feel the same relief, comfort and joy that I do! I will just hang in there a few more days to see if it's too good to be true, or if it is a reality! I just hope you have given yourself enough time to satisfy the questions in your head, and to come full circle with complete peace of mind so you won't EVER have to deal with this again!!!! You deserve to live a completely

HAPPY life! (IS there such a thing?!?!?) I don't want to go out shopping with you and have you looking at certain stores, and have it start all over again! You NEED to be SURE it is DONE, and your questions are over! I don't want you to ever have ANY doubts. You NEED to be sure NOW that it will be gone....FOREVER, never to haunt us again!

I told Matt tonight that you have worked through your problems and that you are coming home for GOOD! He was soooo, soooo happy, and jumped up and down and said "Yaaaaaaaaaaaahhhhhhh"! He loves you and needs you as much as I do, and I know you need us in your life to make your life complete! I told Matt the three of us belong together and we deserve to be HAPPY! I told him to say his prayers and thank God for the loving parents he has....and I told him that our family is what is most important in life! I also told him that he has been blessed with great parents, and a very strong, brave, loving, hard working father. We just can't wait to have you home for good.......I will hug you and love you more than ever, and I may never let you go! It was so hard for me to let you go for the past three weeks..... especially not knowing what would happen in the end. I guess all of our prayers were answered.....we belong together and we WILL be together, the way it is supposed to be! Matt seemed so relieved to have us talking to each other! He made me laugh because he said......"This morning you were crying because you were sad and mad at Dad, and tonight you are crying because you are happy and can't wait to see Dad! I just don't get it!"

We have sooooooo much to catch up on...so much to share. I will NEVER forget getting that dreaded letter in the mail over a year ago, when this whole mess began for us...and I will never forget this phone call telling me you were coming home as Dave....to STAY! Now I just can't wait to embrace you and play catch up with our lives...TOGETHER!

As I have told you all along, I love you more than life itself. As you and I have both found out, (the hard way) life just isn't the same without us being TOGETHER!

Well, my eyes are swollen shut from all the tears I've shed. I'm looking forward to going to bed tonight with a smile on my face...instead of crying myself to sleep.

Whether the decision was rash or not, good or bad, right or wrong...I felt as though the world had been lifted from my shoulders, too.

In the days that followed I had my breasts removed, leaving red, angry jagged scars to mark their short participation in this sad circus. I had all my hair cut off, leaving me with a very short men's haircut. I had my acrylic nails removed. And I moved back into my house.

For my part, I felt an incredible array of mixed emotions. In fact, I was flooded by emotions for days and days. After being under so much pressure over the past several months, stepping back into *safety* was a huge relief. But in the weeks that followed, the sorrow at losing my boobies...after feeling so much pride in them for so long, would consume me.

The following Monday was to have been Donna's first day at work. Instead, Dave returned after three weeks off. I was still very tender and sore from my surgery ordeal, with bandages on my fresh sutures and the breast drains still collecting bloody fluid under my baggy shirt.

There were no comments that my hair was suddenly much shorter, and appeared much darker, than when I left. Or that my nose was somehow different. Or that I had lost a noticeable amount of weight. Rather, people seemed happy to see me and welcomed me back, oblivious to the life-or-death odyssey that had just occurred.

As a guy, I had never been a good loser. I think that's one of the things that made me successful as an athlete, as a student, and even as a consultant. I remember a saying on a T-Shirt: SECOND PLACE IS JUST

THE FIRST LOSER. This was a mentality that I could easily understand, and even identify with, as it is the mindset we teach our sons from an early age. I consider myself to be an over-achiever, and I feel a strong need to not only succeed, but to excel, in the things I do.

My capitulation to the pressures I was facing was a crushing defeat for me. I had never experienced anything like it. Trying to understand what had happened and how to deal with it consumed me for weeks. The calm that I felt in having all the pressure removed was punctuated by this dull ache of failure that continued to gnaw at me.

email from: Dr. Sheila Dickson

Hi, Donna,

I do not see you as having chickened out. I see you as having gone as far as YOU could go. You had to stop at the point where it was necessary for others to come with you. Brian stepped aside and it doesn't sound like the Specialist from San Francisco was able to help the situation. Keep the trapeze in mind: you can't fly from one to another if there's no team to catch and throw for you. Think of this as a valuable lesson for your son: there is strength, intelligence and consideration for others in not committing suicide, and that is metaphorically speaking what it would have been—your trying to do it all by yourself, especially in a physically weakened condition.

Maybe this picture will help: you climbed up to the high dive, walked to the end of the board, bounced, lifted your arms, bent your knees and on looking down at your target, saw there was no water in the pool. So you stepped back, climbed down, and will practice until the time that there is sufficient water.

Be gentle with yourself. S

In the weeks that followed, I knew that I needed some time to recover from all that had happened. I distanced myself from everything that was somehow connected to Donna. I stopped taking hormones. I stopped going for electrolysis. I broke contact with all of my TS friends. I needed some down time to recover.

Maria did see me briefly, however. I will never forget the look on her face when she saw Dave come into her office. It was as if she was watching a ghost walk through her door. Her mouth was open, her eyes huge and unbelieving, and her hands were on both sides of her head. It was as if seeing me as a guy for the first time would cause her head to explode. She kept saying "Oh my God. Oh my God. Oh my God...." and staring at me.

My *time out* would not last long.

I moved back into the house, and even back into our bedroom. Very little was discussed about what had happened. It was almost as if any discussion of it might cause one or both of us to reconsider things. Perhaps it was all better left alone for the moment.

Elizabeth wasted no time in reclaiming her husband. She took immediate steps to rid us of Donna's household, as if retaining any part of Donna's life provided a continued threat of re-infection. She began ransacking my apartment to return all the items that I had bought.

At first I watched helplessly as Donna's belongings were returned or given away, one by one. It only took a short time for me to become defensive, and then angry about what was happening. These were not her belongings! She was returning things that weren't hers! I started to argue about what was happening, which suddenly raised suspicions in Elizabeth's mind about whether this was really over yet or not.

I had tried to explain to her that being transsexual is something that doesn't go away. It doesn't heal. There is no cure. It is part of who I am. I tried to explain that part of the reason things had gotten so desperate was because I had had no outlet for expression of Donna, and going forward we needed to discuss and address that. Things could not go back to the way they were, because this could not be an all or nothing situation. Donna needed some space in this world, and I would do what I had to do to make sure she got it. The fact that I had returned from the brink of a full-time life as Donna did not mean that I could live a life without her in it at all.

The most significant source of contention was my apartment. Elizabeth wanted me to cancel the lease. Because of all the penalties that would be involved if I broke the lease, the money was lost whether I cancelled it or not. I could not see the need to hurry, or perhaps I just didn't want to give it up.

In an odd way, the apartment came to symbolize Donna. Elizabeth wanted it gone completely, while I wouldn't and couldn't let it go. Before long this issue became a splinter in our joyous honeymoon period. Perhaps I still felt I had issues to resolve, and wanted to keep it handy as a safe haven, just in case it was needed. I quickly got the sinking feeling that this splinter would soon become an infected, open wound.

THE JOURNEY

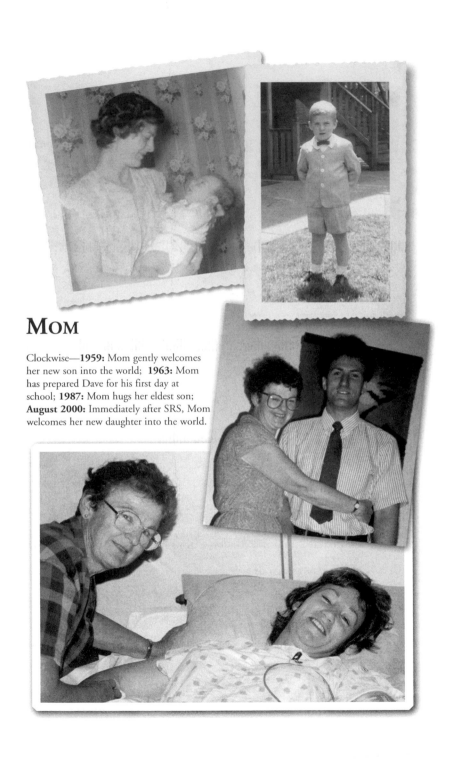

MOM

Clockwise—**1959:** Mom gently welcomes her new son into the world; **1963:** Mom has prepared Dave for his first day at school; **1987:** Mom hugs her eldest son; **August 2000:** Immediately after SRS, Mom welcomes her new daughter into the world.

DAD

Clockwise—**1959:** Dad roughhouses with his baby son; **1989:** Dad visits our house; **1997:** Before dad started getting too sick...; **February 2000:** At Mirror Lake in Yosemite, after bringing Dad to a final resting spot.

Sis

Clockwise—**1964:** Jude adoring her big brother, Dave; **1979:** Jude graduates from high school with Dave there to congratulate her; **August 2000:** Jude visits her new sister in the hospital shortly after SRS.

BRO

Clockwise—**1962:** Dave welcomes his little brother; **1984:** Just brothers; **2000:** Jay welcomes his big sister.

FAMILY

Clockwise—**1963:** The three kids ; **1967:** Mom's favorite picture of her young children; **1977:** A rare family portrait. Dave was a high school Senior; **1975:** Dave wore his hair long in high school.

SIBLINGS
(1979)

Below—**1992:** Jude stands between her two brothers.

Above—**Christmas 2002:** Jay stands between his two sisters.

July 5, 1980

This doesn't really look like me does it — little nose, cute little chin green eyes. But if this innocent little happy knew that he would be so in love with you he would be smiling so big you couldn't fit it in the picture. If love brings happiness, then you've already brought me a lifetime full. I love you Dave

BUFF

Just before I got married, I was in perhaps the best overall shape of my entire life. Love gave me a motivation for living like I had never known. I gave this 4th grade photo to my soon-to-be-bride, personalized with a heartfelt message on the back.

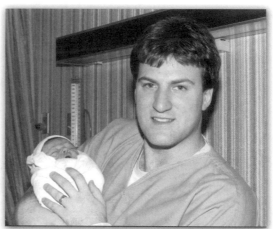

SON

1985: The day my son was born remains one of the happiest days of my life. As my son grew, we developed the special father/son bond I had always dreamed of having. It was strained to the breaking point by my transition, as we had little or no contact for nearly seven months.

Left —**July 2000:** Slowly but
surely, my son came to accept
Donna in his life. By July of
2000, when this portrait was
taken, we had reconciled to a
point where our bond actually
seemed to have been strengthened
by our separation.

FIRSTS

Left—**January 1999:** My first support group meeting was the first time Donna ventured out into the world. Prior to any surgeries, this is the very first version of Donna.

Right—**February 1999:** My daylong visit to the mall with Julie marked the first time that Donna was actually seen in public.

Above—**August 1999:** A month after my FFS, Donna went to visit her family for the first time.

Left—**October 1999:** My first day at work as Donna was a mixture of pure joy and sheer terror.

Below—**August 2000**: The first post-op picture of Donna immediately after SRS.

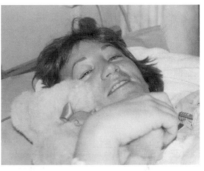

Left—**August 2001:** At the San Francisco Ren Faire.

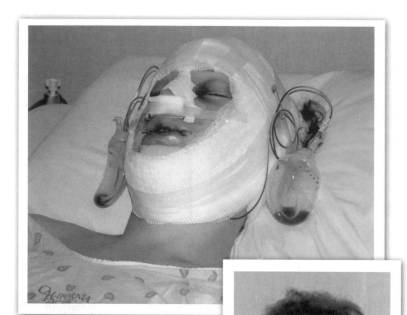

SURGERY

Clockwise- **July 1999:** The fresh trauma of Facial Feminization Surgery (FFS) leaves a patient looking and feeling as though a train hit her; **July 1999:** A week later, as the bandages are removed, much of the swelling has gone down; **February 2000:** My Forehead Revision procedure was more substantial than I anticipated.

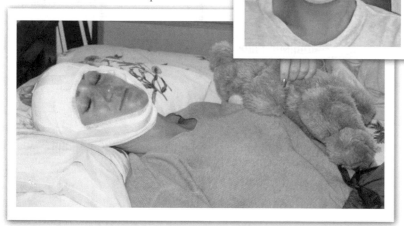

Left- **February 2000:** Once the bandages were removed, I displayed the stitches from my forehead surgery—just before my eyes got swollen to the point of not being able to open them.

Right- **August 2000:** Recovering from Sex Reassignment Surgery (SRS) involved being confined to bed for six days following surgery. Some of my bedside companions were a teddy bear, a pink topiary, and a box of pink bubble-gum "It's A Girl!" cigars.

MOVING ON

All I wanted out of my transition was to be able to live my life in peace, allowing what the world sees on the outside to reflect who I knew myself to be on the inside. I wanted to be able to blend seamlessly and comfortably into society—just like everyone else.

The top picture is *plain* Donna. No makeup. No adornment. It's how I look after getting out of bed and taking a round brush to my hair. I show it to demonstrate that it's not hair, or clothes, or wigs, or makeup that make a person. It's heart.

Part III

Resurrection

CHAPTER SEVENTEEN

ABORTED HONEYMOON

As for acceptance from you, or anyone else for that matter....that is not my ultimate goal. My life will continue with or without it. My ultimate goal is acceptance within myself. If others can accept that...I'm happy. If not, then in my mind it is more a reflection on them than it is on me. If you do end up "writing me off," then in my mind you become as big a hypocrite as I feel most people are; full of rosy words and wonderful concepts about being yourself and spirituality and freedom. But when push comes to shove the true colors come out. It becomes, "Conform or else!" or "Be what I want you to be!" And the realization will be right there...plain as day...that instead of being a Neil Young, you're a Backstreet Boy."

— EMAIL TO MY BROTHER-IN-LAW

I call them purges. Transsexuals or cross-dressers occasionally purge themselves of all their female belongings, vowing never to indulge again like a teenager recovering from a painful hangover. Often, this newfound resolve is very strong at first, but eventually it weakens to the point where it eventually becomes a mere memory, until the next binge-induced purge.

This can become an expensive proposition for some. Expensive gowns. Shoes. Makeup. Jewelry. They do everything they can to rid themselves of this unwanted and intruding segment of their lives, and throwing out all of their female finery symbolically represents turning their back on their whole female self.

During her years in working with the gender community, Maria has seen it happen countless times. She has seen husbands run back to their wives. She has seen transsexuals flee the pressures of their female existence for the relative safety of their old male lives. Once the pressures are off, things are happy and relaxed. She refers to this time as the honeymoon period. As with any honeymoon, it rarely lasts.

Maria wished me a happy honeymoon, but realistically predicted that my honeymoon would last for six months...tops. Sadly, it didn't even last for six weeks.

As I recovered, physically, spiritually and emotionally, from my nearly disastrous transition experience, I started to realize that nothing had changed in me. I had not proven that I was meant to live my life as a man any more than I had proven that I was **not** meant to live as a woman. I gradually realized that I had buckled under pressures that I had put on myself in my misguided attempt to live up to the mental image that I had formed of the woman I expected to be. I had tried to manage my transition based on what was convenient for my employer, and not based on my own needs. And, I was playing it far too safe, hoping to maintain some semblance of my male life just in case I needed to flee back there, as I had just done.

This gradual realization caused me a tremendous amount of concern and confusion. Where was my life heading? What could I do now?

JOURNAL ENTRY

> I started crying this afternoon. I couldn't help it. For some reason, the enormity of what I had done kinda snuck up on me, and all of the sudden it felt like an elephant on my heart.

I'm getting more and more confused as time goes on. Not just about Donna. About EVERYTHING in my life. I'm questioning whether I even want to be married right now. I don't think I still want to be her husband anymore. I want to be a dad for my son. I want to live in my house. I want to be Donna. I want to be together with her SOMETIMES. I want to follow-through with some of the plans we've built for the future. But I don't want to be a husband anymore.

I'm very disappointed at having gotten so close to my transition, and not being able to follow it through. I see my wife's tactics (then and now) as basically emotional blackmail, and it makes me angry more than anything else.

After six weeks back home I had confirmed to myself that I really hadn't done what I had set out to do. I had turned back on the path of self-discovery too early. I felt outside pressures, which influenced the decisions I needed to make about me and about my life. I realized that it wasn't that *what* I was doing was wrong…it was *how* I was doing it that was flawed. Looking back on everything that happened, it was obvious that I had gone into this unprepared, uninformed, and naïve. The result was a dangerous mixture that was doomed for failure from the very beginning.

I hadn't told my family. I hadn't told my son. I allowed others to manage my transition at work, and it had become apparent that the *Big Bang* just wouldn't work for me. The cumulative weight of these compromises, miscalculations, and stupid decisions was more than my transition could bear.

I wrote to Brian to let him know what was happening.

email to Brian

Brian:

I've been thinking a lot about my aborted transition attempt lately, and realized that I never really had an opportunity to thank you for all your efforts on my behalf. Once all the pressure was off, everything kind of slipped back into the groove, and we never had a chance to talk about it. Sometimes life's currents tend to sweep you along, and it's just something I need to do before the current picks me up again.

Your friendship and humanity towards me during my most difficult of times have, in a very real way, renewed my faith in humankind. You are the first "friend" that I told about my situation, and that experience in and of itself was one of the most difficult things I have ever done. But your reaction, and your continued support and friendship, were truly forces that helped me to survive.

Your gestures helped me more than you will ever know, and there is no way on earth I could thank you enough. I will never forget them.

My life continues to reel with turmoil and confusion. Make no mistake…the things that drove me to the brink of my transition have not gone away. They have not magically disappeared. I would have gone through with it if I could, but in the end I just wasn't ready. My inability to follow through fills me with deep disappointment and I constantly think back to things I could have done differently. Everything was in place, and everything seemed perfect. You were supportive. HR was supportive. Our group is full of fantastic people. I had been able to move out of my house. I couldn't have asked for anything more.

But no one will ever be able to comprehend the pressures I had placed upon myself, and in the end I could not handle them all. I was overwhelmed by the demands of my change in lifestyle, by the isolation of being alone, by the terrible sadness of leaving my home and my family and everything I had known, by my inability to work, by the immobilizing fear of how my friends and family and co-workers will react to me. I didn't do what I did because I wanted to, as it is a path I think no one would choose unless it was a last recourse. I did it because I felt compelled to do it in order to live the rest of my life in peace. Inner peace is something I have not known for a long, long time, and I fear I will die before ever knowing it again. And that thought fills me with sadness.

If and when I attempt this again, I will not make the same mistakes.

In many ways, I am a different person now than I was before this experience. My life will never be the same. Relationships with those who have been closest to me (i.e. Elizabeth) have been strained to a point where I fear they will break. Relationships with others who know about my situation (i.e. you, my sister, Karen) have been strengthened. I have no idea what to expect in the future, but I see change in the wind....

Do not think I have given up on Donna. Her spirit is as alive and as active inside of me as it ever has been. And in some way, shape or form, it will come out. The struggle to bottle it up for so many years has taken too much out of me, and I have neither the strength nor the willpower to try to do it any longer. It's finding a way to do it that fits in the parameters of my life that is difficult, but what will be will be. Donna is me. I am Donna. And in a perfect world, that would be enough. To be accepted for who and what you are without judgment and without question. But this world is far from perfect, as am I, so I'll just have to accept that and do the best I can.

Brian stopped by my cube one afternoon shortly afterwards, and said that the email didn't really surprise him. The Specialist from San Francisco had indicated that, although the previous chapter may have been closed, this book was far from over. He suggested that I talk with Lin in HR. I told him that I had already made the appointment.

> I had my meeting with Lin in HR at 10:30. The gist of our conversation is that this "drive" doesn't go away, and although I am very disappointed that things didn't work last time, in the end I just wasn't ready, but it will happen again. I talked about the things that I felt went wrong last time, and all the things I've done, and plan to do, to ensure that doesn't happen again. She said she expected that we'd have this talk eventually, and it was fine by her. She just wanted to make sure I was getting the support I need, and I told her actually, except for at home, I was.

Now, it was time to set things right…

How does a father tell his son that he is really a woman? What kind of a reaction should he expect? Why should it be so hard? Those questions had paralyzed me during my previous attempt to transition. This time, I had no hesitation in telling him. The only question was how.

I had discussed it with my psychologist, who felt that kids are far more aware and accepting than we give them credit for. She said that I needed to have faith in our relationship, in our bond, and in our love. I told her that's how I tried to approach this when I first told Elizabeth, and look where that got me.

I had hoped that Elizabeth and I could tell him together, but that was obviously my own fantasy. I had come to the conclusion that he could either learn the truth from me, with compassion and love, or, he could learn from Elizabeth, out of anger and bitterness. Either way, it wouldn't change the plans I was making, or the decisions that needed to be made.

At the time, Matt was taking Tae Kwan Do lessons. The drive from our house to the studio usually took about a half hour. It was during these drives that I started, little by little, to set the stage.

One day, as we drove, I asked if he wanted to know why things had been so unhappy in our house lately. Why mom and I couldn't stand to be in the same room, why mom had wanted to divorce me? What she meant when she said that my family was all fucked up? I asked him if he wanted to know the big secret that we had been hiding.

"Yes, of course," he said, suddenly interested.

I told him that before I could actually tell him, I needed to explain a few things.

He was curious, and eager to listen.

I asked him whether he felt that people who were born with birth defects really *wanted* to be that way. If someone was born blind or deaf, or had a hole in their heart, or was mentally retarded…was that their fault?

He said, "No. Of course not."

I explained that the things that caused those birth defects happened while the baby was developing inside the mommy.

"There are many things that can go wrong while a baby is being made," I explained, "some of which you can see as soon as the baby is born, and some that you can't see until the child gets older. "

On a subsequent drive, we talked about boys and girls, and what actually makes a boy a boy, and a girl a girl. Are you a boy because you have a penis, or because you *feel* like a boy? Did you ever think that maybe it was both? What happens if a person has a birth defect where they have a penis, but they don't feel like a boy? Is that their fault?

He said, "Of course not."

Just because a person wears a dress, or has long hair, or likes the color pink, does that make them a girl?

"Of course not."

I explained that being a boy or a girl was partly based on your body, but also based on your brain. Some girls like boy things, and some boys like girl things. That doesn't mean that they want to be the other sex, it's just the way they are. But, there was a birth defect where a person's body could develop into a boy, but their brain felt that it should be a girl.

Here we were. We were on the brink. It was time to push us over the edge.

I told him that *that* was my problem. I had been born with that birth defect. I was born with the body of a boy, but I didn't feel like a boy. I had tried my best to be a boy, but it just wasn't working for me. I needed to figure out if I could be a girl, and the only way to do that was to try to live like a girl and see how that feels.

He thought about it for a few seconds, and said words that I will never forget as long as I live. "Does this mean that you're going to have your *schlong* cut off?" he asked.

I told him I really didn't know.

I told him that his mom did not think it was a birth defect. I told him that she felt it was sick, and wrong. I told him that she felt I was choosing to do this, and would try to make him think that I was selfish. I told him that, no matter what, I loved him and wanted to be with him and hoped he could understand.

"Are you going to get divorced?" he asked.

I told him I didn't know. I told him that I still loved his mother, and that she still loved me, but that it was a possibility. I told him that she wanted me to fight the birth defect, but that I couldn't fight it any longer. I told him that she would say things about me that might or might not be true because she was angry, so if he had any question to feel free to ask me *anything*.

We talked about treatment for people who have this birth defect, and some of the things I was planning to do. I asked him if he thought he would have a problem with any of it.

"I don't really care," he said.

We drove silently for a few minutes. I could tell Matt was thinking.

"I think you'll make an ugly girl."

I smiled. I had a picture, and asked if he wanted to see it. I watched his eyes as he studied it, looking for some reaction. He really didn't have one. Then he asked another historic question.

"Where did you get those boobs?" he asked.

Of course, Elizabeth was absolutely furious that I had disobeyed her order that Matt not know about my problem. At that point, there was nothing she could really do about it.

After yelling at me for a while, she immediately went to quiz him....

JOURNAL ENTRY

> Sometimes things happen in this whole mess that really catch me by surprise. They are truly defining moments, and today was one of those times.
>
> Apparently, after Elizabeth and I had our little "chat," she ran right off to interrogate Matt. Based on what I've heard so far, the conversation went something like this....
>
> Elizabeth: So, I understand dad told you all about his "problem."
>
> Matt: Yep.
>
> Elizabeth: It's really sick, don't you think?
>
> Matt: No, not really.
>
> Elizabeth: What do you mean no? It's really pretty sick.
>
> Matt: No it's not. It's not his fault. It's the way he was born. Kinda like when I talk too fast. I was just born that way. I don't want to do it, but I can't help it, and he can't help it either.
>
> Elizabeth: I heard he showed you a picture.
>
> Matt: Yep.
>
> Elizabeth: I'll bet he looked ridiculous.
>
> Matt: No, not really.

His support would not last.

Telling Matt, and his apparent acceptance, was another incredible burden off of my shoulders. Over the next couple of weeks, I started to make transition arrangements again. I felt invigorated, as if suddenly finding a new sense of purpose. This time, I was not in a hurry. However long it took to get ready, that's how long I was ready to wait.

The timing of my next assault on the gender barrier would be centered on an appointment to see Dr. O.

The doctor had recommended quite an extensive laundry list of procedures to enhance my feminine appearance. Since the money that my dad had left me was enough to cover the entire battery of surgeries, I decided to book them all at once. I called the doctor's office, and earliest date I could get was July 21st, which was four weeks away. I immediately sent them the money to reserve the spot.

The schedule we discussed included a full week of recuperation at the hospital in San Francisco after the surgery. I would be released from the hospital the following Friday, and fly home to Phoenix.

I immediately met with Lin to tell her about the arrangements.

During our meeting we negotiated dates. I wanted the company to tell everyone at work about my transition while I was still in San Francisco, but I did not want to begin living full-time as Donna until a couple of months afterwards. I wanted that time to do the things I did not have the time to do last time such as finishing electrolysis and spending time becoming comfortable as Donna. Since everyone would be aware of what was happening, I would not have to hide all the visible changes that would become apparent as soon as I returned from the surgery.

By the end of the meeting, the plan was all set. They would tell everyone about my transition that Friday, before I returned from my surgery. I would continue to appear at work as Dave, and my private time as Donna, for eight weeks until the beginning of October. October 4, would be my first day at work as Donna.

It was show time. Again.

I spent quite a bit of time and energy thinking about what had gone wrong in my previous transition attempt. Perhaps it is my project management background, where we often do a lessons learned process after each project to assess the things that went right so that we can do them again, and the things that went wrong so that we can fix them for next time.

One of the main things that had become obvious was the difficulty I had in making good decisions. I had no guide to work from. I had no experience to help me decide what to do. I found that I often felt paralyzed by indecision, and that bothered me. My first attempt to walk in the mall alone was a perfect example.

As a result, I decided that I needed a guide. I needed a set of rules. I thought back to the Hebrews who wandered aimlessly in the desert until Moses found the Commandments that would help them to give their lives the direction and the structure they needed to live as a society. I needed something similar. I needed my own commandments.

I drafted a series of rules that I felt would have helped me during my first transition attempt. I thought about it for quite a while, and after considerable rewriting and refining, I developed my five rules to successful self-discovery:

My Rules

Rule 1. Do not allow fear to dictate your life. If you want to do something, do it. If not, don't. Do not base that decision on fear alone.

Rule 2. Manage your expectations. Besides fear, the most destructive emotion is disappointment. Disappointment is based on our own pre-defined expectations of things, and not on actual outcomes. Our level of satisfaction or disappointment is based on how the results measure up to our expectations, and not on the merits of the outcomes themselves. By carefully keeping my expectations low and realistic, I could minimize any feelings of disappointment.

Rule 3. Live with dignity. Dignity is a core concept in my life. I needed to make sure that it is reflected in the decisions I make, and in the life that I build. Even when things are going to hell in a hand basket, maintaining a sense of dignity is key, and something I would not allow to be taken from me by anyone or anything. Dignity is non-negotiable.

Rule 4. Be honest with yourself and with others. Hiding my situation and disguising my intentions had gotten me into trouble. A major part of the self-acceptance process is honesty. A person cannot be honest with others until they are painfully honest to themselves. I vowed to strive to do both.

Rule 5. Experience Everything! I truly felt that I was embarking on a new life. I did not it want to be saddled or restricted by the decisions that Dave had made during his reign in this body. Life can be a very sensual feast for those willing to experience it, and I wanted to ensure that Donna made her own decisions. This was true with the foods I ate, with the types of movies I liked…all the way to my decisions about sexuality. The only way to know is to try.

Perhaps the most important attribute, the glue that keeps all of this together, is discipline. If I could keep my discipline, maintain my focus, keep a cool head, put myself in situations where I would not feel overwhelmed, and follow my rules, I felt I would have a good chance to be successful. Of course, thinking that is one thing; actually putting it into practice is another.

Elizabeth and I had made arrangements to go back to upstate New York over the Fourth of July holiday. We had lived there for 15 years, and I still considered it home in many ways. Both our families still lived there.

This trip made me a little nervous for a lot of reasons.

First, it would be my first trip home after my dad's death. I did not know how that would affect me.

Also, I knew that I looked different. My mom hadn't mentioned anything during my visits to Dallas, so I hoped that the change would be too subtle to need explanation. I also knew that the effects of the hormones on my face and on my body had been dramatic, especially for people who had not seen me in a while.

The afternoon before we planned to leave I stopped by the bank to get some money for our trip. I wanted to withdraw a couple of hundred dollars from our saving account for our spending money.

Imagine my surprise when the teller told me that I could not withdraw the money, as the account had been closed. Our joint savings account had been closed! The account that held *all* of our money…including the money that my dad left to me and in only three weeks would be paying for my new face…was gone. I asked the teller if she was sure, and she double-checked and said that Elizabeth had closed it at the end of April.

As I left the bank, I was livid. I was madder than I can remember being at any time before or since, and I rushed home to confront my wife.

She was in the backyard cleaning the pool when I got there, and I immediately started yelling at her.

"How the HELL could you do this? You took all of our money, all of the money that *my* dad left *me*, and you felt free to *steal* it all for yourself?" I yelled.

She denied doing it. "I moved the money into an account with a higher interest rate," she explained. "I told you about it months ago."

"BULLSHIT! How come you never asked me to sign a signature card? How come I have to learn about it by going to the bank and having them tell me our account is closed? How come my name isn't even on the God-Damn account?" I ranted.

"Where the hell do you get off stealing all of our money?" I continued. "Just who the hell do you think you are? If you're looking for World War III, then you got it!"

"You are so wrong," she sobbed. "You sound like a lunatic!"

"Who the hell is a lunatic here?" I countered. "The money my dad left me is my money! *My* money! Not *yours*! Not even *ours*!"

She offered to write me a check for the entire amount that my dad had left me, and to put my name on the account. I made her do it right then and there.

We put on a pretty good *happy* face for our friends and family. Nobody would know that we were absolutely devastated, and that our marriage and our lives were hanging by a thread. We had gotten far too good at giving the outward appearance of marital bliss despite all the inner upheaval we were both feeling.

The highlight of my trip was finally disclosing my situation to my mom.

The thing I felt most awkward about was timing. Between my dad dying, and my sister having a baby with birth defects, our family had been through some very difficult things over the previous several months. If it's true that bad things happen in threes, then my little revelation would just be icing on the cake.

I think that, no matter how well we think we know our parents who can say for sure what their reaction to news like this will be? I have known gals whose parents have completely disowned them as a result of this news. Although I did not expect outright and total rejection, I did not expect the news to be greeted with welcome arms, either. That left a whole lot of room in between.

My sister knew about my plans to disclose my situation to Mom, and was ready to do damage control. "If she does go off the deep end, I'll do my best to help her get back to shore." That reassured me, and as the day that I planned to tell her arrived I felt as ready as I would ever be.

I had arranged for the two of us to go out to breakfast on Saturday morning. We sat down, ordered, and started to chat. She could tell that I had something important to talk about. I had dropped subtle hints that we needed to have a talk for several weeks, and I'm sure she was curious about what I had to say. I wasted very little time before I started right in.

I spent a half hour doing my best to explain. I talked about the difference in physical gender and mental gender. I explained what happens when there is incongruence. I explained about treatment options and my plans for the future. I explained my feelings since early childhood. Somehow, I think I got it all out.

She listened carefully, mumbling an occasional "Uh-huh" from time to time. I scanned her face for reaction as I talked, but was both relieved and concerned that I really didn't notice one.

Once I had finished, I asked her if she understood what I was trying to tell her.

She thought for a second, and then replied. "Are you telling me that you're gay?"

"No!" I said. I explained that this had *nothing* to do with sexuality. So I tried again, using a more in-depth explanation. When I was done, I asked her is she understood.

She replied, "So are you telling me that you are bisexual?"

With that, I knew that I could not give her all the information she would need to comprehend my situation.. Perhaps her generation sees these things through a sexuality-tinted lens. Luckily, I had brought a copy of *True Selves* with me so I gave it to her. I asked her to read it, and perhaps then she would understand. I assured her that she'd have questions, and I told her to feel free to ask me anything.

As we sipped our coffee, I could see that my mom's mind was churning.

"What are you thinking about?" I asked.

"I'm just searching for clues that I might have missed that should have indicated this to me a long time ago," she replied.

"I doubt you'll find any," I told her. "I was very good at being a guy, and there were very few chinks in my armor. Elizabeth didn't know. Judy didn't know. And although I can tell you a few times where things happened that were related to this, if you didn't know the entire story you 'd never be able to put two and two together."

We sat a few more minutes.

I spoke. 'It's not your fault, you know. It's nothing that you did, or didn't do. It's the way I was born."

She was silent.

"I looked for reasons for years and years, racking my brain why this should happen to me. I am comfortable now not needing to find the reason or the cause. I just know that it is, and I'll deal with it."

As we left breakfast that morning, I knew she would be okay. I was relieved that another burden had been removed from my shoulders. I knew that, despite my awkward attempts to explain, that she would eventually understand. Granted, it was not easy, and it took a bit of time, but I felt incredibly proud.

Near the end of our trip, Elizabeth and I spent an afternoon hiking in Green Lakes State Park. It is a nearly round, deeply wooded, lake located near Syracuse. The defining feature is the distinctive vibrant deep green color of the lake.

We went there together on this July afternoon to walk around the lake and talk. It was the first time we had talked *to* each other and not *at* each other in a long time. I could sense her fear and frustration, and her feeling of helplessness to *save* me or stop me. I could see defenses up and armed where not too long ago there was comfort and intimacy. We even held hands for a short while, and I think that this was the last time we shared any physical level of intimacy at all. Those feelings would soon fade.

Once we returned from our trip, there was less than two weeks to prepare before my trip to San Francisco for my facial surgery. I took care of the last minute details at work. Maria took a break from working on my face. I restocked my apartment.

And, home life still sucked.

JOURNAL ENTRY

Last night I went home so we could have a "family dinner." Elizabeth decided that she was in bad mood, so it turned pretty sour. Later in the evening, she was going through some receipts from my buying gas for her truck (since mine is STILL broken in the driveway). She noticed that I bought gas on two sequential days and started accusing me of driving here and there....it was totally asinine. But from this little spark, a huge eruption sprouted. I told her that it was totally innocent and that I resented her accusing me, and one thing led to another, and the next thing you know, she was crying and telling me to file for divorce and to take Matt and the dog and get out of the house and that I am going straight to Hell for this.

Matt has born the brunt of her unhappiness lately, and has been trying his hardest to avoid her. He heard all this, so he and I grabbed some stuff and left. We had a very good conversation as we drove to my apartment, and he said he feels that my "problem" has brought us closer together. I was dumbfounded to hear him say that. He wants out, and thinks that the two of us would be good together no matter how I want to live.

Four days later, on July 21, 1999, I left for San Francisco. I had already said my good-byes to Matt. I left Elizabeth another note telling her I was leaving. However, this time I left not with sadness or with fear. It was with resolve and with confidence and anticipation. I was on the right path. I could feel it.

CHAPTER EIGHTEEN

A NEW PHYSICAL SELF

"I saw an angel in the marble, and carved until I set her free."
— MICHELANGELO

Davies Medical Center sits atop a hill in the Castro section of San Francisco. I arrived the day before my surgeries to take care of all the pre-op details that needed attention. I sat down with Mira, Dr. O's office manager, to review everything that was going to happen.

Our conversation turned to my chest, and the still fresh jagged lines that were left from my aborted breast augmentation. Mira thought the doctor could lessen the scars, so it took very little prodding to add another, smaller set of boobs to the already lengthy laundry list of surgical procedures for the following day.

During our pre-op meeting, the doctor began a process known as informed consent. Facial feminization surgery (FFS) is major surgery. He described, step-by-step, exactly what he was planning to do, and all the possible complications that could result.

He started at the top; the forehead contouring and scalp advancement. He said that he would slice across my entire forehead and down behind my ears, and bring the skin down to work on the forehead. They were going to smooth (as in, shave off the bone) my entire brow bossing, which was so pronounced that it would expose my sinus cavities. He told me how he would shorten my forehead, and advance my hairline to a more feminine level. He described how he would change my nose, which needed to be completely redone to fit seamlessly with all of the other changes he was doing. He explained that he would shorten my chin and round off my jaw from inside my mouth by making an incision all along my lower gums. After that, he planned to shave down my trachea by making an incision just under my chin. Finally, he explained how he would put my breast enlargement under my chest muscles.

He described all the possible complications...from short and long-term numbness, to the possibility of cutting muscles and nerves. He explained that, following surgery, I would have staples and sutures and drains and gauze covering most of my face, and much of it needed to stay in place for most of the week. He explained that much of my face and forehead would be numb following the procedures, but that sensation should gradually come back.

He wanted there to be no doubt that this was *major* surgery, that I would be in the operating room for at least 12 hours, and that recuperation would be long and difficult, not so much pain, but what he called "discomfort." I understood.

When all was done, Mira gave me a pen (I affectionately refer to it as my $34,000 pen) to sign the check and pay for it all. We hugged...she wished me luck...and I was off to contemplate what was about to happen.

At 7:00 a.m. I was wheeled into the pre-op area. As I lay on the gurney outside of the operating room I was calm and relaxed. I felt totally comfortable and at peace with what was about to happen. I knew that the events of this day would forever change my life, although I had no idea as to the magnitude of what was to come.

As I was wheeled into the operating room, I made a special effort to avoid making eye contact with the power tools that would be used to re-landscape my face. Some things are better left not known. I was introduced to the staff there as they busily prepared for our very long day together. As I felt the anesthesia begin to pull me into unconsciousness, I repeated Elizabeth's name over and over just in case I didn't wake up, until gradually all was dark.

The surgery itself actually lasted 13 hours.

I awoke in my hospital room. It was night. I was alone. I was a mess. My face and upper torso were completely and tightly wrapped in gauze. I had seen pictures of other patients on the Internet, and the best way to visualize it is to imagine what someone who is beaten with a baseball bat to the head might look like.

There were tubes and wires and machines everywhere. Drain tubes. IV tubes. A catheter tube. Wires leading to the monitoring machines. A Demerol pump. Beeping and buzzing noises were coming from the bank of machines surrounding the bed. It was quite an impressive set-up.

I took stock in myself to see what was what. I found that, as long as I lay still, I seemed to feel no intense pain from any particular part of my body except for a throbbing, dull headache that grew stronger and sharper as the night wore on.

The inside of my mouth was a mess. Incisions had been made around my entire bottom gum line to give access to my jaw. At first I thought that there was cotton packing all along my lower gum line, until further inspection with my tongue confirmed that it was all swelling. I could feel the ends of the tied off sutures. The nasty taste of dried blood and nameless other seepages was something I am still trying to forget.

My entire head was wrapped like a mummy, and the only exposed area of skin were my lips and around my deep purple swollen-shut eyes. The rest was either wrapped in gauze, or held in place with tape as though pieces might fall off if I wasn't careful. I was afraid to touch anything.

The night crept by...second after long second. The nurse stopped in every hour or so to change the bandage under my packed nose, empty the bloody fluid filled drains hanging from the bandages on my jaw, and check my vitals. As I tried to breathe deeply to clear my lungs of thirteen hours-worth of anesthesia, I ended up hacking up globs of phlegm and blood. I'm sure I looked even worse than I felt. I just wanted to die.

At some point, I sat up in the darkness and swung around so my legs hung down over the side of the bed. I held my bandaged head in my hands, and bemoaned my sorry situation. Here I was… all alone…in pain…in the dark…and for what? I was afraid to cry, for fear of damaging some of the surgery that had just been done, so I struggled to control the flood of emotion that I was feeling. What had I done?

I counted the minutes until daylight arrived.

Later that morning, both Dr. O and Mira stopped by. As they entered my room and approached the hospital bed, Mira had an alarmed, pained look on her face. I'm sure she has seen many of us like this, but I'm also sure that it doesn't get any easier to see us in this state of self-inflicted trauma.

Dr. O said that all the surgeries went beautifully, and that I'd be moving to a recuperation room the following day. He said I would have stitches taken out during the week, then staples removed as well as the nose packing and drains…little by little I'd get back to a normal state as parts healed. He told me that he had put me on a soft diet until my mouth healed, and that the best thing I could do for myself over the next several days was to rest.

Although I made a conscious decision to avoid looking at myself for as long as possible, I accidentally caught sight of myself in the mirror on the second day after surgery. What I saw made me sick to my stomach. I wanted to puke. The sutured line across my forehead looked like something out of *Frankenstein*. The bruises around my still very swollen eyes were an intense purple and magenta color. My chin and jaw were swollen to three times their normal size. The extent of the damage was absolutely astounding.

I spent the week recuperating as best I could. Besides being in pain, and dealing with the packing that would stuff my nose for nearly a week, I soon learned that the surgeries had sapped me of every ounce of strength and stamina. The simple act of getting out of bed to go to the bathroom and back was absolutely exhausting. I got stir crazy on Sunday and walked a mile to the store to buy a newspaper, and it took me two days to recover.

The healing properties of the human body are amazing, and there was little else to do but to let time, and Mother Nature, work their magic and help me heal.

JOURNAL ENTRY (FFS+2 DAYS)

I'm up and about for a few minutes, so I figured I'd try to write something. I'm certainly not at my best, but I'm feeling the littlest bit better every day. I have lots of healing to do. I have staples in my head, sutures all throughout my mouth, packing up my nose, drains in my boobs...various tapes and bandages hiding some pretty dramatic looking bruises...all in all pretty spectacular. It's hard to believe it's me behind all that construction.

The healing life is a boring one. Sleep. Pain pills. T.V. Walking around. I met with some of the other girls on the floor for an hour last night. They were just great. I'm in pain, but at this point it's a dull overall ache rather than any particular place. The first day felt like my head had been hit with a sledgehammer, so this ache is far more acceptable.

JOURNAL ENTRY (FFS+4 DAYS)

I'm actually feeling almost human again today. I don't look so hot, in fact I look like hell, but at least I can finally move around a bit rather than just lie in the bed in a moaning stupor.

The surgery really took a lot out of me. I sat through some of these past few nights wondering if I'd even make it through them...I was just so miserable and time seemed to creep so slowly. But now I'm able to walk around, and I spent some time visiting with some of the other girls on the floor. I'm not in quite so much pain (they prefer to use the word "discomfort" around here), so there is light at the end of the tunnel.

Today is Sunday, and there's not much happening around here. They discharged me from my hospital room yesterday to my "guest" room on the third floor. They have me on a "pureed" diet due to all the sutures inside my mouth, and I must say it's pretty nasty. For lunch they sent pureed chicken and mashed potatoes and pureed beans....basically it was baby food. I haven't seen Dr. O since yesterday morning, and I don't think I'll see much improvement in my situation until Tuesday. That's when I think they unpack all this stuff out of my nose, and take out the staples in my head, and hopefully I can take a shower. My eyes are still very swollen and get tired pretty easy, so I can't really concentrate on anything requiring my eyes (like reading) for too long. There is a nice view of the bay from the back of the hospital, so I've gone down there just to sit and enjoy the wind in my face a couple of times. It has helped to deal with the monotony.....

The gal here from Belgium is Sally. Her wife offered to wash my hair for me this morning, and I quickly accepted. I have a bunch of stuff out this afternoon—staples or sutures or packing, but someone to carefully wash my hair at this point would be a penny from heaven. It is solid with dried blood and all kinds of other gook from the surgery, and to have it clean would be a big step towards feeling human again.

I talked to my mom for half an hour yesterday. I didn't tell her I was coming [to San Fran for surgery] before I did it, and my sister told her. But she seemed fine and we had a nice talk...

The night before I was to be discharged from the hospital, some friends from the Bay area offered to take me out for my first normal

203

meal since my surgery. My soft diet at the hospital had long since lost any charm it may have had at the beginning, when I looked forward to its three daily arrivals like a child waiting for a present in the mail. I quickly accepted, and a small group of us decided to go down to Fisherman's Wharf.

One of the gals was a friend named Carrie. She was very tall, very gangly, and certainly of *questionable* gender. At nearly 6'6", her height made her conspicuous, and her large Adam's apple and mostly masculine features were difficult to hide. Despite the fact that she was wearing her wig, and a very pretty dress, the waiter at the restaurant still referred to her as Sir, which of course pissed her off to no end.

After dinner we decided to enjoy the late summer evening ocean air with a stroll along the wharf. We walked casually from store to store, enjoying the evening.

Behind us, we heard a teenage boy yelling. It took a few seconds, but we soon realized that he was yelling at Carrie.

"EXCUSE ME! SIR?! YOU IN THE DRESS! CAN YOU PLEASE TELL ME WHAT TIME IT IS?"

As I turned I noticed a group of five or six teenagers that were giggling. We kept walking. They kept following, and taunting.

"SIR?! YOU IN THE DRESS! WHAT TIME IS IT?"

I could see that Carrie was getting flustered. I, on the other hand I was getting angry.

I stopped to turn and face these kids.

"No!" Carrie said. "Just keep going! Ignore them! They'll eventually get tired and leave us alone."

Every ounce of testosterone in my body wanted to throw that kid into the ocean. But I knew that I needed to learn to control that. Plus, I had just spent a lot of money on my new face and didn't want to do anything that would threaten to mess it up. So, I slowly turned and continued to stroll, hoping that the kid's interest in us would wane before my self-control expired. Thankfully, the kids went off on their own a couple of minutes later.

On Friday, July 30, the final sutures were removed from inside my nose, and I was discharged from Davies Medical Center. Although the bruising and swelling had subsided substantially, I was very weak and tired easily, and healing from my surgery would take upwards of six months.

I had a 3:30 p.m. flight from San Francisco to Phoenix, and got to the airport with plenty of time to spare, not wanting to have to rush in my still weakened state.

As I sat in the departure lounge, waiting to board my plane, I was well aware of what was happening in Scottsdale at that very minute. Lin had gathered the 50 or so people in my group in a meeting room to disclose my situation to them.

Following is the letter that I wrote, and that was read, to my entire group at work. Once this letter was read, nothing could ever be the same.

Dear Mail Team:

I am writing to you today to discuss a very personal issue. It is one that has plagued me for my entire life, and one that I have been attempting to avoid and suppress for as long as I can remember. If I had any way to spare you, or myself, this disclosure, I would certainly do that. But there comes a time when a person assesses their life, and they find it's time to face their situation with honesty and courage and integrity, rather than fear and shame and guilt. I have reached that point.

My particular situation deals with gender. Although I am physically male, I feel that I have been "miscast" in life. Although the body says "male," the heart and the mind and the soul say "female." And although this may sound stupid and incomprehensible to some, it has been the source of so much confusion and pain in my life that I cannot even begin to describe it. The clinical name for this condition is "Gender Identity Disorder," and it has taken me many years to finally accept the fact that it is me.

There is a stringent internationally accepted protocol to guide doctors and psychologists in helping patients deal with this condition. It has been proven that there is no "cure"…no way to make a person feel more male or more female on the inside. Once a person's gender identity has been developed, it is there to stay. Rather, the focus is on helping the person come to terms with this incongruity, and to helping them to feel comfortable in their own body by modifying it to more closely match their inner spirit.

The first step in this process is to meet and talk with a psychologist who specializes in gender issues. I have been doing so for well over two years. Patients are carefully screened, and those who are clinically diagnosed are referred to a medical doctor for administration of female hormones. These hormones have a variety of mental and physical effects, and help a person determine if this is the path on which they feel they should continue. I have been on such a regimen for two years.

Once a person feels comfortable enough with themselves, they are allowed to begin a phase called the "Real Life Test." This requires a patient to live full-time in their new gender role. It requires them to change all legal documentation to reflect their new name and new gender, and to try to exist in society in that new role. This is a very difficult and terrifying task, and it is the point at which I find myself now.

My father had a saying … "For those who believe, no explanation is necessary. For those who don't, none will suffice." There is no way I can explain this problem to you in hopes that you will understand. Rather, I am hoping that your compassion and your professionalism and your humanity will help you overcome the stereotypes and the prejudices that society has created, and will help you to see that underneath it all is a person who is still trying to find their path in life, hoping that it will lead to eventual happiness.

Writing this letter to you has been very difficult, but not as difficult as some of what I have already done. I doubt that any of you will know what it's like to try to explain this to a 13-year old son to whom you are the ultimate role model and friend. I doubt you'll know what it's like to try to explain it to your mom, when she has already faced the death of her husband only 6 months before. I doubt that you'll know the pain of trying to explain this to your wife of 18 years, who feels betrayed in a way that I cannot even describe. If there were ANY way for me to continue as I am and avoid having to face this, I would do it. But there is not. I thank God for the strength He has given me, and the friends that I have, as everyone who has learned of my situation has provided me with strength and support.

Over the next few weeks, I will be preparing for my Real-Life test. I am telling you this so that you will know what is happening, and so that the outward signs are not taken out of context. I am planning to begin my transition here at work on October 4. My name will be legally changed to Donna, the gender on my driver's license indicate that I am Female, and I plan to live and work full time in that role. Please treat this with the sensitivity that it requires.

The coming months will bring many challenges to the Mail team. We have a tremendous team with tremendous people. It remains imperative that we keep our focus on the tasks at hand, and not become sidetracked along the way. We all have a job to do, and I am confident that this team can continue its work without missing a beat.

I am entering a world that is totally foreign to me, and I have much learning to do. I plan to take things slowly, but I feel confident that I am finally on the right path. I finally feel a peace within myself that has been absent for a long, long time. As I begin this process, all I ask is for your patience and your tolerance. Anything else will be icing on the cake.

Sincerely,

Donna Rose

I had no second thoughts. I felt no pressure. In fact, I actually felt an odd sense of comfort and of achievement, although nothing had really even happened yet! I think the abortion of my transition attempt only four short months before added to my appreciation of this milestone. I was on the right path. I could tell. I could *feel* it.

CHAPTER NINETEEN

OH...MY...GOD!

Trying to pass as a "male" is becoming harder and harder. I never, ever, ever thought I would be able to say that. But I need to heal, to grow out my whiskers, to build my wardrobe, and build some confidence, so I'll have to endure this twilight zone between genders for a little while longer. But no matter how you slice it, there is no way to make this look totally male.

— JOURNAL ENTRY

Thanks to my surgical adjustments, I was now firmly entrenched in a very odd and uncomfortable role. My facial features, although still swollen and misshapen, were undeniably female. I had substantial breasts. I had sport-length acrylic nails. But I dressed like a guy. I had short, male-styled hair. And I maintained a constant stubble of remaining facial hair to make it easier for Maria to remove. I suddenly found it difficult to pass convincingly as *either* gender.

On my trek to cross the gender-line in the eyes and the mind of society, I now found myself firmly straddling it. By day I planned to live and work as Dave. However, during evenings and on weekends, I would live as Donna. It would allow the opportunity to ease into my new role that I hadn't been able to enjoy last time.

I also found that, somehow, my sensitivity to what others around me might be thinking about me seems to have diminished. I really wasn't all that worried about what other people might think when they saw this curious person of questionable gender.

The Monday after my return from San Francisco was my first day back at work after my two-week "vacation." It was a day I had both looked forward to, and feared, for a long time.

Apparently, the meeting with the group on Friday had gone well. There was certainly surprise in the announcement. I'm told that there were a couple of questions, but nothing to get too upset about. Lin emphasized that there was a zero tolerance policy in effect, and no harassment of any kind would be tolerated.

As I prepared for work in the dark of the early autumn morning, I really wasn't all that nervous. I wasn't really sure what to expect, but I knew that the possible scenarios I could dream up would probably be far worse than what would actually happen throughout the day. I could not let myself get distracted by fear, or by appearing tentative or unsure. I made it a point to keep my head high, and maintain my dignity no matter what happened. I also planned to stay in or around my cube as much as possible during the first few days, thinking that was probably the safest and most sensible thing to do.

I did my best to treat this just like any other day, which was difficult considering the fact that I knew that it was actually unlike any other day that had come before.

JOURNAL ENTRY 8/2/1999 [TITLED "The Day"]

OMIGOD...OMIGOD...OMIGOD...

I can't believe that today ever happened. Not that it was terrible. As far as I could tell, anyways.

Last night Brian called to see if all was still a "go." I told him I was calm and ready. He asked that I be at work at 7:30 so we could plan on a definite time for the first day, so I told him I'd be here. I knew that I had to be up at 3:45 to be at my electrolysis appt. by 5, so I went home and went to bed. I actually slept okay, which is an indication of how tired I was considering all that was about to happen...

So the alarm went off, and I got ready. My regular work clothes. Pants. Sports Shirt. Sports bra. And off I go to electrolysis. Maria was just GUSHING. She said I would make an interesting sight, as my face (in her opinion) now had a mostly feminine flavor, but the swollen jaw will take time to go down.

I was at work at 7:30. Work clothes. Strapped down boobs. Long polished (clear) nails. Puffy, bruised face. A very interesting sight. The last thing I did before getting out of the car was to say a prayer. And then I just went.

On my way in I ran into one of the younger guys in the group. He was very nice, and we actually walked in together. It made it a little easier. I made it to my cube, and have actually been here most of the day. I feel like a turtle, and my head will eventually pop out, but right now this shell is my safe haven. I have had maybe a dozen people or so come by to chat and offer support. I also got a very nice voice mail from someone that I barely know who doesn't even work in our group anymore. He's all the way on the other side of the building, so word traveled fast.

I've just spent the day doing my work. I turned off my cell phone so I can concentrate without interruptions. Lin from HR stopped by to see how the day was going, and I thanked her for her efforts.

It has been a long, grueling day. But I also have a sense of satisfaction for having faced this day, and for having dealt with it. There will be rough days, but today was a milestone, and I'm actually kinda proud of the way it went.

The rest of the week passed similarly. I had envisioned two very different scenarios: one in which I was totally and completely shunned and found myself suddenly immersed in a very hostile situation, and the other in which friends and co-workers actively approached or contacted me as a gesture of our continuing friendship, and to help me feel comfortable. Of course, neither of those actually happened. A few people actively attempted to make contact with me, although most kept their distance. I didn't feel that they were avoiding me, necessarily, but even if they were that was certainly their right. I hoped that time could soften that barrier and the awkwardness that now separated us.

JOURNAL ENTRY — DAY 3

Work has been quiet. I'm determined to talk to a couple or three people each day to kinda "break the ice," and have done that this morning. Nothing earth shattering, but it's a start.

I'm starting to settle into this groove a little bit. It's much easier to deal with than last time. I don't know why. When Karen stopped over on Saturday she said something that intrigued me. I was talking about the fact that I'm still searching for where I fit in life, and she said that she thinks that I'll eventually find peace before this is all over, and that my place is as a female, and that I'll be a good one. It was an odd statement, so I called her yesterday to ask what she meant. She said that the first time, I just didn't seem "at peace." I seemed to be doing things in such a way that it gave her an uneasy feeling, and caused her to worry about me. She says that this time I have a peace and calm about me, and that the difference is like night and day, and now she's comfortable for me, too.

Elizabeth called me last night. She doesn't like the fact that many of my friends are transsexual. She said that she thinks

I'm spending too much time with "those freaks" and that they're sucking me in blah blah blah.... I told her that those people are not freaks, and that I am one of them, and as long as she can't understand that then she'll never be able to move forward. We are all trying to help each other get through this. She got a bit more perturbed, and I ended up hanging up on her, because I don't need that right now.

Throughout the week, a few people offered various gestures of support. One of my coworkers asked me out to lunch. Another stopped by my cube and asked if I had plans for dinner. Most, however, left me alone.

News of my situation spread through the company very quickly. As I worked, my back faced the entryway to my cube, but I could see by the reflection in my computer monitor that a steady stream of curious gawkers made their way past my cube, nonchalantly peeking in to see the *freak*. I was more amused by this sudden notoriety than anything, wondering just what made all of this so interesting to people.

By mid-week, the entire campus was aware of the transsexual in their midst. I got a phone call from a friend in one of the other buildings on campus for a friendly "long-time no-see" chat. I knew right away that there was an ulterior motive for the call.

"Is there something you want to ask me?" I eventually asked, trying to make this easier.

"Weeellll...I don't know," he replied tentatively. "I will say that there is a rumor floating around here about you, but I put no credence in it at all."

I thought about it for a second. "Hmmm. A rumor. Well, I don't know exactly what the rumor is, but I can guess. I'm also sure that there probably is at least some grain of truth in it."

He was silent.

"Can you share this rumor with me, so that I can either confirm or deny?" I asked.

"Well," he said, choosing his words carefully. "The word that is spreading over here..." he paused, "is that Dave has boobs."

I smiled. I should have known that the "Dave" message had zeroed in on the most sensational aspect of what I was doing. It wasn't about my transition; it was about my chest. Too funny!

"I can confirm that," I said, just waiting for the next group of *looky-loo's* to make their way past my cube to catch a glimpse of the guy with the boobs.

To say that they were uncomfortable, I think, would be an understatement. As the days and weeks passed, the awkwardness and discomfort expressed itself in the most ridiculous ways. For example, one of my coworkers, who managed our fantasy football league, sent me an email asking if I still wanted to participate. I sensed that the real reason for the note was so that I would say no and leave. In fact, I made it a point to stop by his cube and ask if my situation had anything to do with his note, and he reluctantly admitted that some of the guys in the league did not feel comfortable about my participation. I told him that I wasn't looking for a confrontation, so that if it would make things easier for all the guys I'd resign, and I did.

I learned early that I couldn't afford to let the pressure of everything I was feeling affect my productivity at work. If anything, I needed to do better work than I had done in the past, which would be difficult to maintain given the circumstances. I didn't want to give the company an excuse for getting rid of me, although I was all too aware that they could do that without an excuse any time they wanted.

One day, as I sat in my cubicle and worked with my headphones on, a sad song caught my attention. I listened to the lyrics, which suddenly filled me with a tremendous sense of sadness for the terrible pain that my family and I were enduring. I started to cry softly. I couldn't help it. It wasn't a sobbing, face-all-red, chest-heaving kind of cry. It was more like a soft, tears-gently-running-down-your-cheek kind of cry. Wouldn't you know that someone walked into my cube to ask me a question, and I hurriedly composed myself to answer.

A few days later, Brian stopped by.

"Listen, Donna. I'm just giving you a head's up. Someone said that they stopped into your cube the other day and you were crying."

I tried to explain, but he really didn't want to hear. "You need to stay focused and effective here at work. You can't be crying in your cube. Understood?"

From that moment on, I knew that while I was at work, I was all alone.

Elizabeth was not handling things well. I urged her to get some help. I implored her to tell friends, or family about what was happening, as she needed support and comfort just as much as I did. But she was so embarrassed and ashamed about what was happening that she continued to hold out hope that I could come back home as Dave, and nobody else need know what had happened, so she didn't tell anyone. Not her parents. Not her friends. Nobody.

She wanted assurances from me. She wanted timeframes. How long would it take for me to know if this was the right course for my life? How long would it take for me to realize that this was all one huge mistake and come home to be Dave again? Although I knew that I couldn't give timeframes, one thing I did know is that the life I had known as Dave was long-gone.

EMAIL TO ELIZABETH

Honey:

You left me a voice mail today. It was heart wrenching to listen to you. I am going to philosophize for a moment to tell you what helps ME through each day in hopes that it will help you, as well.

My "situation" is something that I must deal with. For years and years and years I have fought it and tried to pretend that it didn't exist. I was afraid of what would happen once it became known, as I was comfortable in my own little world. I was able to walk through life with my eyes half closed, always keeping up a stiff guard to keep out the pain I knew was inevitable. As I fought and fought against it, I became to dislike the person who I was, and that affected everything about me. It affected how I felt about myself, how I related to you and Matt…everything about me. I became unhappy. I began to lose hope.

The turning point for me, and you have a long way to go to get there (if ever) is acceptance. To finally realize the truth for what is IS, and not what you WANT it to be is a major threshold, and has been a key moment in my life. To finally accept that there IS something that has been a burden to my soul, and that it needs to be addressed and dealt with in order for me to proceed as a person, was a very, very difficult thing for me to do. But I have done it, and although I am scared and lonely right now, I am at peace with myself for what I am doing. I am working through my situation as best I can. I am trying to maintain my integrity and my dignity and my humanity and my love in the face of tremendous hardships. I know that your heart has been broken, as has my own, but I refuse to ever lose faith.

I have done everything I can to spare you and Matt from participating in my journey. You have said that you cannot accept this part of me in any way, shape or form in your life. But the reality of the situation is, it IS a part of MY life. And if you are involved in MY life right now, it will be part of YOUR life. So in the same fashion as I have accepted myself, and can move forward to whatever awaits me, you are facing choices of your own. But the reality of the situation is that you don't have to make ANY decisions right now. You are not going to make this go away no matter how hard you wish it, or how hard we both cry. I have no desire to lose you, or to lose our love or the lives we hoped to build and live together. But I accept me for me right now, and if you want timetables and you want decisions right now, I cannot give them to you, and if you are in that much of a hurry to move on with your life

then so be it. In the same way that it took time to get where I
am now, it will take time to work it out, and I will do that.

Time is the key ingredient here. If you cannot accept that, then
that in and of itself will be the barrier that we cannot overcome. Time. And love. And support. And acceptance. And the
understanding that Matt is BOTH our responsibilities in order to make sure he grows up to be a good, loving person. I
will end up wherever I end up whether you call me every day
to tell me you love me, or if you curse me. It just makes our
journeys that much easier or more difficult. I stopped last time
for the wrong reasons. I will not this time. It is not fair to you,
or me, or Matt.

If you are looking for timeframes, or assurances that I will be
back totally as "Dave"…I cannot offer you those now. I would
be lying to both of us.

I will continue to talk to you in hopes that you will talk to me.
I am through arguing. I am through fighting. I have a difficult
enough time getting through each day.

Stay strong. Know that I love you. You have not lost me. And I
pray that I have not lost you. You once said that love was not
enough, but I think it is. Have faith in that and see where it leads.

The only person in my family who didn't know what was going on
with me was my brother. My mom was pressuring me to tell him about
it all. I had plans to visit Rochester at the end of that month as the
entire family was gathering there to celebrate her seventieth birthday,
and she wanted to make sure he knew before then.

I'm not sure why I delayed. Perhaps it was because I had learned
that, for some reason, the women I knew seemed to take my news
better than men. After a while, I developed a litmus test to gauge just
how well the men I knew as Dave accepted me as Donna. If they
attempted to shake hands, or if they kept their distance, then I assumed

that they had difficulty with it. If they actually hugged me, as they did with other women, I immediately knew that they felt comfortable with me in my new role.

My brother and I certainly had our fair share of sibling rivalry, but I had always been the older one, the athletic one, the confident one, and the loud one. I think that relinquishing the Big Brother role was not as easy as I originally thought it would be.

At the beginning of August I wrote a long, rambling email to tell him. I forfeited my crown as the eldest son, and acknowledged him as the only male in our family now.

I sent it to him on a Thursday, expecting to hear something back by the next day. I got no response on Friday. Or on Saturday. Or on Sunday. On Monday I called Mom and Jude to ask if they had heard from him, as I was getting a little anxious that he hadn't called either of them.

He finally called me on Tuesday. Apparently, he had been out of town for the weekend so he had not seen the email. He told me he loved me, and he could learn to live with whatever made me happy. I was happy. I was relieved. I cried after the call.

One of the things that had been most difficult for me during my initial attempt to transition was the intense feeling of isolation and loneliness that had consumed me. My cold-turkey separation anxiety had overwhelmed me more than I ever imagined possible.

This time, I was ready. I had an extensive support network to help me. Intially, I talked with Matt regularly, which provided a tremendous sense of satisfaction and strength. My family called often to make sure I was okay. Maria was there for me. Other TS friends checked on me regularly. The isolation at work was balanced by the support I found in the rest of my life. I did not feel confined to my apartment, and made it a point to get out and about with the rest of society.

Perhaps more importantly, though, I found this newfound sense of calm helped me to turn inwards. I slowly realized that my time alone could actually be a good thing for me, and I gradually learned that there was a significant distinction between being alone, and being lonely.

As a guy, I was always in motion. I always needed something to do, someplace to go, somebody to be with. Others told me that I could be exhausting to be with. As I slowly released my grip on that old life, I tried to curb that drive. I used my time alone to actually get to know myself, and to let the peace and quiet of that time give me energy instead of fill me with emptiness.

After a long day at work I would sometimes return to my apartment for an evening of spiritual healing. I would light several candles, turn on some smooth jazz, open a bottle of good wine, turn out all the lights, and spend some quality *me* time.

Sometimes I would just curl up the living room floor, surrounded by all of my pillows. Other times, I would take a long, slow bath. I would close my eyes and let my mind wander; breathing deeply as if putting myself into a trance-like state of relaxation. I lost track of time, and would often come back to the here and now with the sudden realization that the bathwater had gotten cold, or that my candles were burning dangerously low.

I considered this time to be a time of spiritual healing and preparation. As I considered all that was still to come, I knew that I needed to maintain that sense of spiritual calm that was so evidently lacking from my previous transition attempt. I had never allowed myself the time or the opportunity to do it before, and perhaps that had been one of the problems in the first place.

A major step in my continuing evolution occurred during a support group meeting in August. It was the first meeting I attended since returning from surgery, and the reaction from friends in the group was universally positive.

At that point, my hair was still very short, having been sheared off during my brief retreat home in April. For some reason I thought that made me look like a boy. As a result, I continued to wear my poofy brown wig when out in public as Donna.

219

As this meeting progressed, my wig became more and more uncomfortable. It hurt the suture line along my forehead. It made my scalp itch. It made me hot, and it caused me to sweat. It felt like a costume, or a crutch, and before the meeting was over I'd had about all I could stand.

As I sat there, thinking about what to do, I made a snap decision. I yanked off the wig, exposing my short matted brown hair. I decided that my hair was my hair, long or short, and that's what I'd work with. It was almost with a sense of pride that I realized that I had outgrown it, and that my days wearing that big brown wig had come to an end.

The next day I went to the salon and let the stylist work his magic. I was pleasantly surprised to learn that I could look pretty good with a short cut. A new version of Donna was born.

Several weeks after surgery, I went to Dallas to visit Mom. It was the first time that she spent any time with me as Donna. Plus, it was my first opportunity to show off my new face. She seemed pleased.

My mom spends weekends at Goodwill buying clothes. Her closets are absolutely stuffed with them. She takes a great deal of pleasure in buying a nice dress for a couple of dollars, whether she really needs another dress or not.

During my visit, Mom wanted to get an idea as to what styles of clothes looked good on me. She thought it would be helpful for me as I compiled my own initial wardrobe. Plus, I think she saw this as an opportunity to demonstrate her support, and to bond with me in a new and unique way.

She brought dress after dress into the bedroom, and I tried each one on, modeling for her and listening to her comments. She liked this one because it was slimming. She didn't like the next one because the color wasn't right. I listened carefully and patiently, really appreciating her help and direction.

As I stood in front of her, modeling a dress, I couldn't help but be struck by the entire surreal scene. If anyone had ever told me that I'd be trying on dresses, and my mom would be helping me, I'd have told them they were absolutely insane.

I realized right then and there how truly fortunate I was to have a parent who was doing her best to be supportive. I realized that the bond we could form as mother and daughter was even stronger than the bond that she had built as mother and son. And, I realized just how much I loved her.

Chapter Twenty

Epiphany

> *Confusion is a constant companion. Am I doing the right thing? Is this really the path for my life? Am I succumbing to a temptation of some kind? What about my life ten years from now? Will I have friends? Will I be loved by anyone except my family? Questions. All valid ones. But in the end, there is no one to answer them. You have to go by your feelings. You have to go by your own instincts. If you know them to be true, then those first tentative steps along this path become more determined and more deliberate. To the point where it becomes a comfortable jog...*

— EMAIL TO A FRIEND

I think it started on a treadmill. To be honest, I do some of my best thinking there. A mind/body disconnect is an important skill for an athlete, as it allows the mind to wander just to keep some distance from the punishment and fatigue that the body is enduring.

Over the course of the next few weeks, I took the seed that I had discovered, and I considered it from as many different perspectives as I could. Slowly but surely I found that it began to make sense. I found that I could put my mind around the essence of my "problem" in ways that helped me to visualize exactly what I was dealing with, and provided explanations where I could find none before.

The question, "Why am I this way?" suddenly seemed to have some answers, or at least reasonable explanations, which was more than I had ever gotten before.

The key, for me, was to completely rearrange my way of looking at this apparent gender mismatch between body and mind. I find that trying to consider questions that are outside the general paradigms of common thinking are naturally restricted by looking for conventional answers. Unconventional problems require unconventional thinking. Dad expressed it well in his book, *Life Itself*, when he wrote that the problem wasn't necessarily that we didn't know enough to answer any particular question. It was equally as probable that *"we simply do not properly understand what we already know."*

I had always examined my gender problem as strictly that—a *gender* problem. I spent hours, days and years trying to explain this apparent mismatch between my body and my mind that was so powerful that it could completely derail an otherwise happy and successful life. The turning point, the missing piece of the puzzle, was to analyze exactly what gender is, and how we apply that to ourselves. Once I had done that, expressing it as simply "gender" related suddenly seemed inadequate and inappropriate. A human personality is far too complex, and far too inter-connected, to accurately support that kind of simplistic thinking. Rather, a personality is a dependent whole, and when one thing changes dramatically, everything else changes as well. In my dad's terminology, it is a *system*.

I found the answers to my questions in my dad's work, a place where I had never thought to look before.

My father was a brilliant man, and I had always considered his work and his theories to be in a stratosphere so high that most of us can't even see it from down here. All it took was one peek at the complex mathematical formulas that used to express his work to convince me that it was all way over my head, and that trying to understand was doomed to feelings of pathetic inadequacy.

During the last years of his life dad began to take his scientific work, and to apply it to every-day problems. Throughout this process, the connection between theory and real-life application helped me to understand what he was trying to say. In other words, I'm a visual person, and once I saw his theories in action, I could grasp the concepts that he was trying to convey.

One topic that my dad wrote about extensively over the last several years of his life is something that he calls *complexity*. As I considered what I knew of my dad's work, and applied it to real-life situations, I realized that *complexity* is a concept that seemed to be the missing piece of the puzzle! It provided basic explanations to questions I had been asking about gender, its role in the overall scheme of a person's psyche, and the root meaning of what it means to be transsexual.

I'm not in any position to give a lesson on complexity, but I'll give my interpretation in a single paragraph. In its most basic form, complexity implies that systems are complex, meaning that there are several discreet, but related things happening all at the same time. They key concept is that everything is interrelated and has relationships either directly or indirectly, with other things. As a result, the behavior of any individual part is as dependent on the state of the whole as it is to the conditions of things that are directly related. Quite simply, the whole is more than the sum of its parts.

In a human body, not every single cell is directly connected to the heart. However, if the heart dies then the organism as a whole dies as well, which will in turn affect every single cell whether it has a direct relationship to the heart or not.

According to common thinking, being transsexual is about sex and/or gender. In fact, most transsexuals are seduced by this kind of simple reasoning, and once trapped, getting out is extremely difficult. "I feel like I should have been born as a woman." "I feel trapped in the wrong body." Both are common statements made by transsexuals who try to track down and localize the source of their discomfort, and gender seems to be the all-too-obvious culprit.

My discovery is that being transsexual is *not* just about gender. In fact, it's just a small part of the issue. Certainly, gender is the most obvious indication of being transsexual, but human beings are far too complex to be reduced to one-dimensional explanations for anything, much less something as highly integrated into our overall psyche as our gender. Rather, gender discomfort is just the symptom of a much larger situation.

If we take a step back and look at things through an unprejudiced lens, it becomes apparent that being transsexual is about *self*. It is about the need to express yourself in a way that feels comfortable and natural. It is about being accepted by others in a way that is congruent with how you see and accept yourself. People do that every day of their lives, and as long as it is done inside the paradigms that society has defined as *normal*, it is rarely given a second thought.

Gender is a social construct that exists solely by providing do's and dont's, or can's and cant's, that are based on a person's physical sex. That's it. That's all it is. Somehow, these cultural gender norms have grown to a point of such seemingly universal acceptance, that it's almost as if they were mandates from God.

Transsexuals are people whose overall sense of *self,* or of self-expression, is more closely aligned with the roles and expectations commonly associated with people whose physical sex is *opposite* their own. To be free from prejudice and stigma, what's wrong with that? In a world where we encourage and appreciate the incredible diversity of nature, and where we encourage individuality and originality, when it comes to gender expression, we somehow clench so tight that we lose sight of the fact that people are complex creatures.

Whether the reasons for this incongruity are based in neonatal development, rooted in psychology, or are some combination of the two. What difference does that make? Certainly, scientists are always asking *why* and feel the need to find answers that they can prove. For some reason, many people seem to feel that providing scientific explanations to various questions, which lends credibility to the very answers that they derive. But I would argue, that any attempt to find answers inside the strict paradigms of male/female, masculine/feminine without considering exactly what that is, how it is connected to a person's personality, and how each of us interacts in a society, will fall short.

To insist on reducing a person to a single aspect of their total self… whether it is their gender, sexuality, or even something as mundane as their occupation, is to completely lose sight of the bigger picture. People are not that simple.

Early in my struggle to come to terms with my confusion, and while we were still on speaking terms, I tried to talk to Elizabeth about my feelings in an effort to sort things out, or at the very least to explain myself. Although I had viewed Dave and Donna as two distinct personalities struggling over the same body for a very long time, it eventually dawned on me that they were just two names for different parts of the same person.

I once asked Elizabeth a philosophical question: If they could devise a surgery to remove the portion of my brain that made me need to express Donna, would she want me to have it, even if it were dangerous and my life would be at risk? Without hesitation, she answered "yes!" She really seemed to believe that by removing the part of the brain that was responsible for Donna's intruding thoughts, as if it were a tumor, what remained would be the Dave that she thought she knew and loved.

I tried to explain that someone's personality is much more complex than a tumor, and that one part cannot be removed from all the others so cleanly. The aspects of my personality that she felt were Donna, were actually the things that made me different from all of the other boyfriends she had had. I told her that my ability to communicate with her, to be sensitive to her, and to empathize with her, were all parts of my personality that could be considered as feminine traits. In the end, if the traits that she considered to be Donna were removed, the end result would not be Dave. It would be someone totally different. Furthermore, I didn't think that she would like that person very much.

No matter whether a person is transgendered or not, their sense of gender is so deeply interconnected and intertwined with the rest of their personality, and sense of self, that any changes to one will certainly affect everything else. There's no arguing it. Realizing this, and accepting it, is a critical step in coming to terms with the confusion and the magnitude of the change that changing gender entails.

Although transsexuals are often viewed as having contempt and disregard for the norms and rules of society, the truth is that we are actually doing our best to conform. That's what transition and sex-change is all about. Instead of living in a gender *twilight zone* of our own making, we do our best to comply with the gender rules that society has defined. The fact that the rules we are trying to follow are those that have been established for the *other* gender is really not the issue. It's just the symptom.

CHAPTER TWENTY ONE

THE FAMILY MEETS DONNA

When I started this, I talked with my psychologist about this path I am on. We embark upon it with the understanding, or at least we THINK we understand, that we have the possibility of losing EVERYTHING in our lives. Our family. Our friends. Our wives and children. Our homes. Our jobs. EVERYTHING that we knew from our lives is at risk, and whether we keep any of it or not, in a large sense, is not up to us. I have not seen my wife since June, nor my son since Labor Day. I have a house full of my stuff, and a garage with an Infinity SUV and a Mercedes in it. I have all the toys and trappings of a fairly successful middle-aged person. But those things pale in comparison to the love and the support that I have gotten from my family

— EMAIL TO A FRIEND

By August, Elizabeth and I had not seen each other in six weeks. My face, and my entire physical appearance, had undergone a dramatic change over those 42 days.

To her credit, Elizabeth did make an attempt to actually see me after the surgery. I was not expecting it, and it turned out to be a disaster.

I had made arrangements to stop over at my house on a Saturday morning to sign a few things, pick up some mail, and give the dogs a bath, which was one of Dave's jobs. I knew she would be home, but she said she planned to be sleeping and would stay in the bedroom until I left, and I respected that.

I arrived at the house and let myself in. It was strange to see "our" house and all of our possessions after being apart from it all for so long. None of it *felt* the same anymore.

All of the things that she said she would leave for me were piled on the island in the middle of the kitchen. On top of it all was a letter, talking about her trying to be able to work this out with me. As I stood in the kitchen, reading it, she came around the corner behind me. I heard her, and turned. And that's when she saw my face.

After only three weeks of recovery from major facial surgery, my face remained swollen and misshapen. The bruises had faded away, but I'm sure I looked like hell, especially to someone who expected to see the same, old male-looking face. If she anticipated that I would look anything like I did before my surgery, seeing me at that point was a shock.

As I looked up, she stopped dead in her tracks, put her hands to her mouth, and screamed, "OH GOD!!" before turning and running back into her bedroom. I followed her, trying to comfort her and explain, but she had started to sob uncontrollably.

"Oh my God! Oh my God! What have you done?" She wailed.

I hugged her from behind, explaining that I was still healing and all should settle down over the next few weeks.

"What have you done to your face? Why did you do that? You ruined your face!! Oh my God!" She was inconsolable

I think Elizabeth expected a *little* change; something that she might be able to explain in case I came back. But this change was total and complete, and there was no explaining it. I looked much different. The reality was that my change was permanent hit her like a ton of bricks.

"You look like a mongoloid!" she yelled, crying harder and louder.

Later, she barricaded herself in the locked bedroom. She was still sobbing loudly, and nothing could make her stop. My presence there only seemed to cause her more pain. Eventually, I yelled through the locked door that I loved her and left, wondering if we could recover from what had just happened.

It was to be the last time we would see each other.

Journal Entry

Why does this have to be so hard?

It was hard to tell my family. It was hard to tell my work. It was hard to show up last Monday. I can, and am, handling those things. But knowing the pain I am causing Elizabeth is killing me.

She called me this afternoon while I was in class. She was hysterical. She was sobbing and trying to talk and was just inconsolable. I asked her if anything had happened and she said no, that she had just lost faith that things will ever, ever get better. I told her she needed to keep faith. Not in me, because I can't guarantee her anything right now except that I love her. She needs to keep her faith in life. She said she had lost her faith, and hung up. It was horrible.

She could blow her brains out for all I know. But I absolutely cannot go back now. I cannot. I cannot. I will not. I have done things to forever change me and my life. And whereas Elizabeth feels I am playing into the hand of the devil by succumbing to temptation, I feel that I am following God's plan. I don't know why this has happened to me, but to think that it is all for naught would be more than I can handle right now.

My mind races at times like these. I just want to run away. I don't want to face her, or her wrath, or her family. Those thoughts fill me with pain. I can deal with my own world, but having to carry hers as well is just too much for me to manage.

At the end of August, I traveled to Rochester to visit with my family for a week. It was to be the first time anyone in the family officially met Donna, face to face. I was determined to spend my entire week there in my new role, which was to be my most extended exposure as Donna up to that time. My nervous anticipation of the trip made the weeks leading up to it seem to fly by.

At that point it had been only six weeks since my facial landscape had been rearranged, and everything seemed to be healing nicely. There was still a bit of swelling in my jaw, and the barely noticeable scar along my hairline remained a little pink, but otherwise there was very little to indicate the extent of what had happened. I was gaining a new appreciation for the healing powers of the human body.

The good news was that nothing hurt. There was no pain anywhere. Of course, the reason may have been because much of my face was still numb to some degree or another, but as far as I was concerned that was a blessing. I was slowly but surely regaining sensation in my nose, and on my chin, which still felt as though an inattentive dentist had mistakenly injected them with an errant syringe full of Novocain.

Everything seemed to be well on the road to regaining normal feeling, except the top of my head. The entire crown of my head was still completely devoid of sensation, so washing my hair felt like I was giving my dogs a bath. I couldn't feel a thing. This didn't really pose a problem, except that my clumsy attempts to learn to use a curling iron on my still short, short hair sometimes inflicted nasty burns to my senseless scalp. The only way to realize the damage I was doing was either the appearance of a nasty scab, a faint sound like sizzling bacon frying, or the sickening smell of searing flesh.

The main reason for the trip was for the entire family to get together to celebrate my mom's 70th birthday. She approached this milestone in a celebratory, upbeat mood and I didn't want to do anything that might steal her thunder. Of course, having the oldest son show up in a dress somehow seemed to be hard to top.

I don't know if everyone practiced their parts or what, but once I arrived I quickly felt accepted and at ease. I seemed to slip seamlessly into the fabric of the family as if things had always been that way. My nieces and I went shopping at the mall together. My sister-in-law offered to clean out her closet and give me things she never wore anymore. My sister and I spent afternoons going to lunch, and talking as though we had forty years of catching up to do. It was absolutely unreal.

The day before her birthday my mom took me aside and told me that she had brought a pretty black and white dress that she thought would look good on me, and she would like me to wear it out to her birthday dinner. I tried it on, and we both agreed that it did look nice. I told her I'd be proud to wear it.

Although my mom and sister seemed to be comfortable around me, which was both a relief and a source of pride and happiness, I had still not yet seen my brother. He had been out of town during the first few days of my visit, and his first glimpse of Donna would not happen until he arrived at the house to pick me up to take me to the restaurant.

I was in the kitchen talking with my sister when he arrived. I heard him come into the front hallway, saying "hello" in a loud voice to announce his arrival. I had primped for an hour, and was actually a little nervous to greet my brother in makeup, pumps, and a dress. He came around the corner and saw me. I really didn't know what to say. What *was* there to say? So I said the first thing that found its way to the tip of my tongue.

"Hi, bro," I said with a look on my face that probably said "I'm sorry about making you feel awkward but I feel awkward too and hopefully things will get better."

"Hey," he said. "Hi, sis." We hugged.

Jay drove me to the restaurant, and we chatted a bit to break the ice. I think we both realized the irony and the humor of our situation, although I must admit that the sense of humor that seems to run in the family has always been a bit off-center. When in doubt, humor works.

At the restaurant, it seemed strange to be celebrating a family event of this magnitude without dad. His absence was only one of the many significant recent changes in our family, and I think we all celebrated Mom's special day with a real sense of pride in the resiliency and cohesiveness that we had shown. For a family that I would never have described as close, I don't think I had ever felt closer to everyone than I did on that day. I did not want it to end.

JOURNAL ENTRY

> It's 4 p.m. and I'm starting to pack to leave. I am finding it a very emotional thing, as I have felt so accepted and comforted and loved here that the thought of leaving upsets me. I have been crying on and off all day.
>
> I was out as Donna all day today....no makeup or anything. Just me. And Rachel. I always have someone to be with me here, to do things that I have always dreamed of doing but have been afraid to do alone. That is not true so far away. These people and this place are good for me, and I will make sure to be back to return it to them before too long...

Pain and rejection patiently awaited me upon my return home. My relationship with my son collapsed.

In all honesty, I didn't see it coming. Had I fooled myself into believing that everything was okay, when it would soon become so obvious that everything was *not* okay? Maybe Matt had been effective at telling me what he thought I wanted to hear, for fear of hurting my feelings, for as long as he could. The axe was about to fall.

Over Labor Day weekend, he and I were supposed to spend a full day together. We planned to go out for brunch, and then maybe shopping, or to the movies. But when I called the house the day before to finalize our arrangements, he told me that he had made plans to spend the afternoon with friends instead.

I was disappointed. I was hurt. I was angry. I looked forward to spending time with him, especially after being out of town for a week, and it was obvious that he didn't really care about spending time with *me*.

Maybe it was because he was uncomfortable being out in public with me with me because of how I looked, and I suppose I certainly couldn't blame him. Perhaps my fears that he was being brainwashed at home were actually coming true. And then maybe it was because he just didn't know how to relate to me anymore, that I was changing so much on the outside that I just didn't look or seem like his dad.

Whatever the reason, we still met for brunch, but a tension seemed to have crept into things that I didn't remember being there before. As I dropped him off at home from our aborted day together, I watched him walk from my car to the house. Little did I know that it would be the last time that I would see him for nearly seven months.

JOURNAL ENTRY

I have been calling home every day this week. Not to talk with Elizabeth so much as to talk to Matt. He started school on Tuesday and I want to know how he's doing. How things are going. She has the ringers turned off on all the phones. I leave messages to have Matt call me. I send him emails. I haven't heard a thing. Last night, Elizabeth sent a snotty message saying that until I decide to come home as Dave they don't want to talk to me.

JOURNAL ENTRY

I was at electrolysis yesterday afternoon and got a call from Elizabeth. I had sent several emails to Matt, and had called several times, and have not gotten a reply all week. I sent her a "nastygram" telling her that I resented her trying to come between Matt and me. She called to say that it was not her that was the reason for not calling. She supposedly passed along all my messages. She said that Matt didn't want anything to do with "this," and had chosen by himself not to return the calls. She went on to say that he cannot and will not see or deal with me as Donna, and that when she asked him about who he wanted to be with in case anything happened to her, he picked her brother first, her parents second, and me third. She tried to put him on the phone to tell me himself, but he didn't want to talk.

It was September 13, 1999. Name-Change day had arrived.

For transsexuals, a name change is a *big* deal. To finally have a recognized, legal, gender-appropriate name that matches our inner selves is absolutely huge for us. What's more, to finally have a legal document, such as a driver's license, with our new name, our new picture, and an "F" in the gender box, it almost too overwhelming to consider. In many states, as far as the law is concerned, *this* is your sex change. Whether you continue on to have the actual sex change surgery or not, from this point forward *you are female* according to the legal documentation of the state.

Very few of us actually have the opportunity to name ourselves. I am sometimes asked why I chose the name Donna. My son once questioned why I didn't choose a *cooler* name, like Jennifer or Megan or Ashley. The answer is actually pretty simple. I wanted to keep my same initials, DGR, so the first name needed to begin with a "D." I had a cousin named Diane, so that was out. I did not *feel* like a Debbie, or a Doreen, or a Darcy. For some reason, Donna immediately felt right. I even liked the way it looked when it was written. So that's the name I had given to the feminine side of my personality.

As for my middle name, my mom chose that. She had asked if she could, and I was touched that she wanted to participate in my re-naming. It was a pretty simple gesture, but it was significant in demonstrating just how much she loved me and truly accepted what I was doing.

I had already narrowed the list of "G" names down, and as I waited for her to tell me what middle name she had chosen I must admit that I was a little nervous. Donna Gertrude? Donna Grace? Donna Gabrielle?

They just didn't sound right, but who could guess the way my mom's mind was working? Maybe she would want to exact revenge for all of the grief I had ever given her, and would choose something so hideous I wouldn't even be able to pronounce it! To my relief, she called to tell me that she selected a name that happened to be one of the finalists that I had identified. Donna Gail.

The rules and procedures for name changes, and for changing the gender designation on a driver's license, vary from state to state. Often, the second of these two tasks is the far more difficult one, sometimes even requiring the intervention of an attorney. Thankfully, in Arizona, the process was relatively straightforward and simple.

In Phoenix, there is a court dedicated to nothing but name changes. I had waited several weeks for my day in court, as had 30 or 40 other people judging by the size of the crowd that was waiting to get into the courtroom. I had filed the paperwork at the county courthouse, and had been scheduled for a hearing date. I had also obtained the necessary supporting letters from my doctor and my psychologist to provide to the DMV.

LETTER FROM MY PHYSICIAN (ADDRESSED SPECIFICALLY TO THE DMV):

RE: DAVID ROSE aka DONNA ROSE

TO WHOM IT MAY CONCERN:

Donna Rose has been treated for transgender through our office and has been receiving appropriate counseling and hormonal therapy and is at this time deemed irreversible in her gender reassignment.

At this time we are requesting that her gender be switched on all appropriate documents including Social Security and driver's license.

Thank you very much for your kind assistance.

FROM MY PSYCHOLOGIST:

TO WHOM IT MAY CONCERN:

David Rose aka Donna Rose, DOB 02/22/59, is in treatment with me for Gender Identity Disorder (302.85). The patient is undergoing standard medical treatment for the condition.

As part of treatment, the patient is required to present and live at all times in the female gender role. Treatment has progressed to the point that changes are now irreversible, and it is appropriate for her legal documents to reflect the new status.

After all of the buildup and all of the waiting, it was all over in a little less than an hour. According to a legal proclamation from the state of Arizona, signed by the judge, David Rose was no more. My new name was Donna Gail Rose!

I took my official court order directly across the street to the DMV to get a new driver's license. Although I had heard horror stories about getting the driver's license information changed, the clerk was pleasant and helpful, and everything went smoothly. I got my picture taken, and within a few minutes I received my brand new Arizona driver's license with a not-too-unflattering picture of Donna, my new name, and a big capital "F" in the sex box. I was absolutely thrilled to death. I couldn't stop looking at it all night long.

I spent the next several weeks contacting every place that I could think where the old name needed to be changed. All my credit cards. My school transcripts. My Social Security card. My frequent flyer accounts. My retirement accounts. Eventually, my new credit cards started to arrive in the mail. It reminded me of the excitement I felt when I was in college and I got my first credit card…that I was now officially *somebody*. To see a shiny new credit card with DONNA ROSE imprinted on it provided the ultimate in validation.

JOURNAL ENTRY

I got my new Bank Card in the mail yesterday. It says Donna Rose on it. I haven't gotten any credit cards yet, but I go running home at the end of the day (however late that may be) to check my mail. It reminds me of when I was a kid and was expecting something in the mail, and I couldn't wait to get home from school to see. I remember one time when I got the addresses for all the NFL football teams. I wrote letters to every one of them. I rushed home everyday to see if they sent me anything. And I did get lots of good stuff. Photos. Stickers. Media Guides. It's almost like being a kid again....

People have been writing/calling asking if I am nervous about 10/4. It is so close. Funny thing is, I have been closer before. When I pulled the plug last time, it was the Tuesday before. Things are so different this time around....When I think about 10/4, I don't really think about what it will be like. I think more of the things I have to do to get ready. I have to finish electrolysis. I have to seriously expand my wardrobe for work. I am going to have my hair done next Saturday. I don't really have time to dwell on it. But I'm sure I'll think about it as it gets closer....

I like to minimize things by saying that the hard part is over. Showing up the Monday after everyone was told, and having all the changes out there for everyone to see, was a major hurdle. And in one breath, I figure that showing up here as Donna on 10/4 will be anticlimactic after that. Almost a yawner. But in another (and more realistic) way, I think that (just like divorce) knowing about it is one thing, and actually seeing it is another. For me to show up here in woman's clothes and a new name and a faceful of makeup will be a major thing. People who may have gotten fairly "comfortable" to the idea of Dave/Donna will now have to get comfortable again. It will be that Monday all over again. No matter how hard I try, there's really no way around that. I survived it the first time, and will do so again....

Sadly, my relationship with my son had become almost non-existent, and that hurt me deeply. He didn't respond to my phone calls. He didn't respond to my emails. I originally felt that Elizabeth was keeping him from responding, but I eventually realized that he just wasn't comfortable with me, especially now that I had change my name. In time, I hoped he would change his mind.

Ironically, my relationship with my sister, and with my mother, was closer than it had ever been. There was a connection between us that had never been there before. Mom and I actually said "I love you" at the end of our conversations. Dave never did that.

My mom's main concern for me at the outset of my transition was that I would be lonely for the rest of my life. It is a concern that I shared as well, although I never admitted it to her, or really even to myself, for that matter. I really couldn't do anything about it, however, so I hoped that by being myself, and by learning what I needed in life, I would find someone to love and who would love me back. I almost felt selfish hoping to find a second soul-mate, when there seem to be so many who never even find a first.

My intimacy needs were not necessarily based on sex, as there was a chance I would never be able to have an orgasm as a woman. Rather, they were based on my need, which I think is a fairly universal human need, for a deeper level of intimacy; a spiritual intimacy, an emotional intimacy.

JOURNAL ENTRY

> I don't really think about sex all that much. I don't know if it's the hormones, or the feeling that my sex life is pretty much in limbo, or what. This may sound odd, but I haven't had sex in so long that I think the prospect of it happening frightens me a little bit. I don't know how I would react. I have not ruled out the possibility of "exploring" at some point. But I have serious questions as to who would be the partner? What interest would they have in me?
>
> My lack of intimacy hurts me more right now than anything. I have been very alone for a long, long time. And I suppose

like anything else, you get used to it. But the thought of needing and having someone and sharing intimacy is something
that I try to avoid thinking about too much because it makes
me feel very lonely and empty.

Chapter Twenty-two

A Brave New World

I have dreamed about this for most of my life. And the fact that it is happening continues to be surreal sometimes. It continues to surprise me. It continues to make me happy. And I hope that feeling of being thrilled with who I am in the world never goes away.

— Email to a friend

By the end of September, my days of having to live the lie that had become David Rose were down to a precious few. I did not mourn the passing. I did not see this as the end of one life, and the beginning of another. Rather, I viewed it more as a natural progression, sort of like spring follows winter, or morning follows night.

I felt at ease. I felt confident. I felt at peace. I had no second thoughts, which was a significant difference from how I was feeling at this same point just six months earlier. At that time, all the pressures I had placed on myself nearly killed me. Now, the same events held none of those pressures…only anxious anticipation.

From: The Management

Subject: Mail Team Announcement

Date: September 28, 1999

ITD Mail Team,

I wanted to give all of you an update regarding the next major step in David Rose's transition. David has legally changed her name to Donna Rose. Beginning next Monday, October 4th, Donna will take another step in her transition by presenting herself as a woman at work. You will soon see her name change effective in email and voice mail as well. Don't forget to update any mailing lists you have at that time.

Thank you —

Although my initial disclosure at work had occurred some two months before, I was well aware that my debut there as Donna, in makeup and a dress, would spark renewed interest, curiosity, and perhaps even hostility or resistance. It was like going all the way back to the awkward beginning all over again. Lord knows what rumors would end up circulating this time. Just for fun, I thought that perhaps I should start by floating a rumor that I was pregnant, and see how far that went.

At that point, there wasn't anything I could do about any of that. I made up my mind to keep my head high, to appear confident, and to go with the flow. I couldn't let the little things that were bound to arise get me down. I needed to save my energy and my stamina for the big battles that I knew still lay on the horizon.

As the Sunday before my debut as Donna arrived, I really wasn't all that nervous. Family and friends called all weekend to see how I was doing, and to wish me luck. I had started living full-time as Donna the day before, so in a way I was relieved that the half-hearted attempts to keep some semblance of Dave alive were done. It was *finally* time to move on.

To this day, October 4, 2000, my first day at work as Donna, seems surreal.

JOURNAL ENTRY

How long have I talked and dreamed about this day? I can't believe it's here. I can't believe this is me. It's as if I were just a spectator watching this person do these things, and to realize that it's me is really amazing to me. I have no idea where I have gotten the strength/ courage to actually show up here today. It has built itself up over time, because I know it wasn't here too long ago. It's one thing to want it and talk about it, and another to do it. And still another to feel comfortable about it. How many people actually follow it through? Pretty amazing.

I actually slept pretty well last night (in bed a little after 10), but was up early. Like, at 3 something. I found a lot to do to keep myself occupied. Like iron. And put away clothes. And straighten up my ever-increasing wardrobe in my big closet. I was tired last night, and decided to put off most of this stuff until I had a little time. And I had the time.

I also had to decide what to wear. I ended up choosing a pair of Anne Taylor slacks (kinda gray green...Julie calls it "Sea Foam") and one of my Anne Taylor silk blouses (ivory). I thought about wearing a jacket, but felt I would be more comfortable without, so I passed it up. I originally had on a pair of black Naturalizer shoes with a pretty low heel, but my feet were sore by lunch so I went home to change into a more comfortable flatter pair...They're doing better now....

I didn't expect to see much of a reaction, and that's what I got. We had three new people start today, so I got introduced to them. I was originally supposed to go over and get my new id badge photo at 8 this morning, but I wanted to be here in my cube for most of the morning, so I rescheduled it for tomorrow.

243

> I made a promise to myself to keep my head up, and look people in the eye, and display on the outside the happiness and satisfaction I feel on the inside. So far, I have done that. And when this day is over, those are the things I will remember. Not necessarily what I wore, or what I did at lunch....but how I felt. I will never forget this day.

I gained confidence as the week progressed. I spent quite a bit of time each morning carefully choosing my clothes, and being especially careful with my makeup, to make sure that I walked that fine line between causing too many waves and being too careful. As I drove to work, I'd look in the rear view mirror at myself, still unable to believe that the reflection staring back was really me, and that I was going to work looking like this. Where had I found the courage? When had I finally become so comfortable?

Thankfully, the entire week passed smoothly and seemingly without incident.

JOURNAL ENTRY

> This is Day 4. So far, so good. I don't think I could have asked for much better. It's not like a marching band greets me at the door or anything, but I have no problem being me and no problem with who I am at work. If others have a problem....I haven't heard about it. But it wouldn't surprise me.

At the end of the week, Brian called me into his office to chat. He asked how I was feeling. I told him I was feeling great, and I thanked him for all his help.

"How have things gone from your perspective?" I asked.

"Great!" he said. "The entire week has been almost incident free, which is nothing short of amazing."

I know that he was as relieved as I was.

"Almost?" I asked, suddenly picking up on that word in his answer. "Is there a problem that I don't know about?"

"Well, a couple of people have mentioned that your makeup is a little heavy. And one person said something about a dress that you wore the other day."

"That's it?" I asked. "That's the only negative feedback?"

"For me, yes. I'm not sure if Lin has talked with anyone or not. Everything seems to be going well. We are all very relieved."

I can assure you, nobody was more relieved than I was.

JOURNAL ENTRY

> I got a phone call from Elizabeth at work this afternoon. She is angry, and started in on me again. She wanted to know if the Dave that she thought she knew, and the dad that Matt thought he had, would ever come home. I told her no. This person is different in a lot of ways. But that's not acceptable to her. In any way, shape or form. She wants our old life back, but that is gone forever. I told her I did not want to discuss this here at work. She knows I can't reply here. I ended up hanging up on her. It hurts me more than I can say to know the pain I have caused her. And Matt. And although I can sometimes move that out of the front of my brain because of the joy I am finding in things I have dreamt about for my entire life, the realization that she can find no joy tends to jolt me back to my reality.

The main responsibility of my group at work was to support our company's mail order pharmacy business. A mail order pharmacy is a huge warehouse of drugs where we filled prescriptions and mailed them out to subscribers around the country. It was a totally mechanized operation where conveyor belts carried empty containers to machines that would automatically drop a specific number of pills into each bottle. It was actually pretty impressive to watch it all in action.

After less than two weeks at work as Donna, something happened that was to have a profound effect on my role at work, and on my transition in general.

I was called into a conference room with Brian and two of the managers. I thought that perhaps somehow there was a problem related to my transition. Nobody likes to be asked into a conference room with the boss, not knowing why, and I watched nervously as they closed the door and sat down across the table from me.

Brian started speaking. "We have a bit of a crisis."

Apparently, the consulting company that we had hired to build and manage the software that controlled all of the drugs in our warehouses had abruptly decided to leave over a payment dispute, and we needed to identify someone on our team to analyze it, learn it, and take ownership of it. Pronto. They thought I could be that person. Actually, as I was to learn later, they really didn't have anyone else available so I got it by default, but at the time I felt honored that they had chosen me.

As it turned out, it was the best thing that could have happened, both for me and for my group. It would require me to spend most of my time traveling to our warehouse locations around the country, and very little time at our headquarters in Scottsdale. I wouldn't have to be around them, and they wouldn't have to be around me. Although I had never been a road warrior, I was to learn about the lifestyle in very short order.

I spent the next several weeks and months traveling back and forth between Scottsdale, Fort Worth, and Birmingham, Alabama. In my new role I worked directly with the staff at each location, and after only one week an interesting revelation started to become apparent. Although I'm sure news of my situation had preceded me to the warehouse in Fort Worth, it didn't interfere with my day-to-day work there. Everyone was friendly and professional to me. Everyone treated me like Donna. There were no mistakes in pronouns. There was no uncomfortable undercurrent. There was no *attitude*. It was wonderful!

I think one of the main reasons for this unquestioning acceptance is that very few of them actually knew me before my transition, so it was easier for them to accept than it was for folks who knew Dave. Whatever the reason, the resistance, the discomfort, the awkwardness, and the general attitude that I had noticed at work in Scottsdale during my two weeks there as Donna, seemed to be non-existent on the road.

I almost hated to go back to Scottsdale sometimes. I seemed to be a source of unending morbid fascination and curiosity. I had to schlep halfway across the campus just to use the bathroom. In contrast, my trips to Ft. Worth were full of invitations to happy hour, and to lunch, and I was treated as a valued and respected member of the team. I suddenly found the validation for Donna that I so very much needed.

My travels were not without their humorous moments.

At one of the early support group meetings that I had attended someone asked whether I had noticed any personal space challenges yet. I told them I had no idea what they were talking about. They told me I'd know it when I felt it.

I was on one of my business trips, waiting in line at the airport, and there was a man behind me and just off to my right. I noticed that he was uncomfortably close. In fact, if I didn't know better, I would have thought he actually knew me, he was that close. I took a small step forward to try to put a little distance there, but he moved forward as well…seemingly oblivious to my discomfort. And then it hit me; this was what she was talking about! Men and women are afforded different amounts of personal space, and now that I was perceived to be a woman mine was suddenly smaller.

Even simple things take a little while to adjust to. For example, when there are several people on an elevator, the women get off first while the men usually wait their turn. I have gotten on an elevator more than once, and when the door opened, we all just stood there until I realized that the men were waiting for me to get off first as the only woman in the crowd.

It also took me quite a while to become comfortable with wielding the awesome power of a woman's chest. Large breasts are almost magnetic in their ability to attract and hold a man's attention. It is the oddest experience to be talking to a man, and to have him making eye contact with your chest, almost as if talking to the *boobs* instead of directly to *me*. I certainly understood the allure, as I still appreciated a shapely woman's body as much as the next person. At the time, however, I had not yet harnessed the apparently significant power of my chest, so the stares and attention that it received was a source of anxiety and discomfort for quite a while.

Old habits are hard to break. Simple things such as writing or saying your new name, or reacting when you hear it, can become an iffy experience. More than once I signed something, later wondering if I signed my old male name out of habit and not even realizing it. I would hear someone call out "Dave," and I'd immediately looked around to see who was calling me before realizing that they were actually calling someone else.

New habits are hard to form, too. For example, I had never learned to carry a purse. Most women make carrying a purse seem like second nature, and never seem to leave it somewhere or lose it. During the awkward couple of months between the time that they announced my transition intentions at work, and that I actually started there as Donna, I used a fanny-pack as a surrogate-purse. I put my wallet, and keys, and a few other necessities, in it, and brought it with me wherever I went as though it were a purse. I needed to get used to having something to carry, so by the time I began my life as Donna I had already become somewhat purse-aware.

It also took me several weeks to settle into my new daily routine. As a guy, it took me 20 minutes, tops, to get up, take a shower, grab a quick bite of breakfast, and get out the door. I could set my alarm for 7:00 a.m., and be out the door ready to face the world 30 minutes later.

In my new life, the typical morning routine was much more elaborate, and took much more time. To get up, shower, shave my legs, do my hair, draw my face, get dressed…it all took well over an hour. Some days, I'd spend 20 minutes fussing with my hair before finally admitting defeat, realizing that some days are destined to be bad hair days. The hair gods can be very fickle.

Ironically, as time went on, I realized with more than mild surprise that I really enjoyed this part of my day. It was the only real *me* time that I could find some days, so taking my time and enjoying the attention I gave myself made it a very relaxing, healthy way to start my day.

Chapter Twenty-three

Reactions

There will be those who will accept you and understand and take it in stride and of course there will be those that shun you for various reasons like religious beliefs, peer pressure, and just fear of the unknown.

— Email from a friend

Little by little, people that I knew as Dave were learning of the new direction in my life. Some learned through emails or phone calls that I made to tell them. Others learned through word of mouth, as this kind of news tends to be hard to control. It was like watching a fire grow, or a virus spread.

The reactions I got were fairly universal. Everyone was shocked. But everyone expressed support and concern, at least at the beginning.

The Topolskis were neighbors during the entire time we lived in Rochester.

They are among the most caring people I have ever known. To me, they were the epitome of good neighbor. I remember waking up on cold, snowy winter mornings. There would be a foot of fresh snow on the ground, often piled three times that deep at the end of the driveway, where the snowplow dumped it as it drove down the street. Mr. Topolski would have already stopped over and cleared the driveway with his snow blower before going on to help other neighbors dig out.

At the time we moved into the house, they had two young kids…Danny and JoElyn. We watched them grow up, become adults, and eventually move out to pursue their own lives.

I called each of them to tell them about what was happening. They each responded to me in an email.

EMAIL FROM: JoElyn Topolski

Hi there-

Okay- Let's get a couple of things right out there in the open—

1) Was I shocked? That would be an understatement!!

2) Does it make me love you any less? Not one bit!! It doesn't change my feelings for you one bit!!

3) Will I be able to call you "Donna" from now on? Yes, with a little practice and probably a few slip-ups…(calling you 'Dave' a few times when you come visit us at Thanksgiving)

4) Do I understand all of this? Not really but I am willing to listen and learn!

5) Do I think that you make a good-looking woman? HELL YA! AND You better stay away from my boyfriend because I get extremely jealous and violent for that matter…just kidding!

SO THERE! I hope that you are relieved that I feel that way and I want you to know that no matter what has happened (with you, you and Elizabeth, etc) I would never, EVER stop talking to you! Dav— ooops— I mean— DONNA, I am a very open minded person and I owe it all to my parents, my church and my faith in God! They have all taught me what it means to love and accept people for who they are no matter who they may be! If you feel that Donna is more the REAL you then I can't wait to see her face to face...because I already know who the real Donna is "inside," and I love that person very much!

I know that you have been through 'a lot' but I truly hope that you are happy— especially just being yourself for once!! It must be a huge relief. I can't imagine keeping that inside all this time. I will pray for you, Elizabeth and Matt because I know that the road ahead is a long one- and I will do EVERYTHING in my power to help them try to understand and accept all of this—I think that it will come in time (I am hoping anyway) because both of them need you as much as you need them.

I love and miss ya tons...

JoElyn

EMAIL FROM: DAN TOPOLSKI

What's going on Donna/A.K.A. Dave,

How is everything going? I know your life took a 360-degree turn so I can imagine you are still adjusting to the entire change in your life. First of all when I heard about this entire situation, of course I could not believe it. It took a long time to sink in. I think that it was the fact that it was so unexpected. But after I heard the entire story of what happened and thought about it, I knew you would never do this on purpose to hurt Elizabeth or especially Matt. So I knew that something else must be going on, or that you have been battling with this for quite a while. So I went on the one internet site and read just about everything I could on what you are going through. I think it did a very good job of explaining your entire situation. I know personally that these types of things are

252

not something that you personally want, but I know for a fact that its physiological and has to do with your overall chemical makeup. (or what you call gender imprint—I think?) I also know from talking with many gay people (thanks to my mom!) that no one wants this, it is just they way they are. All they want to be is the person they feel they really are. I understand this. So to make a long story short, I trust you, and I know you would not do this intentionally, it's just the way you were meant to be. Even though I hate to see you and Elizabeth separate ESPECIALLY because of Matt, I support whatever both of you think is best. The one thing I hope is that you and Matt stay close, like you have always been. I don't think it matters if you're a man or woman, he needs you either way. I hope Elizabeth and Matt see it the same way too.

During my years in Rochester, I started and managed a small video production company. My original college major was in broadcast communications, and although I enjoyed doing that work I found there was much more demand and money for computer programmers so that's the direction that my career took. The highlight of my formal video production career occurred during a college internship in Syracuse, New York, when the Phil Donahue show came to town for a week. I was a member of the production crew, and have a picture of Phil posing with the rest of us, my large muscles making it easy to pick me out of the group.

In mid-1980s I started video taping weddings, more as a hobby than a long-term money making venture. At that time very few people owned VCRs, so business was slow. However, as years passed and wedding videos became more and a more popular and accepted, those of us who had been doing them for quite a while suddenly found ourselves very busy.

As my business grew to a point where I was turning down more weddings than I could accept, I brought in students from the local universities to help me with my weekend productions. I trained the students on my production style, provided equipment, and did all the marketing. They, in turn, spent six or eight hours on Saturday video-taping weddings, gave me the tapes to edit at the end of the day, got paid, and had fun in the process.

Mark was a tall, muscular, handsome kid fresh out of college. He had an infectious smile and a twinkle in his eye that could disarm even the orneriest and pickiest of clients. He was dependable, fun, and was the type of person I was proud to call a friend.

One day while I was at work, Mark telephoned. I was surprised to hear from him. He explained that he had met a woman, had fallen in love, and had recently gotten engaged. He had spent weeks trying to track me down to ask if there were any chance that I could videotape the wedding. The ceremony was scheduled for the day after Thanksgiving, and he thought that perhaps I would be in Rochester to visit over the holidays.

I was very happy for Mark. At the same time, I didn't quite know how to respond. I could have easily said no, and that would have been that. But for some reason, I didn't want to decline. I was genuinely touched and honored that he would have gone through all this trouble to find me, and felt that I owed it to him to be honest.

I told Mark that I would consider it. I told him that there were a few things he needed to know about recent events in my life before making this commitment. I said I would send him an email with the specifics.

I sent him an email explaining everything to him, and waited to hear back. One day. Two days. Three days. Four days. By then, I figured I had scared him off, and sort of forgot about it. A week later, I got his reply:

D:

I have been completely immobilized by your email. I appreciate the opportunity to process this offline. I don't think I could have had a dialogue without thinking about this first. My friends know that I am more of a "think out loud" thinker. For me to think BEFORE I speak requires a lot of effort and quiet time to sort out my thoughts- I've needed a lot of quiet time the last day. This is one of the hardest letters I've ever written.

I have to start by saying I respect you for being upfront with me.

I have been trying to define what I feel. It's been very challenging and very difficult. In a book I read a while ago, I wrote down a quote in my dayplanner "...there is no formal difference between the inability to define and stupidity" I feel really stupid right now.

I realized a way of understanding others by having empathy for them. Not the I-feel-sorry-for-them empathy, but to put myself in that persons shoes and try to feel what they feel & understand their situation, not to rush to judgment. The bible says," ...restore one another in fear and meekness, considering oneself." I have learned and grown with this advice. It has been extremely helpful in personal and professional life.

I have to say I am so grieved for the pain you, your wife, son, and family must have (and still are) going through. I can't say I understand your choice- but I'm a long way from your shoes.

I keep on rewinding to the times we've worked together and I see someone who is intelligent, funny, considerate, has integrity, respect, creativity, sincerity and someone who was patient enough to work with a goofy college kid who needed a job. Whether you realize it or not, you affected my life in a great way.

I have a list of attributes that I collect that describes what I value—you had many of the qualities that I value today. What I keep asking myself is what do I value in people. What is the essence or spirit of a person that I value and how does sexuality fit in?

Simply, I think a person's essence is not in their physical heart, but in their brain.

I did some research and I found a study that I think sums up the sexuality part,"...the organ that appears to be critical to the psychosexual development and adaptation is not the external genitalia, but the brain," Source: *Archives of Pediatrics & Adolescent Medicine* (1997;151:298-304)

"Dave" if we talk- If you don't mind, can I call you "D"? Also, please forgive me if I say something that offends you. I've found the best way understand others is to build a mutual trust so a true alternating dialogue can take place. I hope you will realize that I don't have mean intentions if I slip up.

I look forward to talking with you. Our prayers are with you, your family & friends.

Sally and Ray were former neighbors, living around the corner from us in Scottsdale. They had two grown sons, and seemed much younger than their actual age. Elizabeth first befriended them while taking Matt door-to-door selling magazine subscriptions for school, and we had all become very good friends.

I was actually proud of Elizabeth, as she was the one that told them what was happening. Sally was, of course, shocked to learn about my situation. We emailed a bit to break the ice. I could tell that she was trying to come to terms with my situation, but she was struggling with it. She was a religious person, and even confided in the priest at her church about her confusion. I did my best to reassure her that I was comfortable doing what I was doing, and would be glad to meet with her whenever she felt she was ready to see me.

It took several weeks, but one day Sal called and told me she thought she was ready. So, we arranged to meet over lunch.

Unveiling our new selves to others is a considerable act. People may be accepting when first told the news, but once they actually see the changes, they often rethink their position and back away. In this case, I had had a significant amount of facial surgery in addition to everything else, so I knew that Sal was in for a major shock when she saw me. I just hoped I could put her at ease, and that she'd realize, at my core, I was still me. Only better.

We met in a parking lot outside a busy supermarket, as I had a ton of errands to run before heading out of town again and we thought it might minimize the awkwardness. It was great to see Sal, and we got into the front seat of the car to talk. She was fidgety and nervous at first, and I noticed that she had difficulty looking at me, but as we talked and she became more comfortable, she relaxed.

After some small talk about how I was doing, and about how things were going in our neighborhood, she had lots of questions. How long had I felt this way? What causes it? Why couldn't I wait until Matt graduated from high school to transition? Did I miss sex? I did my best to answer each one.

Afterwards, she wrote to share her feelings about our meeting.

AN EMAIL FROM SAL [EX-NEIGHBOR, AND WONDERFUL FRIEND]

Amazingly enough, I feel so much better after seeing you. I really wasn't expecting that reaction, but you are definitely more at peace with yourself and I think I understand that this was so huge that you couldn't control it. I have always known that you did not reach this decision lightly, many years of thought have gone into your decision to change. You are the same caring, funny person on the inside that you have always been. Since seeing you yesterday and talking with Ray last night, I have talked with my sons, my Mother and my sister and told them. I seemed to be holding back, but after our visit, I realize that I must deal with the "This is" and it isn't going to change aspect and then go on, and my verbalizing the situation makes it easier to move forward. But then, I have

257

always thought talking about anything that bothers you is the best way to help you move forward. Everyone of course has the initial shock that we have all gone through and I am sure my reading and research have helped me to get where I am with this today. Bottom line is that I am glad we met so I could see the new you.

I will keep you and your family in my prayers.

Love, Sal

~

EMAIL FROM: an ex co-worker

Re: Our phone conversation where I told her about my situation

Hi There,

The night after we spoke, all I could do was think of you. You really knocked my socks off when you told me about your life in the past year. I have such strong feelings about our society and how we judge people instead of looking at what their needs and feelings are. Because of knowing you and the person you are, only makes me feel stronger about this subject. What you must have gone through all these years. I feel glad you decided to become the person you are. I'm also sad cause I know this can not be an easy transition.

~

Elizabeth and I had started talking to a divorce mediator. We had hoped to be able to end our marriage amicably with as few hassles as possible, but after one session with the mediator it became apparent that this wasn't going to go as cleanly as we had hoped. I suppose if was foolish to think that the divorce could be friendly, as our conversations and email exchanges were strained, at best.

Even more difficult for me, however was the gulf that had widened between my son and me. I had not seen him in almost four months, and at that point I actually wondered if we would ever see each other again. Matt never initiated contact with me, and rarely spoke with me when I called the house to talk with him. The close relationship I thought we had seemed to be crumbling, and there seemed to be little I could do to change that except to hope that time would temper things.

In order to reduce the opportunity for my mind to wander into the painful and scary aspects of my life, I kept busy. I worked twelve-hour days. My schedule was full from morning to night. I used to joke that it was a good thing that I wasn't a born worrier, because if I worried about everything that I probably should be worrying about I'd end up in a coma. I was as driven and focused on my transition and building a new life for Donna as I had ever been on anything. And, for the most part, it worked.

Every once in a while, though, my guard would drop. I would find myself in a hotel room, in a strange city...all alone. This was not a good thing, as it gave my estrogen-fueled mind an opportunity to go places where it didn't need to go. I thought about my wife and son. I was forced to consider a lonely future without intimacy or love. I was forced to face a grim reality that could lie just over the horizon. The price of it all sometimes felt so overwhelming that I'd just break down.

JOURNAL ENTRY

As I enjoy my first few hours of free time in a long, long, time I sit and get more confused. One moment seems to bring clarity, while the next brings the clouds of fear and doubt. I think I know why I have kept myself so busy these last few weeks/months, as down time tends to provide too much time for thinking. I don't know if my attempt to live day-to-day is more an attempt to take life in bite-size chunks, or more out of fear of what the future holds. I think both are equally valid.

When I look in the mirror lately I see myself as looking too "male." Perhaps it is the length of the hair as it grows itself out. Perhaps it is the fact that I desperately, desperately need electrolysis. Perhaps it is all the above. I fiddled with my hair for half an hour this morning before giving up in frustration, deciding that today was just one of those bad hair days....

Also, I am finding myself very lonely lately, especially being on the road like this. No friendly faces around...feeling like a stranger in a strange land. Oh well, I suppose it comes with the territory....

I watched a pay-per-view movie here at the hotel. It was *The Runaway Bride* with Richard Gere and what's-her-face. And as I watch these love story type movies, I wonder about the future. I feel lonely, and whereas most people leading "normal" lives can hope to meet someone and move on, I almost fear that. I wonder how many TS's actually find someone to fill the hole in their lives where a "mate" would usually go. We are plagued by dealing with something so foreign and taboo to most people that it is not uncommon for family and loved ones to disown us. And though we try to ease our mind and the awkwardness we feel in our own bodies....what is the cost? As I sit and contemplate this, I come up with a "damned if you do...damned if you don't" answer.

I try to avoid fear and worry. I find that those emotions are very destructive, and are usually far worse than the reality of what happens. I sometimes joke that if I worried about everything that I SHOULD be worrying about I would be in a coma. But as I sit and cry, I know that I have friends that I could call. I have family. But I don't have someone *here*. I don't have someone to come home to, and to talk about my day with, and to share with. And I have real fears that I never will.

This is probably one of those hormone-induced moments that tend to jump up out of nowhere. It could be the release of all the stress that I have been feeling at work. It could be that I am missing my wife and son, and that the holidays are upon us. I dunno. But I am sad and I am crying and I am lonely right now. I'll get over it. But it hurts.

I went home to Rochester for the Thanksgiving holiday. It was my first trip home since starting to live full-time as Donna. My last trip there, in August, had been a wonderful time when I had felt safe and warm in a protective cocoon of family love and acceptance. By the end of November, I was in sore need of a recharge.

The visit was very relaxed, and was just what the doctor ordered. My nieces and I went to the movies. My sister and I went shopping. I videotaped Mark's wedding. I went to a Buffalo Bills game with my brother. And of course, there was Thanksgiving dinner.

That year we all met at my brother's house. The guys conveniently found their way into the living room to watch football and drink beer, while the women worked in the kitchen talking and laughing and cooking. As I stood, slicing celery for the stuffing, it struck me that this was the first time I had ever been on this side of the wall! In years past, I would have been out watching the football with the guys! But somehow the sisterhood of the kitchen seemed very comforting to me just then, and I realized how much this felt like home.

CHAPTER TWENTY-FOUR

THE 20ᵀᴴ CENTURY FADES AWAY

Today was a very difficult day. I was supposed to be at Maria's
for three hours, but only made it halfway through before I just
couldn't take it anymore. When you're hurting emotionally,
the physical pain just gets unbearable. I left there shaking and
hurting, and cried all the way home. Although I had tons to
do, I just curled up in a ball in my bed and eventually slept for
a little while, and felt a bit better.

— JOURNAL ENTRY

As I neared the end of the year, I started to plan for the new millennium. Specifically, I needed to set a date for my sex-reassignment surgery. Waiting lists are often a year or more long, so getting on a list at that point, and having a specific date to aim for, seemed appropriate.

I had done quite a bit of research, and had narrowed the list of doctors that I was considering to two. I made a trip to Wisconsin to meet one of them and I liked what I saw, so I immediately scheduled the first date that I could.

My rebirth date was set for August 10, 2000.

I had been going to electrolysis non-stop for nine months. I had spent well over 150 hours there to that point, and it was an activity that had become part of my normal routine. I had gotten used to dealing with the discomfort, the aftercare of my sore, sad skin, and the mounting financial burden that I was facing.

Because of all my traveling for work, I wasn't able to keep up my usual electrolysis schedule, so I had to fit it into any free time that I could find. My brief weekend trips home to Scottsdale often consisted of unpacking, cleaning my clothes, repacking, running errands, paying bills and going to electrolysis.

By this point, my face was very clear, so electrolysis sessions usually consisted of clearing any regrowth that popped up, and we could usually get through most of the face in a single session. It was an incredible feeling to be able to run my fingers over my cheeks and chin, and feel nothing but a smooth face. I remembered back to only several months earlier, which by then seemed like a lifetime ago, and how I used to marvel at the small but growing circles of cleared area.

Now that I had set a surgery date, we were about to start on a new process that made the old one look tame in comparison.

JOURNAL ENTRY

As I sit at work and write this, I am totally physically and mentally drained. After two days of intense electrolysis, we actually started working on the "surgery area" this morning. Oh my God. Just thinking back to it makes me want to cry.

The main premise of modern SRS surgery, known as penile inversion, is to create a cavity in the pelvis and turn the penis inside out to form a vaginal canal. Usually, the skin of the penis is insufficient to provide the necessary vaginal depth. As a result, skin grafts are often needed to add onto the end to increase the length of the inverted canal. In the early days of sex-change surgeries, the grafts often came from the patient's hips, leaving unpleasant scars. I have heard some early SRS patients complain that recovering from that skin graft was as painful as recovering from SRS itself.

263

During the late 1990s, as surgeons perfected and extended SRS techniques, another source of the tissue for this skin graft was identified, and became widely used. This skin was found to be pliable and perfectly suited to provide the extra depth that was necessary. Furthermore, it was sensitive, so it provided added sensation to the vaginal cavity. And perhaps best of all, it did not require making any additional graft incisions, so healing was substantially quicker and less traumatic. It was ideal.

It was the skin of the scrotum, which up to that point had been deemed unsuitable for use and had typically been discarded.

I'm not quite sure how to put this delicately, so I'll just be blunt. Unless all the hair is removed from the surgery area in preparation for SRS, the new vagina will end up with hair on the inside. As a result, most surgeons suggest that the area be cleared of all hair in order to provide smooth, hairless skin in and around the vagina.

This involves electrolysis. Needles are inserted into each follicle containing hair on the shaft of the penis, on the scrotum, and surrounding the entire surgery area, electricity applied, and the hair pulled out at the root. Even worse, since this skin will not be visible and scarring is not a consideration, maximum voltage can be applied in hopes of killing the hair with one jolt.

For my first session to prep my surgery area, I arrived at Maria's for our usual 5:00 a.m. appointment. I had taken a pain pill in preparation, but no other medication was involved. First, she shaved the entire area down to nubs. Then, the *fun* began.

Unless you have been through this, there are few words to describe it. Let's just say that if this had been a form of torture devised to loosen a subborn tongue, I would have confessed to anything a dozen times over.

After three grueling hours, our session was over. I slowly put my swollen, red, painful private area back into my panties. Puss was seeping from the wounds, and I had trouble walking. The puss eventually dried, so every time I had to pull them down to go to the bathroom, it was like ripping a band-aid from a newly formed scab.

When I got to work, Brian noticed my distress. I am not sure what was the bigger give-away…the pained grimace on my face, or the funky way I was walking.

"What happened?" he asked.

I explained what I endured that morning, in gory detail. He looked at me in horror, his knees clenched together as if imagining such a fate himself. And he said to me words I will never forget.

"Donna, I can honestly say that you want this more than *anyone* I have even known has ever wanted *anything*!"

The holidays are often a particularly difficult time for those dealing with difficult issues or who are separated from their families. The knowledge that Matt's birthday was less than a week before Christmas and we hadn't spoken for weeks, that people were making their New Year's Eve plans, and that the first anniversary of my dad's death was quickly approaching, were never far from my mind.

Sometimes my mind wandered back to a lifetime of Christmases past. I remembered the time less than a week after we had brought Matt home that we didn't even open our presents until mid-afternoon. I remembered the time we bought Matt the electric car racing set, and spent hours setting it up with all the loop-the-loops and twisty-turns. He somehow beat me at almost every race. And I remembered the Christmas just a year ago when we tried as hard as we could to smile and pretend (for Matt's sake, or for our own) to feel the spirit of the season. It all seemed like a lifetime ago, like I was looking at someone else's life.

I realized that, if I allowed myself to be all alone, without plans and without things to keep my mind and my spirit busy, I would most probably become melancholy. My mind was sure to wander where it didn't need to go, especially with all of the hoopla surrounding the end of the millennium. Recovery from a year-end pity party would surely take weeks, and I didn't want to let that happen. So, I developed a year-end plan that was full of spiritual significance.

I planned to spend Christmas with Mom, who was living near Dallas. We had not spent a Christmas together in over 20 years, and this would be a unique and powerful bonding opportunity for us.

Afterwards, I decided that I would spend the last few days of the millennium taking care of the few remaining odds and ends of Dave's life, as the end of the millennium seemed to provide the perfect symbolic end to that existence as well.

Although I had been invited to several New Year's Eve parties, I preferred to spend that evening alone, not out of sadness or of loneliness, but out of the desire for the space and time to contemplate all that had happened over the past year, and all that was about to happen in the next.

Finally, I decided to spend the first day of the new millennium driving up to the Grand Canyon to spread some of my dad's ashes there as a tribute to his life and his death.

I flew to Dallas to spend Christmas with my mom. It was a very quiet and peaceful time.

The day after Christmas we went to church. It was a Unitarian Universalist Church, and I had been there with her a couple of times before. I felt very comfortable there, and found the small congregation to be a very intelligent, friendly, diverse group. They had become a second family to my mom, or maybe they had become a first family for her and we were the second family. In any event, much of her life over the previous few years was spent working for that church.

At the beginning of the service, the pastor asked if there were any joys or sorrows to be shared with the congregation. My mom raised her hand high into the air. When it was her turn, she stood up.

"I want to share my joy, in that my daughter, Donna, is here to spend Christmas with me," she said in a proud and strong voice. "It is the first Christmas that we have spent together for 20 years, and I am very happy!"

The entire congregation burst into applause.

I cannot express how happy I felt at that moment. Some people strive over their entire lives to gain that kind of acceptance, and never live to see it. I felt absolutely and totally appreciated and comfortable, not just by my mom, but by the entire community. It embodies what I felt that religion should be in my life, and reaffirmed my faith in the goodness of people, unconditional acceptance, and selfless love; a faith that had been seriously shaken by all that had happened.

Later that week a friend and I went out to dinner at a seafood restaurant. A small group comprised of two couples was seated at a nearby table. At some point, they took an interest in us…me actually, and we became the topic of their conversation.

It should be mentioned that, up to this point, I had never been aware that others had taken special notice of me. Ever. Not once. For all the worrying I had done during my earliest terrified strolls at the mall, I had never noticed anyone saying or doing anything that led me to believe that I was being scrutinized. I'm not saying that others didn't know about my situation, or that I had not become a target of a comment here or there. The fact is, I had never heard it or seen it, and I rarely thought about it. Until that night.

As we listened to them, these people could not make up their minds. They would wonder aloud to each other, peeking over at us but trying not to be too obvious.

"Is that a guy?"

"Yep, I think it is!"

"Wait a minute, maybe not."

"Look at the hands. The hands are a give away."

"So is the Adam's Apple. I don't see an Adam's Apple."

Their talk did not bother me. I knew that I was still early in my transition, and probably made an interesting sight for those who looked closely enough. In fact, I think I found their attention more amusing than anything. Eventually, the curiosity began to get the better of them so they started to get bolder.

"I dare you to go over there and ask," one said.

"I can't do that!" another replied.

"I'll give you ten bucks to go over there and ask."

Thankfully, we had finished our meal, and it was time to get up and leave before it got any further. I could feel their eyes on me as I put my purse over my shoulder, and headed towards the door.

My friend was not ready to leave quite yet. He was seething. He stopped over at their table before leaving.

"Yes. She *is* a woman," he said. "In fact, she's more woman than anyone sitting at this table!"

JOURNAL ENTRY

> The most amazing thing about this entire transition so far is not how far I have been able to come on the OUTSIDE, but how I have been able to deal with it mentally. At one point, the thought of being "made" scared me to death. But with the acceptance of this situation, you slowly accept that being "made" is not the end of the world. There will ALWAYS be something to give you away if a person looks closely enough.

> But even as in the case of that table next to us at dinner the other night, they didn't KNOW. They had suspicions, but they also had doubts. The goal of this is not to FOOL everyone....it's to allow what you have on the inside to be reflected on the outside, and the fact that I can pretty much go anywhere without any hassle or without heads turning immediately is amazing to me in and of itself. It just makes it that much easier to be me.

The last step out of my old life occurred during the last week of the century. Perhaps Elizabeth was doing her own year-end "house cleaning" to go through all of the things in the house to purge her space of Dave, and anything that reminded her of him.

She gathered it all up, put it in boxes and plastic garbage bags, and piled them into the garage. There were all Dave's old clothes. There were pages from our photo albums, ripped out one at a time. There was the large photograph of Elizabeth in her wedding gown that was on display at our wedding. There were things that my dad or mom had given me. There were boxes of papers and files. The pile had gotten so big that she couldn't get the car in the garage any more, so she called and asked me to take them away before she had it all taken away as garbage.

I stopped by the old house late one evening and packed it all in my car. There was so much that I was afraid it was going to take two trips, and by the time I pulled out of the driveway my car was filled to the roof! It would take the rest of the week to go through it all.

I spent all of New Year's Eve picking through the remnants of Dave's life, sorting through all the bags full of Dave's clothes and belonging. Some of the clothes had a sense of sentimental value to them. There was the nice suit that I bought and wore only once, for a job interview, but could never fit into again. There were the baggy shirts that I had worn over the last year of *Dave-hood* in an effort to hide my growing breasts. There were dozens of Buffalo Bills T-Shirts that I had collected. There were the many ties that I had received as gifts through the years.

I divided it all into specific piles. One for pants. One for dress shirts, another for casual shirts. One for things I wanted to keep. And when I was all done going through them, I loaded them back into my car. I had decided to give them to charity…in hopes that my last act with a life that had come to an end would benefit someone else.

As the sun went down, and the millennium celebration started working its way around the globe, I was feeling very good about myself. I felt a real sense of closure, even though all I had done was go through a bunch of clothes. I cooked stuffed salmon, and sat down in front of the television to enjoy a nice dinner and a good bottle of wine. I was very content.

Eventually midnight came and went through the state of Arizona. I will forever remember watching it on television, awed by the recorded scenes of incredible firework displays from millennium celebrations around the world as Sting sang his song *Brand New Day* in the background.

I wish I could say it ended there.

At about 20 minutes after midnight, the phone rang. It was my friend Kevin. He had called me several days earlier to touch base and inquire whether I had plans for New Year's Eve. He and Karen, and Elizabeth and I, had attended quite a few memorable New Year's Eve parties together.

I really didn't want to be with anyone, and told Kevin that I planned to spend the evening alone. He said that there was no way I should be spending it by myself. He and Karen hadn't made definite plans yet, but were going to do *something*, and whatever they did he said he wanted me involved. He *insisted* on it! I told him I would reserve judgment until I knew their exact plans, and he told me he would call me back once they were made.

I never heard from him. I assumed they made plans, and I wasn't involved, and that was certainly okay. They had been drifting farther and farther away from me for several months. It hadn't bothered me. But it bothered me now.

If there's one thing I had grown to *hate*, it was when people told me what they thought I wanted to hear, and not what was really going on. I couldn't *stand* that. It was condescending, and demeaning, and I got to the point where I got very sensitive about it. For a while I analyzed everything to measure if people were doing things because they actually wanted to, or actually cared. Sometimes I felt that others felt a sense of pity for me and were trying to make themselves feel better by trying to be nice to me. And that's what I felt was happening.

"What did you do tonight?," he asked.

"Nothing," I replied coldly. "I told you I didn't have any plans so I just stayed home, had a nice dinner, and watched the ball drop across the country on T.V."

"Really? Hell, if we'd have known that we would have called you earlier. We're just over at the neighbors house with a few friends," Kevin said.

"You knew I had no plans! You said you'd call me to let me know once you knew what was shaking, but I didn't hear back so I figured you guys wanted to do your own thing," I replied as I started getting angry.

"I said I'd call you?" Kevin asked in a high voice. "I thought you were going to call *us*!" he said.

"Kevin, why would I call you? You were the one who wanted to include *me* in *your* plans. I was perfectly happy to spend the evening by myself. If you thought I was going to call and beg to please be included you're crazy."

I had known Karen and Kevin for 20 years. I had been a guest at their wedding. We had vacationed, and partied, and matured together. Heck, the only reason that they moved to Arizona is because they had come to visit us during January and had fallen in love with the area just as we had. But I could sense that they could not accept what was happening in my life, and were pulling themselves away. I did not know it at the time, but I would only see them one or two more times before the relationship would break altogether. I suppose it was fitting that that day, that year, that millennium, that old life, and that relationship all end on such a symbolic note.

Chapter Twenty-five

My Father's Ashes

*It's funny....but the more difficult the journey, the more satis-
faction we feel at having made it. That kind of sums up this
journey I'm on, as well....*

— Journal Entry

As the new century dawned, it seemed just like any other day. I don't
really know what I was expecting, but for some reason I thought things
might *feel* different. I mean, the first day of the new millennium had
always seemed like such a huge milestone in the history of mankind. It
always seemed to be so far off in the future, but yet, here it was. I
remember lying in bed as a child, trying to do the math to calculate just
how old I'd be in the year 2000. Would I be married? Would I have
children yet? What kind of job would I be doing? It took me months to
get used to writing a new *year* on things, just think how long is would
take to get used to writing a new century.

I planned to celebrate the significance of this historic day by doing something symbolic and meaningful for my dad. I planned a relaxing and spiritual drive to Northern Arizona to scatter some of his
ashes into the Grand Canyon, giving him the ultimate of eternal resting places.

At mid-morning, the weather in Scottsdale was mostly sunny and cool. Unfortunately, the weather north of Phoenix, heading up into the rocky mountains towards Flagstaff, was very unpleasant and dangerous. It was cold. It was blustery. And, it was snowing.

For some odd reason, I viewed this obstacle as a personal test of my resolve to perform this task for my father on this special day that marked the new millennium. It was as if he had personally asked me to do this for him, although I think that, if he were alive he would have taken one look at the weather and rescheduled the trip to another day when the weather was more accommodating. After all, the Canyon wasn't going anywhere. For some reason, though, I had already stubbornly made up my mind. It *had* to be today.

The drive from Scottsdale to the Grand Canyon is about 220 miles, starting at the desert floor that is the Valley of the Sun, upwards through the cool mountains around Flagstaff. It was a drive I had done many times before as tour guide to friends and family who came to visit us in our desert haven, and most days it took me four and a half hours to navigate.

As I headed north into the mountains, the skies ahead loomed dark and ominous. Flashing signs by the side of the road indicated that slick roads were ahead, and advised drivers to take an alternate route. I began to see cars in the other lane, heading south, that were covered in snow. Soon, it started snowing a little. Before I knew it, I was engulfed by a blizzard.

I had lived in upstate New York for 15 years, and had become a fairly capable winter driver. Most of my winter driving was done on roads serviced by plows and salt trucks that were used to such inclemency. The highway through the mountains of Arizona had become an icy glaze, and there wasn't a salt-truck in sight.

Those of us foolhardy enough to challenge the howling mountain snows crawled along at 30 miles an hour. Some cars had pulled to the side of the highway in hopes that things would let up. Others were not so fortunate, skidding off the highway before coming to rest at some crazy angle, or upside down, in the center median. At one point, I waited for over an hour as snow accumulated on bumper-to-bumper traffic that waited on the mountain highway for a jackknifed semi to be removed so that traffic could pass.

I considered turning back at least a dozen times, my grip on the steering wheel so tight that I couldn't unclench my fingers. My eyes strained from trying to keep my eyes on the road through the howling snows that cloaked everything in a swirling white fog. The muscles in my neck and shoulders were stiff and sore. But for some reason, I felt confident that my dad wanted me to do this. As I drove, I spoke to him, asking that if he were watching to please watch over me. Whether out of faith or folly, I would not turn back.

I pulled into the park as the late afternoon sun was beginning to set. The view across the canyon was as amazing as I had ever seen, dark skies above punctuated by holes where beams of sunlight drilled through the gloom onto the white canopy of fresh snow that covered the magnificent red rocks below. Dark clouds raced across the sky almost as if they were looking for the small outbreaks of blue that tried to peek through the shroud, trying to plug the holes before they had a chance to grow. I paused only briefly to appreciate the magnificence of the panorama. I had other reasons for being there.

I reached into the simple but elegant urn that I used to store his ashes, and scooped out a small cupful. I sat there, looking at the speckled gray dust, marveling at the seeming uselessness of it all. I knew that these ashes weren't my father. The essence that had been my dad had long since vacated this world, leaving behind only an empty husk that we call a body. Still, the symbolic act of bringing his ashes to this place on this day helped me find comfort, and helped me remember my dad. It felt almost as if we had taken this trip together.

I held a short vigil before pouring the cupful of ashes off the ledge and down into the canyon. I watched as they sprinkled and sparkled, floating on the swirling winds almost as if they were flying with unseen wings. I understood why my dad would want to spend his eternity there, and felt a sense of peace and accomplishment that I could do that for him. He would have been proud of me.

I wiped the tears from my eyes before getting back into the car for the long ride home.

THE CHANGING FACES OF FRIENDSHIP

In the end, we will remember not the words
of our enemies, but the silence of our friends.
— MARTIN LUTHER KING

As my transition moved into high gear, and the physical and emotional changes that I was experiencing became more profound and more obvious, I found the way I interacted with others, and the way that they interacted with me, began to change significantly as well.

I think the key to this shift was my own change in perspective, based partly upon the new roles that I felt more comfortable in expressing and partly upon the new sense of vulnerability and neediness that I was experiencing. Friendships that could adapt to my new needs survived. Those that couldn't, ended. As a result, I saw old, established, trusted friendships begin to slip away, while new ones that gave me the validation and support I needed took their place.

I had known Karen and Kevin for nearly 20 years. It was the longest sustained friendship I had ever had, outside of my wife.

Karen had been Elizabeth's best friend as they went to grade school and grew up together. Elizabeth had actually dated Kevin for a brief period as teenagers. In fact, it was Elizabeth that had introduced the two of them in high school so many years before. The first time I met them was when Elizabeth brought me to their 1979 wedding as her date, and over the years the four of us learned that we had a unique chemistry together that almost always led to trouble.

Although we rarely ever lived in the same city, whenever the four of us got together it seems that we felt this unique freedom around each other to drop all of our inhibitions and just let our hair down. As a result, I learned to approach each of our encounters with the expectation that it would most probably add a new chapter to our list of wild and crazy adventures together.

Karen and Kevin had moved to Phoenix a couple of years after we did. As I considered telling friends about what was happening, I decided to start at the top, and that meant Karen and Kevin. They knew us well enough to know that something had not been right in our marriage for quite some time, but obviously had no clue what was at the bottom of it all. Shortly after I told Brian about my situation, I called Karen at work to ask if she wanted to know what was going on, and she immediately jumped in her car and drove halfway across the valley to hear the juicy news.

Karen and Kevin had done their best to accept me as I began my transition. It was Karen who drove me to the hospital for my first breast augmentation surgery. They had invited me out to dinner the night before I called everything off. When I really needed a friend to talk to, Karen was the first person who popped into my head. I'll never forget her prophecy that this transition would work, and that her greatest hope for me was to fall in love while on estrogen.

In the end, though, the lesson I learned was that my best friends were the ones I was most likely to lose. It seemed like the more that I changed into this new person that was becoming Donna, the farther apart we seemed to drift, and the more frustrated I became. After a while I began to feel that their infrequent calls to see how I was doing

276

were more out of curiosity than concern. It reminded me of race-car fans who watch the excitement on the track, not because they particularly care who will win so much as to witness the spectacular crashes that they are expecting, even hoping, to occur. I did not want to be one of those crashes.

As Dave I was a low maintenance friend. I didn't need frequent contact, or even much intimacy, from my friends. And I certainly didn't offer it in return. Guys just don't do that. They give each other funky handshakes and high fives, and talk about sports, hardware, cars, music, or girls. It's actually a pretty short list. For many guys, their idea of an intimate gesture of friendship is to share what kind of power tools they use, or what their favorite sports teams are. As Donna, I needed more. I needed the intimacy of *real* friendship and I was truly hurt by the fact that Karen and Kevin could not seem to be there for me when it was so obvious that I needed them.

As Dave I rarely felt compelled to act upon any of my emotions except anger, which made life very difficult and confusing once I found myself besieged by the cacophony of emotions that my transition unleashed upon my clenched, male-trained mind. Life was a chess match of move, counter-move and emotion only got in the way of making the next tactical advance. A display of emotion, or the obvious need for support or friendship, felt like an admission of a perceived *weakness* that we train our males to resist, even as we criticize them for not being more *sensitive*. It's a very difficult tightrope to walk.

Dave was far too well trained in the manly arts to admit, or to give any indication at all, that he was upset or hurt by anyone or any thing. I was far too macho to actually admit that someone had gotten through my thick defenses to the soft meat that lay beneath it all. Donna did not feel a similar restraint, either because she suddenly felt free to express her emotions in her new role, or because the force of the emotion itself was just that overwhelming. Whatever the reason, the estrogen that surged through her mind caused emotional outbursts at perceived antagonists that even now, years later I look back and shake my head, wondering "Why?"

With Karen and Kevin, I saw our once sturdy friendship slowly sinking into a quicksand of neglect. They never called. They rarely answered my admittedly emotional emails, which probably scared them more than anything. When we made arrangements to spend some time together, they always either cancelled or invited a third person, as though to avoid having to be alone with me. Whether or not my perceptions were accurate or a figment of my extremely sensitive mind, it did not change my perception that the friendship was dying, and that hurt.

In retrospect, I needed friends, and they needed time. I needed people that I could count on, while they needed the space that would allow them to know Donna in their own way. The two didn't mix very well. When they wouldn't or couldn't seem to reciprocate or understand, I let it go. I needed to move on.

Hi Karen:

I am not sure how to respond to you anymore. As I progress through my transition, I have had to assess many things. Not least of which is my needs when it comes to "friends." As I have told you in the past, my needs from my friends, and the investment I make in those friendships, have changed dramatically over the last year. I don't need to rehash all that here, as none of it has changed.

But the bottom line is that I have expectations of certain things, and when those things are not forthcoming, I am disappointed. Through my transition up to this point, some people have surprised me with the level of support and caring, while others have disappointed me tremendously. I would be lying if I didn't put you and Kevin in the second category.

Please don't get me wrong.....I am not blaming you or Kevin for any of this. On the contrary....I blame myself. Disappointment and frustration come from inside each of us. When things do not live up to our own expectations, we feel disappointed. It is not THEIR fault for the perception of failing. It is OURS for setting such high expectations in the first place.

Others (including you and Kevin) have said that it will get better over time. That it will take some time to adjust to accepting Donna where Dave used to be. I can agree with this. But not for people who only see me or talk to me once every 4 months. And I have come to the sad conclusion that those who I felt closest to are the people who display this most. They really do WANT to stay friends. They WANT to be able to adjust. They don't want to hurt me. But they feel awkward around me, and in reality can't be friends, and they do hurt me. So they tell me what they think I want to hear. In reality, they just want to move away quietly and watch from the distance. Instead of using the passage of time to adjust, they use it to gradually drift away.

Eventually, I will leave this city. I will go someplace and start new, and I will cut my ties with most of the life that Dave had. I will build a life where others may know of my circumstances (I make no attempt to hide it), but they didn't know Dave so they have nothing to compare me to. They don't call me D, or Dave, or "he." They call me Donna. That is all they know, and that Donna is a wonderful, warm loving person. They will judge me for who I am, not who I was, or who they want me to be. They will not feel the need to protect their children from me. In my mind, it's not so much running FROM something, as it is running TO something, and when I am ready, that is my future.

I don't know what I am trying to do in telling you all this, except to say that you have been great friends, and I miss you. The spot you occupied in my life remains unfilled. But the feelings you create in me are feelings I do not need right now, so I am doing my best to deal with that and move on. Instead of acceptance and friendship and support, or any semblance thereof, I feel rejection. And even though I accept the blame for feeling this way, it is one thing I cannot accept from "friends." I am not saying that I will always feel this way, and perhaps my feelings and judgment are clouded by the blur of things in my life as they zip by or by the effects of estrogen on a sensitive mind. Perhaps not. But if things really do change over time, perhaps so too will my ability to deal with all of this. We shall see.

Perhaps you are right in that my friendship with you to this date is still based on Dave in Transition. I have only known you as Dave for almost 20 years. That is half of my life!!!! I cannot just snap my fingers and make all that Dave represented disappear. To do so would take convincing myself that Dave was dead. I have tried to wish away the part of you that was this unemotional yet personable and funny guy I had grown to love. I have tried as I certainly like the more intimate Donna, but it is not possible for me to forget Dave. Like the Barbara Streisand song says, "Memories, light the corners of my mind." Dave is there in the corners of my mind, a vivid memory. Donna is a new comer, with no history in my life if I wipe out Dave. Dave has already established himself there and even in death he would not have disappeared from my memories. Although it may not sound it, it is meant as a compliment. Dave existed, he lived, he breathed and although he had his faults (who doesn't), he was still a lovable guy and he made an incredible impact on my life. New friendships typically are slow to form and take much energy to nurture. That is the joy of youth, you had more time then.

I hope when I am dead and gone that you will not forget about me as easily as you seem to expect others to forget about Dave. He lived, he breathed and he was my friend for 20 years. When I was able to see you in the past, it was as you know with much difficulty time wise, but when I did see you, you are right, I always saw Dave in Transition. But I was okay with that. You, obviously, are not. The relationship with Dave was sustainable on long periods of absence as our lives were complicate with jobs, kids, family, distance, etc.

I am sorry you are feeling the way you are about friendships. I am happy however that you are finding new ones that fulfill you. I will continue to hope for the best for you as I always have. I am here always for Dave and Donna, but not just one. I see you as kind of Sybil now. Please don't take this the wrong way. I see two people in one body. One is Dave, who I love dearly and who sustains our friendship and the other one, Donna, the newcomer, who I had hoped to get to know over time as Dave was so fond of her. Maybe in time, I would have, or will, start to see

Donna as the better friend. I wish you only the best and hope our paths will always cross.

Steve was hired at the company shortly after I was. Like me, he was a senior developer in the group. At well over six-feet-tall, everything about Steve was large. From his booming voice to his strong, broad shoulders, thick neck that was nearly as wide as my thigh, and a solid barrel chest, Steve seemed to have gotten extra helpings of *everything*. But for all of his intimidating appearance, Steve was really a sweetheart of a guy. He had gentle eyes, a bright smile, a contagious laugh, and always seemed ready with a humorous story, a funny line, or an astute observation.

When Steve first started at the company, I was his mentor. It was my job to help him get comfortable at the company; to "show him the ropes" so to speak. He was being groomed to become a manager there, and although Steve was at least ten years younger than I was, we immediately became good friends. Perhaps it was the fact that we were both from the East Coast. Perhaps it was the fact that we both seemed to have so much in common. Perhaps it was just because this was one of those times when two people seem to click, so no further explanation is necessary. Whatever the reason, Steve and I soon became "buds."

Sometimes, Steve's wife would make lunch for him to take to work, but when lunch hour rolled around he'd decide to forego the bag lunch that sat, untouched, in the refrigerator at work, deciding instead to head out to have lunch with me at one of the nearby Mexican restaurants. We'd talk about sports, his impending fatherhood, our families, or work. Sometimes we'd just philosophize about everything and nothing at all.

Although Steve seemed to constantly be trying to quit smoking, he'd stop by my cube a half dozen times a day to ask if I'd go out and keep him company while he snuck a cigarette or two. It was there, out by the parking garage, that we had some of our deepest philosophical discussions.

Steve once told me he considered himself to be a "student of the human condition," and he referred to himself as the "people professor." He'd sometimes make a statement about accepting people for who they are, or being open to new things and new situations, and knowing what I did about my own situation I told him he may need to prove those things some day.

During my aborted three-week transition attempt, Steve called me every couple of days to check on me and make sure I was doing okay. Although he had no way of knowing exactly what was happening with me at the time, he seemed to sense that something odd was going on. And when I finally got back to work, Steve was the only one who realized that I looked a little different. He was the only person who said anything about the fact that my nose had changed, although the reasons for it all wouldn't become clear to him until several months later.

As I prepared for my second transition attempt, Steve was the only other person at work (besides Brian) that I wanted to tell personally. We had become good enough friends that I didn't want him to hear about it from a stranger, and then feel hurt that I hadn't confided in him. I hoped that my personal explanation to him would be accepted as a gesture of intimacy, and would help to ease the sense of awkwardness that I expected to creep into our friendship. Truth be told, his seeming depth of character filled me with at least a sense of faint optimism that our friendship could survive the rigors of my transition, and that he would remain a valued ally and friend.

It took me two whole lunchtimes to explain it all to him. There seemed to be no easy way of bringing it up, and my feeble attempts to give him hints and have him guess ended up being pretty futile. How could he know? My own sister couldn't even guess. The fact that I couldn't yet bring myself to use the word transsexual in the discussion was certainly a liability. But Steve was patient. He sensed the difficulty I was having, and that I was doing my best to express things that were having a hard time coming out.

When I finally told him, finally explained everything that I needed to say, it felt like we had just survived a difficult ordeal together. I looked at him to gauge his reaction. His response is one I will never forget. I asked him if he had any questions. He thought about it for a moment or two.

"Actually, yes. I do have a question."

I prepared myself.

"What's your new name going to be?" he asked, with a faint smile.

His seeming "it's not a big deal" attitude actually soothed my frayed nerves. At a time when I envisioned doom and gloom, he was the first person that I spoke with who really seemed to think it would all be okay.

In the weeks after I told him, I actually became glad the he knew! I suddenly had someone that I felt I could talk with about it all, and he did his best to keep me calm.

Once, I expressed the fear that others on the team would distance themselves from me, and how that would hurt.

"I think you're not giving the team, or yourself, nearly enough credit," he replied.

Maybe not.

What I do know is that it didn't last. When I actually started transitioning, and my physical appearance started to change, our lunch-time excursions stopped. He found other people to keep him company while he smoked. Our brief conversations were awkward, and any smiles seemed to be forced ones. I started to feel like the lonely serpent in *Puff the Magic Dragon*.

It got so bad, in fact, that we eventually got into an angry shouting match over the phone about some work-related issue. I got loud, he got loud. I got emotional, he got angry. At some point during the exchange, he made some comment about our group "being a team."

That set me off. All the pent-up anger and frustration that I was feeling towards the team, and especially towards him for abandoning me, came gushing out.

"A team?" I screamed, "How can you dare say that I am part of anything resembling a 'team'? I'm an outcast! I'm treated like a leper! I'm all alone out here, and I don't see no stinking 'team'! And YOU, dear ex-friend, who once seemed so full of optimism, and thought that I wasn't giving the team enough credit; you're the worst of the bunch! You can't even look me in the eye! And you call yourself a 'people professor'? HA!"

Steve later apologized that he hadn't been able to handle things better; that he thought he'd be able to be more accepting, and that he was trying.

That friendship died, too.

~

When Matt was young he and I went out for breakfast every Sunday morning, leaving Elizabeth curled up in bed to catch up on her sleep. We went to the same restaurant every week; from the time he was two years old until he was nearly twelve. Over the years the waitresses there became good friends; we knew them all by name. Our visits became more like show-and-tell as Matt would bring his favorite sports cards, or his favorite cars and trucks, to proudly display to our friends there.

One waitress in particular became a good friend. Mary Beth was a bubbly blonde in her early twenties with a big, happy smile, and always seemed genuinely happy to see Matt and me. We always asked to be seated in her section, and when things weren't busy we'd talk about her boyfriends, her job, her family, football, or whatever else was happening in her life at the time.

After ten years of Sundays, she ended up moving to Phoenix. Matt was crushed. But once we moved there, too, and got settled, we found her and rekindled the friendship. We sometimes got together on Sundays to watch the Buffalo Bills, went to a monster-truck event together, and met for lunch from time to time to keep up on the latest news and gossip from back home.

Mary Beth knew that something wasn't right with my marriage. There had been a long stretch of time when she joked that she didn't believe that I really was married, as Elizabeth never, ever accompanied us on our Sunday morning visits. I called her after I moved out of my house. I told her that Elizabeth and I were trying to work through some difficult issues, although I didn't go into specifics at the time.

A couple of weeks after I got back from my facial reconstruction I called to ask if she would meet me for dinner. I explained everything to her over the phone, even the fact that I had had my face re-sculpted, as I didn't want it to come as a complete shock. She seemed genuinely concerned and sympathetic, and we arranged to meet.

I'll never forget the look on her face when she saw me. It was like she saw a ghost. I'm sure it was a ghastly sight, with the faint outlines of the incisions and sutures, and my face still somewhat misshapen and swollen from the pounding it had taken. She was trying to smile, and trying to carry on a conversation, but I could tell that it was forced, and that I made her uncomfortable. As she ate, I saw her hands shaking. And as we said good-bye in the parking lot, I noticed that her face had become an ashen white. She said she was okay, but I left wondering if we'd see each other again.

I called her several times afterwards, but she wouldn't return my calls. I sent several emails, hoping to hear back, but never received a reply. Eventually, Elizabeth said that she had spoken to her and that she didn't want to hear from me anymore, so I stopped writing altogether.

~

In the middle of January, a prominent transsexual came to Phoenix to speak to the gender community there. Her name was Dana Rivers, and as a man had been a nationally recognized high school teacher. News of her intention to transition on the job led to her dismissal, and her story had recently been featured on national news shows, in *People Magazine*, and she would soon be appearing on Oprah. At that time she was the most visible transsexual in the world. She seemed strong, intelligent, articulate, and courageous. I wanted to meet her, so I went to see her talk.

Dana was a powerful speaker. She spoke passionately about hate and violence towards transsexuals, and how rights that most people seem to take for granted actually protected none of us. At first, her message made me angry, but the longer I thought about it, the more it made me sad.

At the reception afterwards I met Kate. Kate was Dana's press secretary, and had made the trip from San Francisco where they both lived to spend a little time in the warmth of the desert winter sun.

Kate had reams of thick shoulder length-red hair, a wide smile and devilish eyes that seemed more appropriate on the Cheshire Cat than on this intriguing pistol of a woman. Her voice was unlike anything I had ever heard; feminine and sweet to the point that I really think it would have made many genetic women jealous. I was immediately drawn to her, not in a sexual way, but more as a novice drawn to a master; a ready follower is drawn to a worthy leader.

By the time we spent a little time together at brunch the next morning, I had come to realize that Kate's lust for life was unlike anything I had ever experienced in my own sheltered, cloistered life as a family man. She lived in a world of sensuality that was a seemingly endless smorgasbord of opportunity. Whether we were talking about food, wine, or sex, Kate purred with excitement at all the possibilities. She was classy. She was fun. She was exciting. And, perhaps most dangerous to my own situation, she was oh-so-contagious.

The many similarities between our lives seemed almost too strange to be coincidence. She had been married. She had had a very successful career as a software developer and consultant. She had a very successful martial arts background. She had tried her hardest to resist her pull to be Kate, unwilling to live the rest of her life as an outcast and a freak. Eventually, though, her strength just ran out.

Kate had had her SRS just a year before, so she was well ahead of me on the path. At the beginning, I looked at her like a young apprentice eyes a respected master craftsman...full of respect and wonder for all the experience and knowledge that she had gained, and hopeful that I could learn just a mere sliver of it.

Fate has an odd sense of timing. So many times, she seems to arrive just a tad too early, or a sliver too late, almost as if by design. This time, her aim was impeccable. Until now, I had found people to teach me the skills I thought I'd need to know to exist successfully as Donna in society. Now, fate was providing someone to teach me about *life* as Donna. Kate was to become a wonderful mentor, a beloved big sister, and an intimate friend; all when I was to need them most.

As Kate left to catch her plane back to San Fran, I told her that there was a good chance I would be visiting there in February. I was preparing to schedule a follow-up procedure with Dr. O. Plus, I wanted to take some of my dad's ashes to Yosemite National Park, as that had been one of his favorite places. In another ironic twist, Kate said that she used to conduct tours there, and she had the perfect spot in mind for him.

We said goodbye. But I somehow knew that our paths would cross again soon.

CHAPTER TWENTY-SIX

STORMY SEAS

The road I am facing has been horrendously difficult. No one who has not faced it can begin to imagine it. And the hardest part is the roadblocks that continually seem to try to stop nature from taking its course.

— EMAIL TO HR

There were three significant issues facing me as January wore on.

First, I had made arrangements to return to San Francisco and Dr. O in late February for a procedure he called a Forehead Revision. For patients on whom he performed a scalp procedure, he found that if he waited for six months for the tight skin to stretch and heal, he could refine and improve the results with a comparatively minor second procedure. A good friend had recently been there for her forehead revision, and told me it was well worth the effort, especially since the cost was covered by the original surgery so it was almost free. I made travel arrangements to spend my birthday there with Kate prior to the procedure.

Second, at Elizabeth's urging, I started divorce proceedings. Neither of us wanted to be the one to initiate it, but eventually I was the one who actually did the dirty work. It had become apparent that the mediation route just wouldn't work for us, and things between us seemed to be getting worse (if that was possible) instead of better, so it looked as though we'd be settling our nearly twenty-year-old marriage in court.

Lastly, I approached HR at work to make sure that I took care of any loose ends in preparation for my Sex Reassignment Surgery (SRS) in August. Several friends in the Phoenix area had gone through a similar procedure, and although no health insurance coverage was available for expenses related to the surgery itself, their companies had been very accommodating when it came to providing Short-Term Disability coverage for time missed at work, both for the surgery itself and the two or three weeks of recuperation afterwards. Things seemed to have been going so well that I really didn't expect a problem.

I wrote to Lin to officially tell her my SRS date, and to see if there was any paperwork I needed to complete in order to make sure my Short Term Disability (STD) plan was ready for me when I needed it. She wrote back saying that she was sorry, but our STD plan would not cover my absence from work for the surgery, but I was free to use any vacation that I had to cover it, or apply for a leave of absence.

I requested a copy of the plan to see exactly what prevented me from obtaining coverage while everyone else I knew didn't seem to have a problem. She sent it to me in the company mail.

As I reviewed the exclusions of the plan, I was initially surprised to see that there were only a half dozen or so of them. One indicated that injuries sustained while committing a felony would not be covered. That was certainly understandable. Another indicated that self-inflicted injuries would not be covered, and unless they were trying to argue that this procedure was self-inflicted, I could agree with that one. Another said that injuries that resulted from experimental procedures were excluded. Again, that seemed logical.

And then there, plain as day, was an exclusion specifically indicating that time off due to "sexual transformations" would not be covered.

I couldn't believe it. My own company had adopted a Short-Term Disability plan that explicitly discriminated against transsexuals! What's worse, they lumped this situation with all of those other outrageous exclusions. I was absolutely livid.

I wrote to Lin to get clarification on what *was* covered. She told me that anything that wasn't specifically identified on the exclusion list would necessarily be covered. So, if a person was an alcoholic and the doctor recommended that he took a month off to dry out, that was covered. But a person recovering from sex reassignment surgery was not!

As a successful man in our culture, I don't think that I had ever really experienced discrimination. I certainly knew it existed, but it had never stared me straight in the face until right then. The only question remaining is what I planned to do about it.

This meant war.

Hi Lin:

One of the first things I did upon arriving back in Phoenix over the week-end was to go to my desk to get the information you had told me you sent. I cannot tell you how important a matter this is to me, and how disappointed I was at what you had sent to me.

This situation far transcends the $4,000 or so in salary for the 3 weeks that I am planning to be out. It stabs at the very heart of my situation.

I wear a pendant that is inscribed with the Serenity Prayer...."God grant me the peace to accept the things I cannot change, the courage to change the things I cannot accept, and the wisdom to know the difference." It is a motto that means much to me. And THIS is something I cannot accept. It involves principles that I feel so strongly about that I am hoping we can come to a resolution to this before any lasting damage is done.

I am following an internationally accepted protocol of treatment for people in my situation. These steps are supported both by the medical community as well as the psychological community. The medical risks are very high. For example, I am taking a dosage of estrogen that far, far exceeds that produced in a genetic female body (5mg/day + 2cc biweekly injections). I have been on this regimen for 3 years. The chief concern for people in this situation is that the hormones must be metabolized in the liver, and leads to an increased risk of liver cancer. In fact, my chances for liver cancer are at least 10 times what yours are as long as I continue this dosage, and my liver enzymes are monitored every 6 months to ensure that the levels are not elevated. There are only two ways to change this situation. The first is to go off hormones, which is absolutely not an option. The second is to have the surgery, which removes the source of the testosterone, and the need for the high doses of estrogen. So beyond any "cosmetic" or quality of life issues that can be raised by the surgery, it IS irrefutably medically necessary for people in my situation.

I know of a half dozen other gals in the Phoenix area who have had their surgery in the past 2 years. ALL have had their convalescence absence covered by the short-term disability policy of their company. Every one. And all have told me that it was not a problem. If I were to accept this exclusion, I would be alone among them as the only one who did not receive this benefit. The thought of working for a company that would not fight for me in this instance, under these circumstances, would be one I simply could not accept.

The road I am facing has been horrendously difficult. No one who has not faced it can begin to imagine it. And the hardest part is the roadblocks that continually seem to try to stop nature from taking its course. To this point, the company has been wonderful in helping me in my transition. For my own part, I feel I have made a commitment to this company, and remain a valuable asset to it. My users will attest to that. Many transsexuals transition at their job only to leave and start fresh somewhere else. I do not want that to happen. I am hoping that the corporate values that we preach will not fade down the homestretch, and we can all be proud of the way in which it was handled.... from start to finish.

I have spoken with my physician, Dr. Fisher, and my psychologist, Dr. Sheila Dickson, Phd. Both are willing to talk with whomever you feel appropriate regarding my situation. I can also provide names of HR managers at IBM, Honeywell, and Motorola who have worked through this without incident. I am hoping that, based on the overwhelming evidence of specialists respected throughout the United States, and the desire of all parties to continue our relationship, that some arrangements will be made and I will be granted my 3 weeks of paid leave while convalescing. I need that assurance.

Please let me know what I need to provide in order to move things ahead.

Thank You,

Donna

~

HER RESPONSE:

Donna,

Thanks for the update you sent. You are right, I can't imagine what you are going through. I can only try my best to help.

I'm more than happy to continue to convey your concerns about Short Term Disability coverage of sex reassignment surgery on to the benefits committee. However, I don't think that this will be enough information to change the company's guidelines on coverage for an elective surgery. Based on our recent conversations, I thought that you might be able to provide documentation supporting that your surgery is a medical necessity. I'll get it to the benefits committee for further consideration. Without it, there isn't really anything more for them to discuss.

With that additional information from you, I still can't guarantee that there will be a change and the company will support paid time off under short-term disability for your surgery. I'm open to considering an unpaid personal leave for the surgery so you don't have to exhaust your vacation time. Maybe that's another option we should discuss when you're back in town. In the meantime, let me know if you have anything that supports the medical necessity of the procedure and I'll pass it along.

Lastly, I appreciate the info. you sent as well regarding how other local companies have handled your situation. However, I don't need to contact them. We are very confident in the rich benefit provided by our STD plan and we don't feel the need to compare it to others in the valley. How they approach STD doesn't have any bearing on how our plan is administered.

Take care. I'll talk with you soon—

Lin

⌒

My Reply:

Hi Lin:

Thanks for getting back to me.

Needless to say, I do not share the high regard in which you hold our company STD plan. I find a blanket exclusion such as the one you have regarding SRS to be totally unacceptable and ignorant. But I suppose that, at this point, that is neither here nor there.

I have not given up. I am gathering information from my doctor, and from the Harry Benjamin Committee, and from others to help me in my efforts. I will forward the information to you as soon as I have it all.

Thank you again.

Donna

⌒

As a guy, I thought of myself as a formidable opponent. I did not like to lose, which pushed me that much harder to win. I think that's part of what made me successful as a student, as a wrestler, as a businessman, and as a man in general. Life was very much about winning and losing, victor and the victim, about tactics, strategy, muscle, and force. Even simple things in my daily life were perceived at a contest. When I lifted weights, it was me against the weight. To fail to lift it would allow the weights to win. I saw this STD issue as a direct challenge. It challenged my value as a person. It challenged the validity of what I was doing. There were principles involved that deal with dignity, and decency, and to deny those were a direct slap in the face. As I got more and more incensed by it, it almost became a personal assault. One way or another, I was not going to lose this one.

As I developed a battle plan, I saw three options. Either the company could remove the exclusion altogether, which seemed unlikely, they could make a specific exclusion in my particular case, or I would leave. If I left, I assured them that I would *not* leave quietly. The only question that remained: which one would it be?

As a strategist, one of the goals of preparing for battle is to keep yourself from being cornered. Make sure you have options. Don't gamble on something, and then have nothing to fall back on. Make sure you have at least a Plan A, and a Plan B. My dad told me that the first opponent to lose his head is first to admit defeat. So I did my best to keep emotion out of the picture, and to formulate my strategy logically.

The first thing I did was to contact my doctor, my psychologist, several well known transsexual authorities, HBIGDA…anyone who could provide documentation that transsexual surgery is not elective surgery, but a medical necessity. It is part of the treatment protocol for a medically and internationally accepted condition. Lin had already indicated that establishing the medical necessity for the surgery was the key to this battle.

I contacted the state of Arizona to inquire about the legality of this type of obviously prejudiced exclusion. I contacted friends who were in the insurance business to learn about national organizations that got involved in disputes such as this. I started to compile all the information before deciding how to use it.

Once I had those wheels in motion, I started working on Plan B. More specifically, I started making arrangements to leave. I wrote an email to some of the key senior managers that I supported to make sure they were aware of what was going on, expecting that they would bring pressure on the company because of the valuable role I was playing. I called friends around the country that worked in computers, and sent them updated copies of my resume. And, I started responding to inquiries from companies that had been pursuing me for quite a while with a "yes," instead of a "no."

One of these companies was a large computer manufacturer based in central Texas. I had skill with a specific kind of programming language that they used, so they sent Dave email a couple of times each year to ask if he had any interest in a job there. In short order, Donna replied with an updated copy of the resume, a recruiter contacted me, and we began our hi-tech courtship.

Donna,

When will you be back next week? I think it would be really useful if you and I could sit down with the Director of Benefits and talk through your concerns. This isn't a closed issue by any means so let's get together and talk some more.

Lin

Just as I started to feel optimistic that we might be able to work this out, the next salvo was fired at the beginning of February when the managers of the group (including Brian) indicated that they would be changing my role on the team, and that I wouldn't be traveling as much.

It's not that I particularly liked the traveling. In fact being on the road and living out of a suitcase five days a week, three weeks a month, can get pretty old.

Despite the difficult lifestyle and schedule, the trips held two sources of priceless value to me. The people at the remote locations really seemed to care about me. Even the custodians knew my name, and greeted me warmly. Meanwhile, back in Scottsdale, things had become even chillier. Most people avoided me. Some people refused to refer to me using my name, instead calling me "Rose," or "he." I generally let these slip-ups pass. However, if I felt that people were *intentionally* trying to provoke me, or if I happened to be at the low end of my hormone cycle, I was ready to defend myself, firing off a terse email inviting them to stop by to discuss it, or to visit HR.

Perhaps even more importantly, I had gained a tremendous sense of pride in the work that I was doing. The tools that I had developed had improved our physical inventory counting accuracy from just over 50% to well over 90%. I enjoyed it. I felt good about it. I felt that the work I was doing really did have value. I did not want to have it all taken away as some sort of perceived punishment.

In the early days of my transition, all I wanted was to be allowed to show up at work as myself, and be left alone. It was a pretty simple existence, and my expectations were pretty low. It was obvious that that just wasn't good enough for me any more. As I slowly clawed my way up the pyramid that is Maslow's Hierarchy of Needs, I needed more. I needed to feel good about myself. I needed to feel valuable as a person. I needed pride. I needed validation.

At the end of February, as I went to San Francisco for a week I will never forget, I got it.

CHAPTER TWENTY-SEVEN

THE BAY BECKONS

This trip has been nothing short of amazing, in many many respects. Kate has taken the torch as my "teacher" in some ways, and has seen to it that I am exposed to new ideas, new people, and new situations to help me along this path.

— JOURNAL ENTRY

I suppose I should have realized just how amazing this trip was to be from the very beginning. Shortly after arriving, Kate took me to one of her favorite beaches. It was a gray, cool, misty Northern California morning, and strong sea-fueled winds that could have filled even the stiffest of sails hurled mountainous foaming waves of water against the sandy shore. As we strolled bare-footed along the sand, hair flying in every direction, we came upon a bottle half-covered in sand at the very edge of the water's reach. Kate picked it up, held it against the gray sky to try to peer through the dark glass, and noticed a piece of paper carefully rolled up inside. We had found a message in a bottle!

The first order of business on the trip was my continuing quest to take some of Dad's ashes to Yosemite National Park. We spent the five-hour drive getting to know each other, and I don't think there was more than a minute or two of silence for the entire drive. We had so much in common that the words just seemed to flow endlessly.

When we got to the park, it was snowing lightly and it almost felt as though we had the entire park to ourselves. There were no crowds. There was no traffic. It seemed as though all had mysteriously cleared out, leaving Kate and me to complete this quest in total solitude and silence. Kate knew the park well, so we parked the car near the lodge, grabbed a small picnic basket she had prepared and the small vial full of dad's ashes, and we hiked for about a mile to small body of water named Mirror Lake.

The instant I saw it, I knew that this would be perfect. I knew that this would make Dad happy. At the foot of Half Dome, the incredible marble cliffs were perfectly reproduced on the smooth glass surface of the lake, making it seem that the lake were a gateway to a mirror world that lay just below the surface of the water. The silence of the wind rustling through the trees, pushing low hanging clouds across the already gray sky, gave it all a spiritual feel that I will never forget.

Kate left me to complete my task in solitude, so I took the vial of ashes down to the edge of the still water and kneeled there to talk to Dad for a few minutes. I told him that I missed him, but that I took comfort in knowing that he was watching over me from someplace safe. I asked him to show me my path by dropping hints from time to time. I asked him to give me renewed strength to handle all of the difficulties I could sense were brewing even then. And, I asked him to be proud of me, confident that he truly knew what I was doing and why, so that no explanation was necessary.

By the time I sprinkled the ashes on the water, watching them scatter along the surface of the mirror, I was crying. Kate saw me standing at the edge of the water, tears streaming down my face, and came to hug me, and I willingly returned her embrace. I was shaking, and she stroked my hair as I buried it on her shoulder, fighting to stifle my grief while at the same time wanting to let it all out.

Once I had composed myself, we sat at the edge of the water to eat salmon and drink wine, watching the late afternoon darkness begin to descend over the timeless vista that would now be dad's forever. There was no need to talk. Kate touched my hand, stroked my hair, comforted me with a sympathetic glance as I sniffled, as we drank wine and spent the last few moments savoring this spiritual feast with Dad. A warm sense of peace filled me, and Kate and I packed up and slowly walked back to the car, hand-in-hand, in the darkness. In an odd way, we had somehow bonded in a way that I had never bonded with anyone before.

The emotion of the day, and the snow that continued to fall, made a return drive at that hour of the day seem like a sorry end to a very special day, so we got a hotel room near the park for the night. We had a nice dinner. We talked about all that had happened. And then we went to our room.

One of the amazing things about Kate is that she seemed to instinctively know what I needed, and when, even before I did. As we got ready for bed, she called out from the bathroom, asking if I had ever seen a post-op vagina. She said I was preparing to spend twenty thousand dollars on one, but had I ever actually seen what I was getting? I had been to websites that have pictures of them, but I'd never seen one up close.

She came to the bed, and proceeded to give me an anatomy lesson on her barely year-old vagina. It was absolutely amazing. She described the surgery procedure in detail, and showed me the final result. We talked about surgery preparation and recovery. And she told me that she thought I'd really love mine once I had it.

As we fell asleep in the king-sized bed, we were naked. We spooned each other, arms and legs entwined, finding comfort in the warmth and intimacy of being wrapped by another person's body. There was nothing sexual about it. Although it was certainly a new physical sensation for me, the spiritual and emotional growth of the day was not lost in my mind.

Kate spent the rest of the week introducing me to a world I never knew existed. Her sensuality seemed to have no end. During the days I spent with her she took me to wineries, and on scenic drives. At night we hit the town dressed in short black dresses that I would never in a million years have worn out in public without her prodding and guidance. I started to realize that I, too, had a feminine sexuality that attracted others like moths to a flame. The power of it all made me a tad uncomfortable, especially not knowing how to turn it on and off the way that Kate had obviously become so skilled at doing, but I felt confident that it would all come in time.

I celebrated my forty-first birthday with Kate and a small group of her friends who had become my friends. For the first time in my life, as I blew out my birthday candles I felt more than the faintest glimmer of hope that this really might be the last time that I spend my birthday as a boy.

JOURNAL ENTRY

> After all the fun of this past week, now it's time to get serious. Surgery is at 1 p.m. tomorrow, and I am booked there for a couple of hours. Katie will be there to bring me back to her place afterwards.

Dr. O's forehead revision procedure turned out to be much more significant than I had anticipated. In fact, he redid the entire hairline incision…from behind the ear across the entire front of the head. In doing so, he improved the overall shape of my hairline. He removed two metal screws from my forehead, left from the first operation. It was just like starting out from square one all over again!

I think that I might have handled it much better if I had been prepared for the severity of it all. As it was, I must have let my guard down, and I was totally blindsided like a fighter reeling from a sucker punch. In the days that followed, I found myself terribly discouraged by the fact that I was just beginning to get the feeling back to the top of my head, and now it was all numb again! My entire scalp had been pulled tight again, was full of stitches and metal staples again, all encased by a mummy wrap of gauze. The entire procedure had been done under local anesthetic so I could remember with sickening clarity everything that had happened, especially that I could actually feel some of the incisions that he was making. My eyes were swollen shut again. Healing was to be slow and painful.

Journal Entry

> Today is a pretty nasty day. My left eye is swollen totally shut, and I look like death. The pain meds upset my tummy a bit. I had a bit of a weepy fit this morning as well, so I'm spending the day just resting and trying to recover, but it's hard. Kate headed out for the afternoon, so I have the place to myself and will lie down for a nap here in a minute.

There was nothing to do but get up, dust off, and trudge onward. Two steps forward, one step back. As I waited to board my flight home a man noted that I had an *exotic* look. I sure didn't feel exotic. I felt like death warmed over, especially headed back to a difficult travel schedule, a continuing electrolysis regimen, an unpleasant battle with HR over my short-term disability coverage, and a nasty divorce just waiting to explode.

Journal Entry

> Well....it's back to work. Back at my desk. Back to being ignored.

Chapter Twenty-eight

Blessings in Disguise

As far as I can tell, changing genders in mid-stream is the most major change that a person can make in their life.....bar none. It takes a mixture of luck, and of strength, and of physical attributes, and of financial resources, and of support that is a rare cocktail, but once it all comes together it is an unbelievable powerful force. I see my situation as one in a million, and I think that is not very far off. And I thank God to have blessed me with this mixture.

— Journal Entry

My battle with HR had shifted into high gear. I had received letters of support, describing the medical necessity of SRS for people who have been diagnosed with my condition, from noted authorities around the world. One by one, I forwarded them to Lin in HR to support my case. And whereas Lin at first provided little hope that there was anything that could be done to change their decision, as time progressed she began to communicate a little more flexibility, and I gained confidence that perhaps we could actually work through this on mutually acceptable terms that would leave the dignity of both parties intact.

By the end of March, they had reached a decision. I got an email from the director of benefits, saying that a benefits review board had met to consider everything I had sent them, and that they were willing to compromise. If I used some of my own vacation time, they were willing to provide short-term disability coverage for the rest of the time that I would need to recover from my surgery. I had won.

The joy and satisfaction that I felt at having achieved this substantial personal victory, where so few people provided much hope, was short lived. The following week my friend and director, Brian, announced that he was leaving the company.

JOURNAL ENTRY

I talked with Brian before I left work yesterday. He said that they would announce that he is leaving today. He told me who is taking his place, and I know who he is, but little else. This should be interesting. I'm curious to see how this guy will react to me.

In fact, the next six weeks would see a complete shuffle of the entire management team in our area. All of the people who had participated in the planning and execution of my transition would leave, to be replaced by a completely new group who seemed to me to lack the empathy and sensitivity that had helped to preserve my sanity there, and that I had all too soon realized that I taken for granted.

After the management upheaval, I was informed that my new manager was to be a no-nonsense woman named Claire. Claire was older than I was, has fairly short curly hair, and always seemed wired on an intravenous drip of caffeine. She had transferred into the group from some other department, so we were totally unfamiliar with each other, although I was confident that my reputation and situation was pretty much common knowledge throughout the company by that point. Since I was travelling quite a bit, I really didn't have the time or the opportunity to speak with her at length about much of anything, so most of our contact was done via email or during my brief visits to my cubicle between trips.

As my travel schedule was curtailed, I started to spend more time in Scottsdale. One day, Claire came to my cube, her eyes as wide as small saucers and her face white as though she had just seen a ghost.

"What's wrong?" I asked.

She thought for a second, looked around to see if anyone else were listening, and then whispered loud enough for anyone in the near vicinity to hear, "You're a transsexual!"

Apparently, my notoriety at the company was not as far-reaching as I had thought, and she had just found out.

I responded in the same loud whisper. "I know!"

"Oh my God! I didn't know! I didn't have a clue! I feel like such an idiot!" She paused. "Now it all makes sense."

She pulled me into one of the conference rooms where we talked for over an hour, and I explained things to her. I told her how uncomfortable I felt there, and that I was glad she got to see it first-hand. She was incredibly sympathetic, and explained that she had experience working with gays and lesbians, and she would do her best to help. I didn't really think there was much she could do at that point, but I thanked her for the offer.

JOURNAL ENTRY

Some days I feel so good about myself (how I look, my face, my hair), while others (sometime the very next day) I look at myself and am very disappointed. It's really odd. Yesterday was a "not" day. Today is a good day.

One of the side benefits of spending more time in Scottsdale was that I felt it increased my chances of somehow restoring some semblance of a relationship with my son, or my wife, again. The divorce proceedings continued, and conversations with my wife had become even more strained and difficult now that money and property had become involved. Contact with her was like a volcano sitting on a precarious fissure: tense moments punctuated by frequent flare-ups, sometimes resulting in a major eruption.

Even more difficult, however, was the fact that I had not had any sort of contact with my son in nearly seven months, and out of everything that I had endured, that one issue was the most consistent and persistent source of pain. Here he was, growing up without me. What was he thinking? What was he feeling? I would have given anything to be able to sit with him again. I felt helpless to do anything about it other than send him emails on a regular basis, telling him that I loved him and missed him and hoping that he actually read them. Elizabeth screened all the calls to the house to avoid having to talk to me, so I had no confidence at all that any messages I asked her to relay to him actually got passed.

My frustration in their rejection boiled over a couple of times. For example, one afternoon I got a very nasty phone call from Elizabeth who was angry that I had changed the message on my voice mail at work. Initially, I recorded a generic message, but I had gotten tired of people asking for Donna and having to explain that I was Donna, so I eventually changed *"You have reached the desk of Donna Rose. I'm sorry I'm not here to answer your call, but if you'll leave your name and number......"* Elizabeth had called and heard the new message, and it had made her angry. She called to yell at me.

"You are not now, nor will you ever be, Donna!" she yelled. "I'll never call you by that name. I can't believe you changed it, and neither can Matt. It's all just so ridiculous and pathetic! You've gone way too far now! What if there's an emergency with Matt, and the school calls?"

I yelled right back at her. "That name is who I am now! If you'd take your head out of the sand and see me you'd know! You can be in denial all you want, but that doesn't change the fact that I am who and what I am!"

"Well," she replied, regaining her composure, "you can keep deluding yourself all you want. But until you stop being so selfish and start thinking of Matt and me, we won't have anything to do with you." Click. She hung up on me.

Something inside me snapped. Who the heck did she think she was talking to? The only reason that I hadn't seen her or Matt over those long months is because I had honored her wish for me to stay away. But this was too much. It was time for her to face reality. I was going to *force* the two of them to see me.

I left work and jumped into my car, heading up to the house confront her. All logic and common sense was drowned by the blinding outburst of my pent-up anger and frustration. Thankfully, rush hour traffic slowed my trip, and the realization that this probably wasn't a good idea had time to seep in. As time passed, and I calmed down, logic and reason regained control. What did I hope to accomplish? How would a major confrontation make things better? Eventually, I turned around and went to my apartment to reconsider.

Rather than force myself on them, I decided to offer them the opportunity to see me. I decided to wait until it was dark, to avoid having to explain to nosy neighbors, and then pay them a visit. So, with a clearer mind and a calmer demeanor, I drove to my house after dinner. I had not been there in many months, and the drive north through the Sonoran desert was strangely relaxing.

As I pulled into the driveway of the house that was still technically half mine, I saw that although the shutters were closed, the light in Matt's bedroom was on. He was probably in there doing homework, or watching television. I walked up to the front door, and pushed the doorbell. I could hear the dogs barking, but nobody came to answer the door. I rang it again, and to my surprise, the light in Matt's bedroom went off. They had obviously peeked through the shutters, recognized my car, and had gone into the bedroom to hide.

This was so pathetic. Here I was, less than 20 feet from Elizabeth and Matt, separated by only a wall some shutters, and we still had to play this silly game.

I walked around to the back of the house, unlatched the gate, and went into the backyard. One of the dogs was out there, and greeted me warmly, his tail wagging enthusiastically. He remembered me and it was so good to see him. As I peeked through the kitchen window, I saw the other dog inside. I noticed that Elizabeth must have been balancing her checkbook on the kitchen table, and had hurriedly left to go and barricade herself in the bedroom with Matt when I rang the doorbell.

I checked the doorknob on the back door. It was unlocked. I opened the door, and took a half-step inside. All I needed to do was to go into the house, and go to Matt's room, or wait for them to come out eventually. I wasn't breaking any law. As far as I was concerned, I wasn't doing anything wrong.

Or was I? Would this really make things better? What did I think she'd do if I entered her house and forced myself upon them? Did I need her acceptance that badly? Is that the kind of person I had become? It only took an instant for me to answer. No.

"Hey! I know you're in Matt's room!" I shouted, loud enough so that they'd hear. "I had hoped that we could spend a little time face to face, but apparently you're not ready yet. I just want you to know that I love both of you, and I won't bother you here again. I'm leaving now, so you can come out."

I got in my car and drove home.

Several weeks later, after an exile of nearly eight months, I finally had an opportunity to see my son for a few short, but precious, minutes.

JOURNAL ENTRY

Today was a pretty big day. I went home and got to spend some time with Matt.

I had gone to my apartment at lunch. I need to pick up some things from Elizabeth, so I called the house expecting to get the answering machine. Matt answered. He said that his class was out of town on a class trip to Disneyland, and he didn't want to go, so he stayed home today and Elizabeth was at work. I told him I needed to stop up at the house, and I also had something I needed to give him (a Dan Marino rookie card).

He asked how much the card is worth ($400), and that really grabbed him, so he said I could bring it up during lunch. I asked if he thought he was ready, and he said yes....as long as I wasn't wearing a dress. So off I went.

I didn't think that our meeting was too awkward. He has grown up quite a bit, and his baby face is now a pimply teen-aged face with whiskers on it. I went into the house, and he showed me his card collection, and I dropped of what I needed to. The puppies were going nutso, and it was even good to see them, too.

JOURNAL ENTRY

I had a nail appointment this morning. It was kind of a mile-stone visit, as I finally chose a color. Cyndi *[my nail tech]* has been urging me to choose a *real* color, as opposed to light pinks and mauves that I usually wear, and today I did. I picked a deep boysenberry color, and I really like it. In her mind, this signals a shift in leaving behind the old, and the safe, and moving forward. She said she was proud of me. It really is odd to see these nice, dark nails at the ends of fingers that are attached to my own hands.

Despite the fact that the company and I had settled the differences that brought us to the brink of a major confrontation over the short-term disability coverage, the wheels that I had set into motion continued to turn. I had a couple of phone interviews with recruiters at the computer hardware manufacturer in Texas, and apparently the results had been positive enough for them to go to the next level, which was to invite me on-site for an interview. We had already scheduled it for late April to coincide with one of my business trips to Fort Worth, and I decided to proceed with it as planned.

To be perfectly honest, I really didn't expect much to come of it. I was making good money, and didn't expect that anyone would make an offer substantially higher enough to make it worth my while to leave.

Still, the thought of working for a large and respected company, and moving to a brand new community to start my new life as Donna, held more than passing allure, so I rationalized that I had nothing to lose by interviewing with them. If nothing else, it would give me good experience to interview as Donna. Interviewing as a woman would be a new experience for me. As far as I knew, everyone involved was unaware of my unique situation, so unless they brought it up during the interview, and I doubted they would, there was really no reason to discuss it.

While visiting Kate in San Francisco, we had gone clothes shopping together. I tried on dozens of outfits, to Kate's critical thumbs up or down indication of approval or disapproval. One particular outfit, a short black dress with matching blazer, stood out for accentuating my *feminine charms*, and we both agreed that it would be a great business suit for just the right occasion. I decided that this was that right occasion, and I would wear it to my interview.

I flew to Austin, prepared to face an entire day of back-to-back-to-back interviews.

As I dressed for my big day, I slipped into the short black dress, pulled the straps up over my shoulders, and moved to zip it up in the back. Try as hard as I might, I couldn't reach the zipper! It seemed strategically placed in a spot just awkward enough so that I couldn't reach it with either hand.

In my pre-interview disarray, I started to panic. What was I going to do? I remember many times when my mom would ask me to zip her up, but here I was, needing to be zipped, and I didn't have anyone to help. I had visions of running down to the front lobby to ask a bellman for some zipper assistance.

I called Kate. I figured she would know what to do. She laughed at me. She walked me through several possible options, until I finally got the darned thing zipped.

She also had several words of advice. She said that if I was interviewing with a man, and he tried to lock eyes, to look away. She explained that it was a control thing. She explained that I needed to appear confident, but not over-confident or cocky. Although cockiness was sometimes acceptable in men, it is rarely acceptable in women.

She explained that I needed to wear a pair of black pumps, and sit with my legs strategically crossed. She suggested I sit with my back straight, my hands folded, my chin up, my shoulders back and perhaps most important of all, with my chest out. It sounded like the most uncomfortable position in the world.

As Dave, I considered myself to be a good interviewer. I felt confident that I would land any position that I interviewed for, and often became the aggressor in the process. But I never had to worry about how I sat, or how I looked, like I did now. This was not going to be as easy as I thought.

As I took one last look in the mirror before leaving my hotel room, I couldn't believe this was me. I saw a pretty, confident businesswoman in a black power suit. I had curled my hair, and the hair gods had smiled upon me by providing a very good hair day. My makeup looked good. Even my exposed legs looked nice in the black pumps. It was astounding.

Although I was initially very nervous, I eventually settled into a comfortable interview routine. A half dozen people came to interview me, one after another, for an hour at a time. Each had specific questions to ask, and as time passed and I relaxed to the point where I could actually analyze what was happening and how I was feeling. I found that I actually liked the way that they seemed to relate to me better during an interview as a woman than I did as a guy. There seemed to be much less of a sense of confrontation in the air, especially when interviewed by another woman. It was a refreshing change.

After it was all over, I thought that my day of interviews had gone wonderfully. As I drove to the airport to fly back to Phoenix I was really very proud, and very relieved. Whether I was offered a job or not, I realized that the experience had been a good one for me, and that I really wasn't as professionally vulnerable as I once feared I'd be.

JOURNAL ENTRY

> I miss being in love. Not necessarily being loved, although that is certainly a wonderful thing. I miss the tingly feeling we get at the beginning of a relationship when everything is new and special and wonderful. When people can't get enough of each other no matter how hard they try. I think I fear experiencing that as a woman.

As the days ticked by, and I got closer and closer to my surgery date that still lay almost five months in the future, I found myself thinking about it more and more. It didn't make me nervous, and I certainly had no doubts that I was doing the right thing. Instead, I found myself wondering how my life would change once the physical aspect of the transition was over.

One of the biggest question marks in my mind had to do with sexuality. A common misconception is that transsexuals are actually homosexuals looking for a reason to validate having sex with a man, and a physical sex change somehow provides that. Most of the transsexuals that I knew had been heterosexual as males, and their sexual attraction to women did not change after the surgery, so they eventually considered themselves to be lesbians. Certainly, this isn't true for everyone, but it demonstrated to me just how wrong the typical stereotype really was, and that I needed to figure this out for myself.

I really had no idea what my ultimate sexuality would be. I rarely, if ever, fantasized about having sex with a man. I was certainly more comfortable being sexual with a woman. But once I had a vagina, and not a penis…would that change? I thought about that a lot.

JOURNAL ENTRY

> I cannot and will not sleep with a male right now. I do not have the right plumbing. But after the surgery, I WILL have that plumbing. The harder part of that equation is the mental part. To realize that you are a fully functional female, and you can now make love as such with a male partner, takes much

adjusting. To seriously consider a man as a sexual partner where you NEVER would allow yourself to do so in the past is a huge mental barrier. Once it is overcome, however, anything is possible. And in that respect, the surgery has changed how you feel about yourself.

I already see my mind gearing up for the changes to come. Kate says that the closer I get, the more it will occupy my mind. More anticipation than anything. I do not have even the slightest hesitation at what is to come, even though I cannot believe this is really happening. To think that something that I have thought about for my entire life, and that always seemed a total and absolute impossibility, is less than 140 days away, truly and honestly amazes me. To think that I can exist in this world, and feel comfortable in this world, and be accepted in this world, is truly a miracle to me.

At the end of April, I went to visit Kate in San Francisco again. It would be my first visit there that didn't include any surgery or lengthy recuperation of any kind. However, it wasn't strictly a vacation. I had made arrangements to meet with a speech pathologist that worked with transsexuals to help us improve our feminine voice and communication skills. Still, I really just needed some quiet time away, and was looking forward to spending a quiet Easter together with Kate and a few of her friends. As I stepped off the plane, little did I know it was to turn into so much more.

As soon as I arrived, Kate had a shocker for me. She told me that she had arranged for me to go on a "date" with one of her ex-boyfriends. His name was Ralph, he had seen my picture, was apparently well aware of my situation, and was interested in taking me out to dinner. I was speechless.

I think if I had been any place other than San Francisco the thought of going on a date with a guy would have frightened me to death. But Kate assured me that Ralph was the perfect gentleman, and that if the chemistry was right things would only go as far as I felt comfortable. No pressure.

Kate said that she'd come along with us for dinner, but only to provide a sense of comfort. I almost had to laugh, as having Kate as a chaperone was like giving the keys to the jail to an inmate. No matter. I was grateful to have her there, as the thought of being the center of all that sexual attention really did make me nervous.

Ralph arrived to pick us up at seven o'clock. Like any true lady, I wasn't quite ready and continued to fuss with my hair and makeup for an extra fifteen minutes before deciding that things were as good as they were going to get. After one last squirt of perfume, I went to the living room to meet my date.

Ralph was everything that Kate described, and more. At just over six feet tall, with short black hair speckled with grey, a muscular build, and a chiseled masculine face, there was no denying that he was hand-some by any standard. He was courteous. He was funny. And as amazing as it sounded, he was my date.

JOURNAL ENTRY

Dinner was very nice. Ralph was the perfect gentleman for all of us…opening our car doors, helping us in and out of the car, helping put our jackets on, complimenting us on how we looked or on our perfume. It seemed totally sincere, and we all ate it up. He commented that this was every guys dream…to be out to dinner with three wonderful women, and in some ways I think he's right.

Up to this point, it had not seemed like a date. Ralph and I had not sat together. The topics of conversation were general topics, and were pretty comfortable. I did not feel any pressure, and was pretty happy with the way the evening was going.

We got home at around midnight. Lori went to bed. Ralph and Kate and I put on a fire log, and sat around chatting.

Eventually, Kate decided to go to bed, and off she went. So it was just Ralph and I in the living room on the couch.

We talked. And talked. And talked. I don't remember the general topics, but it was a very nice chat. And it got very late. I was getting tired. Ralph lives 40 minutes away, and mentioned that he would sleep on the couch and head home in the morning, as we had all had alcohol during the evening (not a lot) and didn't feel up to driving home. When I first arrived on Friday, Kate gave me the option of making up the bed in the spare room or of sleeping with her, so of course I chose to sleep with her. I offered to Ralph that it was a big bed, and he would be far more comfortable with us, so he should sleep in the bed. Needless to say, he agreed. Well, I went to the bathroom to wash up, and put on my nightshirt, and by the time I was ready he was already in the bed. And Kate was awake.

It was totally dark. I slipped into bed, next to Ralph, and it felt right. Before two minutes were up, I was lying in his arms, and stroking the hair on his chest, and he was playing with my hair. And before two more minutes, we were kissing. Needless to say, Kate heard all the kissing sounds, and decided that if we were going to be noisy, she was going to sleep on the couch. And despite our pleas to stay in bed, and that we would stop....off she went. So here we were...Ralph and I...in bed alone. We started kissing some more, and one thing led to another...

I whispered to Ralph that this was very new to me, and he said that we would take our time, and that we wouldn't do anything I didn't want to do, or feel comfortable doing.

I have no idea how long we played. He played with me for quite a while, and my mind was in a total new thought pattern. I was thinking, and reacting, totally as female. It was one of the most incredible things I have ever felt. Where the thought of kissing and fondling a guy AS A GUY does not interest me in any way, I was feeling totally and completely like a heterosexual woman. And the levels of my own comfort and quest to explore and satisfy my partner shock me even now. I wanted to make him happy. I wanted to make him feel good. And to feel comfortable and happy in doing it.

I have no idea how long we played. It must have been nearly 5 a.m. by the time we collapsed on each other. I slept for a couple or three hours, but not nearly so much as I needed. And when Kate came in in the morning, and saw me lying there in Ralph's arms, looking happy and comfortable (and naked), she was surprised herself at how natural is seemed and how fast it took me over.

Saturday was the "morning after." I have seen it on so many shows. The time when the passion of the night is gone, and the discomfort of what had happened can rear its head in the broad daylight. Happily, this didn't happen. Ralph got up, and gave me a gentle kiss, and hugged me, and told me how happy he was, and I felt happy too.

Easter was a beautiful day here. We decided that we wanted to get out during the afternoon, so we all went to the new U-boat movie. Ralph and I were acting like a couple of teenagers…..holding hands, gentle kisses. It was pretty amazing. Later in the day we decided to go out to Santa Cruz and watch the sunset on the ocean. We had a very, very interesting chat on what was happening to me, and between Ralph and I. There were a couple of guys playing acoustic music, and they were just wonderful. For a few brief moments, all seemed right in the world.

After it was all over, I tried to put into perspective. Trying to figure it all out consumed my mind for weeks.

315

JOURNAL ENTRY

Sometimes things happen in our lives that are of such magnitude that any attempt to try to reconcile them within our own experiences inevitably ends up fruitless. These experiences can cause us to question who we are, and can even call into question whether we really know ourselves, or are we actually strangers with who we really are.

This has been one of those weekends for me.

And whereas I would think that events of this indescribable importance would leave me shaken and confused and upset, I find that I feel exactly the opposite. Although I certainly cannot explain the powers that led me to do and act and think over this past weekend, I find that the "why's" continue to be far less important than the "is." These things happened. I have no regrets. And although I have had inklings of how I might react, the proof is right there in front of me now.

❧

JOURNAL ENTRY

I called home and talked to Matt yesterday. He sounded good. I was feeling him out to see if he wanted to spend some time with me during his spring break, but he answered "Maybe" to most of my questions, which all parents know actually means no. He's not ready yet. It was a nice chat, though.

Elizabeth and I had talked about arranging for me to spend some time with Matt again, and the importance of maintaining at least some semblance of a relationship at this critical juncture. I think she had mentally come to terms with the fact that I wasn't coming home, so it was time to consider the nature of our relationships as we moved forward. She seemed to be supportive of my efforts to spend time with him, and we worked out the details in late April.

We arranged that I would pick him up at the house, and we could spend an evening together. It would be our first significant time together in over eight months.

My plans for the evening were pretty low-key, as I wanted to avoid any possibility of making him more uncomfortable than necessary. I thought perhaps I would bring him back to my apartment, we could order a pizza, and maybe we could watch a movie together.

As I drove to the house to pick him up, I was nervous. I had butterflies in my stomach. How would this go? Would it be awkward? Elizabeth had suggested that I try to look as much like Dave as possible, but that just showed how out-of-touch she was with things at that point. The goal was to get him comfortable with my new direction in life, not some ridiculous charade that I had left behind long ago.

As he walked out to my car, it was great to see him. He had a bag full of stuff to show me. He brought his most valuable sports cards. He had a baseball that was autographed by Barry Bonds. He had a bunch of CD's to play for me. It was almost like show-and-tell.

We had both changed so much in those eight months. He had grown quite a bit, and was very much the young man. I, on the other had, had feminized tremendously, and although his changes were significant, mine were much more so. He seemed to take things in stride, and that was very comforting to me.

In fact, he told me he wanted to go to his favorite pizzeria for dinner. They didn't deliver, so I offered to order it, pick it up, and take it back to my apartment to eat if he didn't want to be seen out with me. But Matt seemed hell-bent on eating it there so I agreed. "This should be interesting," I thought to myself.

As we parked out front, and collected our things to bring into the restaurant, I waited for Matt to get out of the car, but he seemed to be waiting for me to get out first.

"You can get out," I said. "I'll be right there."

"Nah," he replied. "I'll wait for you."

"Are you sure?" I questioned. "If you want to get out, I'll only be a second..."

"What are you going to do?" he asked.

I paused for a second, not quite sure how to put this. "Well, to tell you the truth, I'm going to put on some lipstick, so if you really want to stay here and watch me do that, you're more than welcome. I just thought you might be more comfortable if I did it by myself at this point."

"You're probably right," he said, getting out of the car and waiting for me at the door as I adjusted the car mirror, applied my lipstick, checked my makeup, and got out to join him.

As we entered the restaurant, the hostess greeted us. "Good evening, ma'am. Table for two?"

I thought Matt would split a gut right there. Here I was, his father, but to the rest of the world I was a woman. And as the evening progressed, he saw first hand that I was totally and unquestioningly accepted as a woman everywhere we went. There was no awkwardness. There was no staring and pointing. Things appeared totally normal, and Matt quickly seemed to get comfortable with me. It was a very special evening.

Once we finished dinner, Matt didn't really want to spend time at the apartment, which was certainly fine by me. Instead, he wanted to run some errands, and I happily agreed, pleased that he seemed to feel so comfortable so quickly.

The last stop of the evening was at a bicycle shop; I had a question to ask one of the salespeople. As we entered the story Matt went off to browse some of the bikes there while I went to the back to find some help.

As I stood, waiting to chat with the sales guy who was busy with another customer, Matt saw something that interested him.

"HEY, DAD!" he yelled. "C'MERE WHEN YOU'RE DONE!"

As soon as he said it, he realized just how odd it was, he covered his mouth as though trying to recapture the words that had just gotten out.

After we got outside, we laughed about it. "I'm going to have to find something else to call you," he said.

"You're probably right," I agreed, glad that it was he that brought it up. "You can call me whatever you want. If you want to call me Donna, that's fine. If you want to call me Dad, that's fine too. But my mom and my brother are having the same problem as you are, and they both call me 'Dee.' It's kind of in-between Dave and Donna. 'D' for Dave. 'D' for Donna. 'D' for Dad."

After the success of the evening, we started to see each other a little more regularly. It gave a tremendous boost to my spirits.

JOURNAL ENTRY

It's a paradox, but the more I am with Matt now, the more I miss him. I have seen him more in the past 8 days than I have in the past 8 months, and I kinda got used to life without him. Being with him makes me realize just how much he needs me, and how much I need him.

I didn't realize it yet, but in the following weeks I would make a decision that would separate us by thousands of miles.

Chapter Twenty-nine

Separation Anxiety

*On the home front, yesterday was the first time I mentioned to
Elizabeth that I do not plan to remain in Phoenix. It seemed
to catch her by surprise. She asked when I planned to leave,
and I told her I had no definite plans. She asked me where I
planned to go, and I told her I had no definite plans. I told her
that I refuse to wait in the wings so that some day she might be
able to see me, and then to watch her implode once she sees the
person she still imagines to be Dave. No thanks. She wants me
away, and I will honor that. Far away.*

— Journal Entry

By mid-May, I had pretty much given up on staying in Phoenix.
Elizabeth continued to shun me, and our painful divorce proceedings
continued to drain every ounce of life from me. Although I saw Matt a
little more regularly, I sometimes got the feeling that he did it because
he didn't want me to feel bad, not because he really wanted to be with
me. Our brief time together was a mixture of happiness at being able to
see him, and pain at feeling inadequate and unwanted. At work, Mark
was gone, and the new management seemed to be preparing to put me
into a position that I would not like in hopes that I would leave.

JOURNAL ENTRY

> I wore a skirt today. It was the first time I have ever worn one to work. It was a nice, light, casual, flowing skirt. I'm sure it had people talking. But times have changed from the point of just wanting to be there and not make any waves, to not caring if I make waves. I have been full-time for 7 months. Can you believe that? I can't. And the difference in me now as opposed to the gal who started at work on October 4th is amazing. I met with my psych today for the first time since December, and we talked about that.

In quick succession, the hardware manufacturer in Texas made me an offer. Then, a consulting company at home in Rochester learned that I was available and made me a comparable offer. As I considered the options of moving to a completely new city and having my surgery in secret less than two months after starting my new job, or going home to Rochester to be surrounded and nurtured by my family as I recovered from SRS, the choice really wasn't all that difficult. I would move back to Rochester.

By the end of the month I had accepted the offer, had bought a townhouse (sight unseen) near my brother and sister, and made arrangements to leave Arizona for good.

There was little to keep me in Phoenix. Maria had completed her electrolysis, both on my face and on my surgery area, so I was completely hair free. My meetings with my psychologist, which were originally scheduled for every two weeks, now seemed to happen every couple of months and were more like social calls than counseling sessions. Of course, the thought that I might be running away from my troubles before giving them time to work themselves out didn't seem to enter my SRS-preoccupied consciousness, as my opportunity to leave Arizona seemed like a self-fulfilling prophecy.

The only thing that caused the slightest bit of hesitation was Matt. I sometimes felt the throbbing pain of guilt, feeling that I was abandoning him before we really had a chance to get to know each other again. The dark side of my psyche argued that that day might never come, and I might be shunned by both of them for the rest of my life, and that's the rationale I used to battle the tears that invariably seemed to come during the dark, lonely hours of the night.

I find it ironic that the thing that eventually really started to bring Matt and me back together again is the fact that I was moving away. The two or three days I spent packing and loading the U-Haul represents the longest time that Matt and I had spent together in nearly a year. My brother had flown down to Phoenix to help me pack, and to drive the truck full of my things halfway across the country to my new home. Matt kept us company, helping to carry boxes and furniture onto the moving truck. Although he never really said anything, I could tell that he was confused and unhappy that I was leaving. At that point the decisions had been made, and there was no turning back.

I have never shown more self-control than I did while Jay and I maneuvered the truck, loaded to the rafters with all my worldly belongings and towing my car, out of Scottsdale to begin our drive northward. It was all I could do to keep from telling Jay to drive the truck up Scottsdale Road to Matt's house so I could hug him and tell him I loved him one last time. But what good would that do, except to twist the knife that cut my heart just a little more? I didn't want to dissolve into a puddle of tears in front of my brother, so I mustered the old defenses that had gone unused for so long one last time to keep the flood of tears from flowing.

I had a new house, and a new life, waiting for me in Rochester. My surgery was less than ten weeks away, and there seemed so much to do in such a short period of time. If absence really does make the heart grow fonder, perhaps this really wasn't so much of a good-bye, as "I'll seeya later."

My first few weeks back in Rochester were spent doing all the things a person does when they move. I needed a new driver's license. I had to change all my addresses, and turn on all my utilities. Moving the heavy furniture and boxes from the truck into the house was a job best done by the boys, while the women watched the kids and supervised. Matt even came to visit for a few days, and our time together felt as close to the old days as anything I could remember. When we said goodbye to go back home, it was with pride and happiness instead of guilt and anger. Little by little, all the pieces of my life seemed to be coming together, as if directed by some huge cosmic event that was aligning the planets in preparation for my upcoming rebirth.

JOURNAL ENTRY

> I do find myself thinking of SRS more and more. It creeps into my mind from time to time, with growing regularity, just as Kate had said it would. I look at it with anticipation, although when others ask me about it they ask if I am scared or nervous. Neither of those emotions are part of the picture right now, and I doubt that they will in the future.

How does a person mentally prepare for a sex change operation? It could be argued that the entire transition is mental preparation, but I'd learned that much of transition is as much a test of character and resolve as it is of anything having specifically to do with the surgery. I also think that most of us have little clue as to the profound nature of what is about to happen, and there's really very little we can do to adequately prepare for it even if we did.

By the time I was settled in my new home, I had checked and double-checked that the surgeon had received all the paperwork that he needed, and all that was left was for me to actually show up. I told Matt what I was planning to do, and asked if he wanted to know the specifics, but he said he'd rather know after it was all over; I respected that. I never considered telling Elizabeth about it. We were strangers by that point.

Although there is very little a person can do in terms of mental preparation, I do think there's quite a bit that a person can do to get in the right frame of mind. Questioning is *not* one of those things. If a person is still questioning whether they want to have the surgery at that point, they may have missed the point of the entire Real Life Test

323

experience, and perhaps they need to delay the surgery until they have the peace of mind they will need.

Moving to Rochester was actually part of my preparation. I felt a very strong *nesting* urge to find a home and surround myself by people and things that would love me and nurture me through the pinnacle of my gender journey. I felt like a squirrel in late autumn, scurrying around to scrounge the last few acorns of the season that would help to get me through the coldest days of winter. All my preparations were done early, hoping to avoid last minute problems that might somehow blow up and create unnecessary frustration and tension at the time I was least prepared to deal with it. Preparation. *That* was key.

At the beginning of July I went back to San Francisco to spend the long Fourth of July weekend there with Kate. The main reason for the trip was to get some last minute relaxation, to soak up some Northern California sea air, and to attend a special party that Kate was planning to throw in my honor.

Kate and her friends throw a party for friends as they prepare to leave for SRS. This bon-voyage, good-luck, welcome-to-womanhood party is affectionately dubbed a "Weenie Roast," which was somehow just twisted and ironic enough to be very funny to me. The best way I can describe it is to compare it to a twisted kind of bridal shower. Whereas a soon-to-be bride receives gifts that will help her to start her new household and her life as a wife, a soon-to-be SRS patient receives gifts that will help her in her life as a post-op transsexual woman from others who have already been there. I got all kinds of medical supplies and hand-me-downs that I would need for my post-op care and recuperation: a starter set of dilators, a whole box of lubrication gel, maxi-pads, an inflatable donut to sit on for the plane ride home, and a box of surgical gloves. Just as in a bridal shower, there are also a fair share of gag gifts sure to cause peals of laughter from the entire group: I got my first woman's power tool…a purple vibrator that I affectionately named Barney.

Everyone was all too happy to share her own SRS experience, providing advice and wisdom about the unique experience that they all shared, and that I was soon to experience as well. Of course, this isn't the kind of information that you can find in most books, or even on the web, and it was all very much appreciated.

Once the gifts had all been opened and the chatter had died down, it was time to adjourn to the dining room to eat. Ralph did the cooking honors, and the main course was...of course...grilled wieners.

My relationship with Elizabeth had gotten to a point where we spoke once a month, if that. Lawyers continued working through the divorce, so we rarely needed any direct contact. I had gotten past the point where I felt sorry for her, or continued to wallow in guilt about what had happened between us. If life truly is about choices, and she felt I had made mine when I left in search of my true self, then the ones that were being made at this point were of her own choosing. I felt sorrier for Matt than I did for her, given the fact that he had somehow ended up in the middle of it all.

At the end of July Matt visited me in Rochester. Although he had originally planned to spend just a couple of days there, our time together stretched to over a week.

During his week with me we visited with my family, who were thrilled to see him. We all went go-cart racing. He helped me unpack and become settled in my new house. We spent time talking and getting to know each other again, away from the pressures and distractions that we both seemed to feel in Arizona. Somehow, our relationship felt so much lighter than it had for a long, long time.

EMAIL TO KATE

A funny thing happened last night. I was shopping at a home improvement store with my son, when this guy walks by and gives me a definite double take. I didn't think much of it, and we kept on looking for these chairs we had gone to buy. He walks by again a couple of minutes later, and does it again. This time he stops and tells me that he's sorry for staring, but

I look exactly like someone he works with, and it was really uncanny (is that a line or what?). We started talking and he asked what I did, and if I had a business card. I introduced him to Matt, and in conversation it came out that Matt wasn't living with me anymore, he was just here visiting. We chatted for about 5 minutes, and he took off.

Once he left, I told Matt that the guy had been hitting on me, and Matt asked how I knew. I said it was obvious, and even though I'm new at this, I could just tell. I bet Matt 5 bucks he would call the next day.

Well, he ended up calling me at work this morning before 8:30! He said he was sorry if he had been too forward, but he thought I was just so attractive, and he could sense in me a strength that just drew him to me. I told him I was flattered. He asked if I was in a relationship at the moment....you get the drift. Pretty wild, huh?

Sheesh! A gal can't even shop with her teenaged son anymore without getting hit on! I'm loving life.....

As Matt left to go home, we both realized that we had turned a corner. I think we both understood that my transition and impending surgery didn't change the fact that I would always be his parent, I would always love him, and that I was willing to fit into his life anywhere he could fit me. On his part, I think he had learned that the people who loved the two of us before my transition still loved us, that the world would accept me as my new role, and that I was pretty much the same person that I had always been for him. That's all he really wanted.

To my surprise, instead of feeling elation at the turn in the tide, I felt a quiet sense of peace and satisfaction. I had learned that the key elements for achieving almost anything were time, opportunity, motivation, patience, and hope. The healing of our estrangement wasn't something that could be forced, no matter how badly either of us might have wanted to *fix* it. The fact that all of our efforts finally bore fruit just two weeks before my SRS, after so much disappointment and sadness, seemed to be another indication that all my spiritual loose ends were coming together as if by cosmic design.

Of course, the pessimist in me still feared that everything was going far too smoothly, and that something was bound to go blow up and ruin it all. Or, perhaps it was just the fact that I had stopped taking my hormones in the middle of July to minimize the possibility of blood clots during the surgery, so I often found myself doing emotional back flips for no reason at all.

No matter. The time had come. I had built a timer to count the number of days left before SRS into my computer, and the days ticked down to the single digits. I was ready for the final step.

Chapter Thirty

Renaissance

The cost of this journey has been horrendous. The emotional toll on Elizabeth and her family. On my mom and my family. On my relationship with Matt. The unbelievable amount of $$$ that has me buried under a mountain of debt. But the returns have been beyond my wildest imagination, and I stand at the doorway to the rest of my life.

— Journal Entry

At the beginning of August, I prepared to leave Rochester for SRS in Wisconsin. I was at peace with myself and what I was about to do. There were no doubts, no second thoughts, no uneasiness about what was about to happen.

Perhaps part of what made it easier for me at that point was the fact that this seemingly huge step had somehow become merely another detail, another milestone, in a journey that was full of them. In fact, I already understood that moving through SRS would be a bigger symbolic and psychological event than a physical event for me.

I had already proven to myself that my life was best lived as Donna. The pressures that had boiled in my soul since childhood had gone, replaced by quiet contentment and satisfaction. I had found peace and comfort in a role that I had learned to live in a very short period of time, and I had developed a far richer appreciation for my life than I ever imagined.

Mom had arranged to go to surgery with me. She planned to stay in Wisconsin for my entire weeklong hospital stay, and to return home with me for several weeks afterwards to help during my recovery. Although I was truly touched by the fact that she wanted to be there when so many of us are totally rejected by family and friends, I must admit it had caused me some initial concern. She had once referred to the surgery as "self-mutilation," and that had really bothered me. I felt as though some people held out the faintest of hopes that I could go back to being Dave as long as I still had a penis, and didn't want to let that go.

As far as we knew, Mom had never met another transsexual. Although I was glad that she would have an opportunity to meet more of us, I was a little concerned that she would unintentionally say or do something inappropriate or awkward. Transsexuals can be very sensitive and fragile, and I didn't want her to hurt anyone's feelings by accident.

As my SRS-Countdown reached zero, all that was left was to actually show up.

JOURNAL ENTRY

I am sitting at O'Hare Airport in Chicago, halfway to Neenah. My flight arrived a couple of hours ago, and I am sitting at gate 6B waiting for the flight from DFW with my mom on it to arrive.

It still amazes me that I am here right now....at this point so close to a dream I never imagined had a chance to become a reality. From a young teenager who daydreamed about changing minds and bodies with girls in order to make the universe right, to the career guy who felt more trapped in his life than in his body....it is still amazing that I managed to steer myself here.

The cost has been horrendous. The emotional toll on Elizabeth and her family. On my mom and my family. On my relationship with Matt. The unbelievable amount of $$$ that has me buried under a mountain of debt. But the returns have been beyond my wildest imagination, and I stand at the doorway to the rest of my life. It is odd to me that people tend to define themselves by their genitalia, regardless of anything and everything else. That is the sole criteria that is used to proclaim a newborn as either boy or girl, and I think the impact of this criteria sticks with us throughout our lives. So although I am able to live my life as female, I'm thinking that I will not really able to consider myself as such until that criteria is met. Although the surgery itself is a physical modification, I think the mental changes that happen as a result are far more profound. We shall see....

I have said that I would rather die on the table than continue with this body. I truly mean that. I am ready to die to finish this journey. I have come to that peace in myself, and I am not worried or nervous or apprehensive in the least. I certainly do not look forward to the drudgery of the post-op care, but being near the end of the road (as far as this part of the journey is concerned) fills me with renewed strength and vigor. I can see the end of the road.....and I'm not going to screw it up now.

I was about to say that the last 6 weeks have been a whirlwind....but in looking back at things, the entire last year has passed at absolutely breakneck speed. As has generally been the case, I have filled these last weeks with sooooo much "stuff" that I haven't had much of an opportunity to fret or get too wrapped in what is about to happen. I feel a bit like a bug who is about to hit a windshield...as my life is about to hit the brakes big-time, and I am very much looking forward to the respite.

Sex Reassignment Surgery has changed considerably since the early 1950s when the sensational story of Christine Jorgenson, the ex-GI who became a "blonde bombshell" was featured on the front page of newspapers around the world.

At the beginning, a sex change operation consisted of removing the penis and making a crude *hole* that could be described as a vagina. Very little consideration was given to appearance, sensitivity, or function.

Over the years, that has changed. Surgeons have become much more sensitive to the aesthetics of SRS, and advances in the surgery have dramatically improved the end result. They have refined their procedures to enhance sensitivity, and provide a more satisfying post-op life. Many patients today have full functionality. They are orgasmic. They get moist when aroused. For those of us facing SRS, having a fully functional vagina is an incredible achievement.

Throughout the 1970s, most SRS surgeries in this country were performed in Gender clinics, which were often affiliated with large universities. Eventually, morality questions and financial issues forced these clinics to close, and private practices became the mainstay of SRS in North America.

Dr. Stanley Biber, of Trinidad, Colorado, became the pioneer of SRS. Since his first surgery in 1969, Dr. Biber has performed over 4,500 sex-change surgeries. His popularity became so far-reaching that Trinidad was unofficially dubbed as the "Sex-Change Capital of the World." Dr. Biber's teachings and techniques became the basis of modern day SRS.

Mom and I met up at the airport in Chicago, and flew to Green Bay…the closest large city to Neenah. It seems odd that such an out-of-the-way place should be a hub of sex reassignment surgery, and when I asked Dr. Schrang why he settled there he indicated it was all a matter of timing. He had received his certification for plastic surgery, and had traveled throughout the state looking for a hospital that would allow him to practice there. He ended up in Neenah, and started his practice. His work with transsexuals would not begin until several years later. By that time, he had grown to love the area, so he had no plans of moving to a larger, more metropolitan area.

After spending a little time sightseeing with my mom, I could certainly understand the allure. There was a quaint downtown district, lined with small shops and restaurants. The main street was lined with old, stately looking mansions that had once been home to the early founders of the Kimberly-Clark paper mills, which had been established there nearly a hundred years before.

The hospital where I would be having my surgery sat on the bank of the Fox River. My mom and I spent the last afternoon at the park across the street from our hotel, soaking up the mid-summer sunshine and relaxing before my afternoon appointment with Dr. Schrang that would begin the series of events leading through my SRS. I wasn't tense at all, and mom seemed calm and relaxed, as well. I think mom's training as an RN had prepared her well to be there to support me, and I even sensed that she looked forward to being able to take care of me again, so many years after having left home to live on my own. Once a mom, always a mom.

Dr. Schrang's office is near the medical center, and my intake appointment with him took about an hour. We spent some time chatting. He asked me to get undressed so that he could give me a quick physical and get and idea of what there was to work with. He described what he was planning to do, what I could expect as an outcome, and the risks of the procedure.

As I sat naked on his examination table, I caught a glimpse of myself in the mirror across the room, and smiled. My perky 38C breasts led down to a toned, slender size 10 waist, forged and maintained by thousands of sit-ups and hundreds of miles traveled during my regular, early morning jogs. The only oddity was the small, hairless penis that poked its tired little head above the surrounding pubic hair, seeming so out of place amongst all the other indications of my womanhood. It had shrunk to be no larger than my thumb, and looked to be more like a little boy's penis, or a small deep-cave mushroom, than a prized source of manhood. The three years of hormone therapy, and lack of use, had taken their toll. As Dr. Schrang grabbed it, and stretched it to explain how it was to be reborn, my only worry was that it had shrunk so much that there would not be enough of it there to stretch it where it needed to go. He assured me he'd make it work.

Throughout the entire talk, my mind kept repeating to itself…"I can't believe this…I can't believe this…I can't believe I'm really here." I'm sure he sees girls like me come through his office every day, with starry-eyed looks on our faces, overwhelmed at finally having gotten to that point in our lives.

As my mom and I left his office and headed over to the hospital to complete the admittance procedure, our arms were full. There was all of my overnight stuff. There was my laptop computer. There was a bag full of personal things. And there was a big, brown teddy bear that the girls at my Weenie Roast had given me to keep me company.

JOURNAL ENTRY

> It was almost 4 p.m. at that point. I went to the second floor south, and most of the paperwork had already been done so all I had to do was sign a few things. They put me in room 250, bed A. It was right across from the nurse's station. There was another gal in the bed closest to the window, who had had her surgery two days ago. Her name was Betsy. They told me to get into the gown and stow all my stuff, and the nurse would be in to see me.

The hospital maintains a special section on the second floor reserved for Dr. Schrang's patients. The staff there is well aware of our unique needs, and does their best to soothe our fears, and speed our recovery. Over the course of my convalescence there, they would become true friends, and I always looked forward to seeing my favorite ones as their shifts started and they made their initial rounds.

My evening there was spent preparing for surgery the next morning. The "prep" process took about eight hours, and by the time it was all over, I was exhausted. The goal is to clean out a patient's bowels totally and completely, not because the surgeon has any plans to actually cut into the bowels, but as a precaution just in case something goes wrong and the wall gets breached. There are many things that can go wrong when working in such a sensitive area, so enduring a long, difficult, unpleasant evening really wasn't too much of a price to pay.

It almost got to be funny, although I was far too miserable to find humor in much of anything at that point. Mom had settled in and had started reading one of her romance novels, while I set about my task of drinking a full gallon of unpleasant tasting liquid designed to clear out my bowels.

JOURNAL ENTRY (8/9/00)

> 5:30 p.m. Well…I am sitting in my hospital gown…cross-legged on my bed in room 250…drinking an ungodly amount of GoLytely. They want me to have the entire gallon done by 8….that's only 2 hrs….and there's no friggin' way I will be able to do that. I absolutely cannot see myself drinking that much liquid, but my roommate, Betsy, says she did it (in 4 hrs.) so I suppose it **is** possible, but it's not gonna be pretty. I think I'll explode first.

Cupful after cupful, down it went, like an oral enema. After an hour, my distended stomach made me look pregnant, and the gurgling and groaning down there were an ominous omen of the storm that was brewing. Once it finally started to flow out the back, it came in a steady stream.

This went on for well over two hours. Back and forth to the bathroom. Continuing to drink the nasty liquid. Tummy doing flip flops.

The nurse checked on me regularly, prodding me to hurry up and finish drinking because there was quite a bit to do before we were done for the night. I almost felt like asking what more there could possibly be, but I was a little afraid of the answer so I figured I'd just keep my mouth shut. She said the goal was to have the bowels so clean that the liquid coming out was completely clear, so I kept drinking, and it kept coming.

Eventually, she came into with a small cup of liquid, proclaiming, "Okay. Time for the second course. Now it's time to turn things up a notch."

"Up a notch!? You've got to be kidding." Unfortunately, she wasn't.

JOURNAL ENTRY

> Eventually (at around 8) there was little more than a couple of cupfuls left, she came in and said she couldn't wait any more so it was time to move "to the next level." She had a shot-glass full of mag sulfate, and suggested I have something as a chaser, as it was very nasty stuff. Betsy seconded that suggestion, so I used cranberry juice. The stuff was VERY awful, but she came in with another shot for each of the next four hours.

> Also during that time they gave me an electric razor to shave (Bermuda shorts...from navel to knees). So I did that. She came by to inspect it, and finished up the areas I couldn't see....

> Then, she came in with a jar full of betadyne to paint me. She painted the shaved area, and the stuff was sticky, goopy stuff. Yuck. I had to stand up for a half hour for it all to dry, and had to run to the toilet every few minutes to do my thing in between. The toilet seat was all covered with the Betadyne by that point, too. Yuck.

> By 1 a.m., it was all done. I had been prepped. Now it was time to sleep, so they brought me a pill. I was afraid I would still have to go to the bathroom, but my butt was so so sore by then I was hoping it was all done. Eventually I did drift off to sleep.

Surprisingly, I slept well. For some reason I woke a few times, afraid that I would somehow oversleep and miss my surgery, but it would take a minute to emerge from my fog, get my bearings, and assure myself that I wouldn't miss it before sinking back to sleep.

August 10, 2000. As the sun rose over Lake Winnebego, the nurses in our ward were already bustling with activity. I was had arranged to be the first surgery of the day, not wanting to have to sit around all day, getting hungry and anxious and waiting for my turn. Besides my raw bum, I seemed no worse the wear from all the prepping activities from the night before. In fact, the more I thought about it the more I felt like an athlete who has worked and trained for her entire life, and was about to take the center stage. My moment had arrived.

Once things got rolling, it all happened pretty quickly.

JOURNAL ENTRY

My mom stopped by first thing in the morning, just as the nurses came by to take some blood. Although there was a time (not too long ago) when I was admittedly squeamish about blood, and actually fainted during blood tests, I have become far too accustomed to it to let it bother me now. Shortly afterwards, the nurse came in and said they were ready for me. A guy brought another bed in for me to skootch over onto, they gave me some meds (I think it was Valium), and off we went. Mom, the guy pushing the gurney, and me. Eventually the guy showed my mom where the waiting area was, so we hugged, kissed, and said "I love you," before we left her behind, and he wheeled me to a staging area outside the operating rooms.

It wasn't long before the anesthesiologist came out to introduce himself and explain what was going to happen. When he was done, a nurse came and wheeled me into the operating room, and I skootched over onto the operating table. It was shaped like a cross, and I stretched my arms along the cross bar and they secured them down with velcro. I found it amusing, thinking that perhaps it was just restraints for those who had last minute second thoughts and tried to escape.

There were a half dozen people doing different things,

dressed in surgical garb and masks, and I was introduced to everyone one by one, as if we were meeting for social chat at a cocktail party or something. The anesthesiologist put an iv in the back of my hand, which didn't hurt too badly. I was totally calm and relaxed, and wasn't nearly as cold or as shivery as I have been in other operating rooms

He took a seat up near my head, and things started to happen. He told me he was going to release some stuff that would make me relaxed, and a few seconds later I could feel it. I lay quietly, breathing deeply, letting the warmth that seemed to be coming from my hand spread throughout me. Then, he put an oxygen mask above my face and told me he was going to release the stuff that would put me to sleep, and the next thing I would remember would be in the recovery room. He told me to take deep breaths, and I only remember taking a couple, and that was that.

Although most of the world refers to this surgery as a sex change operation, or simply SRS, the technical term for it is vaginoplasty. The most common technique of male-to-female SRS is known as the penile inversion method. Mucosal tissue gives the new vagina lubrication. A fully functional clitoris, made from the nerve endings that resided in the head of the penis, provides erotic stimulation. The urethra is redirected to the proper location. All it all, it is an amazing procedure, both aesthetically and functionally.

I had been to a presentation containing graphic photographs that showed exactly what was being done. I couldn't look. Although I had listened intently, I covered my eyes to avoid seeing the blood. I really didn't want to know the details. All I really cared about was the end result.

The surgery itself lasts anywhere from three to five hours, depending on the surgeon, what is being done, and any complications that might arise.

JOURNAL ENTRY

I woke up in the recovery room. I didn't know what time it was, or how long I'd been out. I was aware of people moving and talking around me. I was aware of the fairly intense pain in my groin. I was aware that I did not feel sick to my stomach, but also when I opened my eyes and tried to look around, I felt the spins and immediately closed them again. A nurse saw that I was awake and asked if I was hurting, and I said I was, and she said she would get something for me. It helped.

After some period of time they deemed that I was ready to go back to my room, so they wheeled me back there. My mom came right in, and had a big smile on her face. I didn't feel too awful at that point, and she had her arms full of gifts. A book beautiful poems. I pink teddy bear. Some flowers. A card. A box of pink bubble gum cigars that said, "It's a Girl!." I was very happy, and we asked the nurses to take some pictures to capture the moment....

I was attached to machines and contraptions that made a variety of interesting sounds. They gave me the hand-held button for the pain drip. It gives a boost of morphine every 7 minutes, helping to take the edge off the pain. I had a catheter, emerging from all the bandages and packing on my groin, attached to a bag at the side of the bed. I had an iv, in my hand attached to a bag full of saline, and when the drip bag got empty it started beeping. I had an automatic blood pressure cuff on my arm that inflated every so often (early readings were pretty low...60 some over 80 some I think). I had stocking on my legs, as well as inflatable leggings that to keep the blood going, but that also kept me pretty warm. My mom set pillows under my arms and legs, and I was actually pretty comfortable considering....

In all honesty, the physical pain from the surgery really wasn't that bad. I don't know if it's because there really wasn't that much pain, or that the meds were really that good. What did hurt was this thing around my waist called a T-Binder. There was all kinds of packing on the groin, as well as ice bags that the nurses re-filled every few hours. The T-Binder was cutting into my right hip like a knife, and the pain got excruciating. I finally talked the nurses into loosening it a bit (which they were very hesitant to do), and it made a world of difference.

Different surgeons have different post-op rules for their SRS patients. Some prefer that their patients get back up on their feet as soon as possible. Dr. Schrang, on the other hand, keeps his patients immobile and confined to bed for six full days. Some of the SRS stories that I had read on the internet complained more about the boredom and the discomfort of being stuck in bed for so long more than they did about the aftereffects of the surgery.

For my own part, I'm glad it worked out that way. My mom continually shifted a mountain of pillows under my arms and legs so my weight was always evenly distributed. I spent much of the time sleeping, talking with guests who came to see me or Betsy, watching T. V., eating, writing email, adding to my journal, or talking to friends on the phone. Time seemed to pass quickly.

KATE SENT THIS TO MANY OF MY FRIENDS TO ANNOUNCE
THE SUCCESSFUL SURGERY!

Hi all,

I want you to know that I just heard from Donna's Mom and it's official: A bouncing baby girl was reborn this morning in Neenah. Yea!

The patient is doing fine and is in room 250-A.

Kate

As I got to know my roommate, Betsy, I learned that she was a patent attorney. She seemed to be my age, although it was difficult to get an actual reading because most of my memories of her were of lying all the way on the other side of the room in her hospital bed. My first actual glimpse of her everyday self wasn't until her sixth day and she was allowed to get out of bed and move around, and I was stunned to notice just how pretty, and thin, she was. She had a head full of tight red ringlets, and her cute British accent and soft voice was a source of constant fascination.

During our convalescence she had visitor after visitor file through our room, although my memories of specifics are clouded by my week on painkillers. One was a transitioning gal who had been a radio DJ, and who demonstrated the astounding difference in the male and female versions of her voice for my mom. Another was a Female-to-male transsexual, which was the first that mom had ever met.

I think Betsy appreciated my mom being there as well, as her formal nurse's training was a Godsend for us both. She un-kinked the catheter hose when it seemed to get backed up. She helped to adjust our pillows to keep us comfortable. She convinced the nurse to loosen Betsy's T-Binder, which had become so tight as to become unbearable. One day she said, in her oh-so-cute accent, "You're mum's an angel from heaven, she is!"

Dr. Schrang had warned that some patients experience *phantom* pains at some point during their recovery. He said that it was not uncommon to feel an itch, or a twinge of pain, from an area where our penis used to be, only of course it wasn't there anymore so it would be difficult to localize the actual source of the discomfort. He explained that this was probably due to the fact that the skin and the nerve endings had been relocated, but the mind hadn't re-mapped itself yet, so our mind actually felt like we still had a penis.

Several days into our convalescence, Betsy complained to a nurse, "I know it's impossible, but if I didn't know any better I'd swear I have an erection!" She sounded so serious, and so surprised; I almost split my sutures laughing.

JOURNAL ENTRY (SRS+2 DAYS)

Last night I got a fever of 101, and was feeling pretty crummy. They put an icepack on my forehead, and gave me some kind of medicine, and everything seemed much better this morning. My blood pressure is still low...somewhere around 98/60 last I remember, but they came today to take the IV out of my hand, which is a good thing.

The dull ache in my groin is a constant "friend." It is so neat when they come to change the dressings and wipe down there, and there is no penis to get in the way. It's truly and utterly unbelievable. I sometimes really wonder how much of this all is my feeling loopy from the meds, and how much is reality. I still can't believe it. I have really done this!!!!!

I even think the trip has been good for mom in lots of ways. She feels very much needed and motherly, which I think she has not felt for a long time. She has helped not only me, but my roommate as well, who is full of constant praise for her help and concern. My roommate, Betsy, has had 4 or 5 guests who have driven here from Minneapolis to be with her, and mom talks with them all at length. She even goes down to eat with them. I think the feeling of sisterhood that exudes from these relationships helps to ease her worries of my being lonely and alone...

Mom has gotten herself onto a pretty regular schedule. She gets to the hospital at 9 a.m. or so, and stays until early afternoon before heading back to the hotel for a nap. She comes back just before dinner (she actually likes the cafeteria food) and stays until 9 p.m. or so. She is absolutely wonderful.

It seems like we are on a pretty regular routine, as well. We get a menu for meals and circle whatever we want to eat.; no restrictions. In fact, the food is actually pretty good, which is a good thing because my appetite has already seemed to regain its vigor.

341

They come in every couple of days to change the linens on the bed. There is a T-Bar hanging above my head, so I lift myself up while they roll the dirty linens away, and unroll the new ones. I sleep a bit, but not as much as I expected I would..

Throughout the week, little by little, the devices to which I was connected were disconnected and removed. The inflatable leggings that kept the circulation in my legs going were taken away, and I actually felt cold once they were gone. I was disconnected from the blood pressure monitor. They eventually stopped refilling the ice packs that rested on my groin. All the beeping sounds that had almost become routine were turned off, and the room suddenly seemed so much quieter.

At five days post-op, it was time for the unveiling. It was time for Dr. Schrang to remove all of the bandages and gauze packing from inside and around my new vagina. I would ordinarily have been a little apprehensive about this whole thing, but at this point I figured that the worst had passed so the rest should be pretty tame in comparison. Besides, Betsy seemed to have handled it pretty well so I was hoping my experience would be similar.

Dr. Schrang took a position down between my spread legs, and carefully but methodically began removing all the bandages that had surrounded the surgery area since the operation. Layer after layer was removed, until eventually the entire area was bare I got my first glimpse. I was stunned.

I pretty much knew what to expect, but seeing it with my own eyes was proof that it was true. As I look down at my body, there was no penis! In its place was a flat, unmistakably female groin. As Dr. Schrang gave me a moment to look at my new anatomy, I realized the irony that, as he sat down between my legs, this unveiling felt like a symbolic rebirth of sorts, and that a new life would, indeed, be delivered from this new vaginal canal. My own.

The doctor grabbed the end of the gauze that was sticking out of the vagina, and began pulling on it to remove the packing. As I watched,

I was amazed; he pulled and pulled, and gauze just kept coming and coming. It was seemingly endless. The sensation of it coming out was something I had never experienced before, sort of like a monster tampon being slowly extracted by a very long string.

Once all the gauze was removed, it was time for the first dilation. Dr. Schrang took one of the medium sized dilators (1½" in diameter) and pushed it into the new vagina! I was expecting some degree of discomfort, or even pain, and perhaps some bloody ooze to one degree or another. But what I got was a pretty incredible sensation, as it slid deep into the new opening with ease.

My sister arrived in Neenah in mid-week to keep mom and I company. Although I really don't remember her arrival, she tells me that the first thing I said to her after welcoming her and hugging her was, "Do you wanna see it?!"

Of course she did, but she really didn't know how to ask, so I proudly displayed my new anatomy for her. I felt like a child at Christmas who had just gotten a new present, just wanting to show everyone my new toy. Life had suddenly become like perpetual show and tell.

On my sixth day after surgery, I was finally allowed to get up and walk around. As I swung my legs over the edge of the bed, and took my first tentative steps in a week, I felt like a new-born fawn who had just struggled to her feet, trying to figure out just how these darn legs work.

I will never forget the feeling of taking those first few steps, and not having a penis or scrotum between my legs to keep them company. After 40 years of walking, and getting used to having all that stuff down there, the fact that it was gone really hit home once I started walking.

I went into the bathroom and stood in front of the mirror, staring, not believing that this was really me. But it was. Of course, the entire area was still red and raw and pretty nasty looking, but I don't think I'd ever been happier to see anything in my life. And as I remembered that I had initially thought that this wouldn't really be all that big of a deal, I realized that it *was* a big deal. And I cried.

As the week progressed, I found other things that would take some getting used to. For example, when I sat down to pee, I found I sometimes reached down to aim my penis, as I had grown used to doing over an entire lifetime as a guy. Of course, there was no penis to aim, and I sometimes smiled at just how much of creature of habit people really are.

One thing, in particular, symbolized just how this change in my anatomy would affect my life. I know this is going to sound gross, but it needs to be said, so I'll try to be as delicate as possible.

As a guy, when I wiped my behind after pooping, I always went back to front. It seemed as natural as walking to me. I did it without even thinking about it, and it never even crossed my mind that anybody did anything different.

Well, after I went into my bathroom and peed for the first time, I noticed a sign taped to the inside of the door. "FRONT TO BACK" it read. Nothing more. "What the heck does that mean?" I wondered.

I asked one of the nurses, who helped to enlighten me. Apparently, girls are taught from an early age to wipe themselves going from front to back! They need to reach around to wipe in the opposite direction of all of the *equipment* that they have down there, so they need to wipe to the back.

I couldn't argue with the logic; it made sense. But actually remembering to do it, after a lifetime of back-to-fronting, would be a significant behavior change for me. I decided that it would probably be best if I put up a sign in my own bathroom, once I got home, just to help me to remember.

Let there be no doubt, SRS post-op care is a very tedious thing. I know many gals who are more worried about their post-op routines than they are about the surgery. The truth is that there is no getting around the fact that recovering from SRS takes time and work.

As soon as the packing is removed, the key word for any Male-to-Female post-op is dilation. Dilation consists of taking a series of progressively larger plastic dilators, or stents, and putting them into the vaginal cavity. The goal at the beginning is to keep the neo-vagina from healing on itself. As time goes on, a regular dilation schedule ensures that a patient maintain as much depth and width as possible.

The dilators themselves are bullet shaped, about the length of a vibrator, and look like a round of ammunition for a mortar or an anti-aircraft gun or something. There are five dilators in a set, each progressively bigger than the previous one. The smallest one is only an inch in diameter, with the largest being nearly an inch and three quarters. At first glance, the immediate thought is often "I'll *never* be able to fit one of those monsters inside of me." Realistically, most patients will probably be ready to face the largest dilator just a few weeks after surgery.

A dilating session consists of laying down, putting each dilator into the vagina for five or ten minutes, removing it, and then repeating the process with the next largest stent in order to gradually stretch out the area. The entire process usually took me almost an hour. Given the fact that we must do this four or five times a day for several weeks after SRS meant that much of my time awake during the day was spent either getting ready to dilate, dilating, cleaning up from my dilation session, or resting between dilations.

After eight days, it was with a mixture of relief and sadness that I was released from the hospital. We thanked the nurses profusely; they had become special friends and would be missed. We made sure we understood all the post-op activities we should be doing. And when it was finally time to go, one of the nurses brought a wheelchair to take me to the front door, and although I certainly could have walked it the ride felt like a victory arcade; like I had won the Super Bowl or the Indy 500.

I had scheduled to spend a couple of extra days recuperating at the hotel in Neenah before heading home, just in case there were any unforeseen complications once I got up and walking again. Thankfully, there were none.

My minor post-op difficulties were merely due to the fact that I popped some stitches in my perineum during a dilation session, which was more uncomfortable than dangerous. It certainly made for a very tender walk, and I found that staying on my feet for any length of time a difficult, somewhat painful, and ultimately exhausting. I quickly learned that my favorite recuperative position was lying down, so I did my best to accommodate myself as much as possible.

As we packed for our flight home, a feeling of nostalgia had already started to develop around all that had happened during my visit to Neenah. The feeling that something special, something magic, had happened during my time there was so real I could almost touch it. I could tell that Mom and Jude, felt it too.

It had been a long, incredibly difficult road. From that scared, confused child that had first reached out for help, to the newly minted post-op who was preparing to face the world on her own terms, the difference was absolutely incredible. The emotional toll it had taken was staggering. The financial cost of my entire transition was over $75,000. The number of hours spent in physical and emotional pain was more than I could even venture to guess. And even at that, I keenly realized that I had been far more fortunate than most.

My journey had been far more than a test of my commitment, or my courage. It had been a test of my character. It had been a test of my humanity. It had been a test of my adaptability. It had been a test of my heart. And as I reviewed it all, with a quieter mind and a more peaceful soul, I realized that all are attributes most would consider to be universally *human*. Free from all the other labels, that's really all I ever wanted to be in the first place.

At the airport I slowly waddled towards the gate. I was already absolutely exhausted, but incredibly happy, and looking forward to getting home. I knew that my journey wasn't over, not by a long shot, but that a major chapter had just closed. I knew that frustration and disappointment lay in my future, just as it does for each of us. But I felt ready to face it with the courage and conviction that comes from inner peace rather than desperation; a peace that had been earned, not given, and would never be taken for granted.

Epilogue: Dreams

Hope is a waking dream.

— Aristotle

How many people actually make their dreams come true? How many of us actually ever get to a point where we truly believe that the impossible *is* possible, and that mere mortals really *can* make miracles happen?

I feel I have done that. I have overcome astronomical odds to reach my own, personal dream. Whether others agree with what I have done is irrelevant to me, knowing that there will always be disapprovers and nonbelievers who will stand up and say, "Hey, you can't do that!" Fending them off with one arm, while trying to scramble forward with the other was actually the most difficult part of the journey, but in retrospect has added a sense of satisfaction that I doubt I would feel quite so acutely if I had attempted my transition buoyed by universal support and acceptance.

Part of the general petulance, in my opinion, is derived from the fact that most people are so trapped in their own little lives that whenever they see anyone challenging traditional boundaries their natural reaction is worry and anger. It's almost as if they fear that civilization might be so fragile that if we allow people to test things that most people don't define as *normal*, they might actually break it.

On one hand, our society is full of encouragement to "Follow Your Dreams," and to "Dare to Believe," but on the other it is ready and far too willing to judge a person's dreams as acceptable or not. As a result, for those of us whose dreams have been deemed blasphemy in the court of common wisdom, such exhortation takes on an air of hypocritical rhetoric. It actually becomes a direct challenge, and the first decision to make is whether we are up to the task of facing it. Or not.

For some reason, many people seem to anoint themselves as collective sentinels, or enforcers, for society, policing the landscape for transgressors who would challenge unwritten rules based on their own beliefs and prejudices. They seem to forget that one of the key attributes of nature is its ability to define a sense of order, or balance, despite the fact that its main triumph is derived from its unending and amazing diversity.

In nature, miracles happen every day, every minute, every nanosecond. The fact that a cell divides, or that a plant can turn sunlight into oxygen, are miracles of immeasurable proportion. Yet, they are so commonplace in our world that they pass unnoticed and unappreciated. If we were to find similar processes on another planet, the finding would be of such magnitude as to challenge everything we think we believe here on Earth. Yet, it is all so normal to us here that we accept it as common, and we only think about it when something goes wrong. We have analyzed the physical mechanics of it all so minutely that we can explain the general technical process, but is that the same as actually understanding it? Hardly.

Of course, there is a huge difference between people, and nature. In nature miracles are accepted as part of natural processes. They happen all by themselves. For people, they don't. The key component, that cannot be stressed enough, is that people need to actually make things happen in their lives. If we wait and hope that luck, instead of effort, will be the key component of any achievement, we would probably have a better chance of success if we simply gaze skywards and wish upon a rising star. If we sit and wait for some sort of divine intervention, or for fate to run its course, without doing any of the grunt work ourselves, we are often really just stalling...looking for a reason *not* to do something.

I have learned that the value of achieving anything is directly proportional to the effort involved in achieving it, not necessarily in the size of the goal. And I have also learned that the real beauty in an achievement is not always merely in the achievement itself, but in the journey of discovery that leads there. That value *must* come from inside ourselves, and not from others who either cannot or will not appreciate our dreams and accomplishments. As a result, many individual triumphs are best celebrated and appreciated alone.

At the outset of this book I indicated that it is not a step-by-step guide to self-actualization. I think the goals that each of us set in our lives are far too different, and the range of tools we have as individuals is far too broad, to allow for such a simple recipe.

However, I do have some simple advice, culled from trial-and-error, and from learning things the hard way. I have developed some simple tips that, when practiced appropriately, can help dream-chasers be successful in their own individual journeys.

- *Question everything.* The first goal is to really, truly, know yourself and your dream. Why do I want to do this? Am I doing this for myself, or for someone else? In the scheme of things, is this really important enough to me to fight for? If your commitment is tepid, or if your reasons are weak, you have admitted defeat before you even begin. If the answer to any questions is, "Because I'm afraid," search for other answers because fear is not an acceptable answer; it is a barrier to be faced and overcome.

- *Don't be afraid to fail.* This may sound odd, but it is absolutely critical. Success needs to be spurred by the *pull* to achieve something special, not by the *push* of fear of *not* achieving it. Short-term failures are absolutely, positively going to happen, so ultimate success is based on accepting that, and dealing with it. But short-term failures do not necessarily result in ultimate failure, unless we let them.

- *Don't think you can be successful; know you can.* This tenet should not be translated as "Don't Doubt Yourself." Doubt is a healthy response, as long as it is managed. Unmanaged doubt is just an excuse just waiting for a reason to be used. A difficult goal will test your commitment, and your beliefs. It will cause you to question yourself, and to consider compromise short of your dream. If have done your homework, and you truly believe in your goal, you will overcome these obstacles, and they will actually strengthen your resolve.

- *Be resourceful and creative.* When viewing a complex problem, don't rely on common paradigms to find your answers. Uncommon problems often require uncommon tools or creative solutions. Often, it's not the person who wants something the most that actually achieves it; it's the person who is the most resourceful and creative. Plan ahead so that you're not constantly reacting to difficulties that invariably pop up along the way.

- *Define specific goals, and interim goals.* This will help to keep short-term achievements in sight, while the ultimate long-term goal still seems so far away. Once short-term goals have been successfully achieved, take the time to celebrate them and appreciate them before catching your breath, and moving on to the next. Also, don't be afraid to change your course (or even abandon your trek completely) based on the things you discover, both about yourself and your goals, along the way. As we get closer to our goals, the pull to achieve them should get stronger. If not, perhaps our ultimate goal is not as valuable, or as necessary as we thought it was in the first place so we may need to re-evaluate.

- *Be patient.* People have a tendency to want things immediately. Time can either be your enemy or your friend. I strongly urge that you view it as the latter, and not the former. Also, realize that how you are feeling now, or how others might be feeling, will absolutely and positively change over time. That is a given.

- *Be aware.* Know how you are feeling. Know what is happening around you. Perhaps it might be helpful to take the time to actually write it down, as the simple task of expressing it sometimes helps to clarify things in our minds.

- *Actively seek validation and support.* I cannot stress this strongly enough. There is strength in numbers; courage really is contagious. A team of like-minded players is exponentially stronger than any single individual. When you need encouragement, and validation, and an understanding ear, make sure you have identified a support network to provide it. Facing seemingly insurmountable odds alone can be a dangerous proposition. Sometimes, our greatest source of strength isn't in ourselves, it's from the people that surround us. Recognize that, and use it to your advantage.

- *Be Realistic.* This is a difficult one. On one side we exhort ourselves to believe in the impossible. But on the other, we try to manage our expectations to avoid allowing ourselves to be disappointed when the realities of our goals do not match our initial expectations. Perhaps it can best be paraphrased by the saying, "Keep your head in the stars, but your feet firmly on the ground."

- *Once you have achieved your dream, be ready to move on.* This is not an easy task. You have spent so much time and energy working towards a goal, that having reached it can sometimes produce a curious emptiness. There seem to be no more goals in life; no more mountains to climb.

It should come as no surprise that a sex change operation does not solve all of a transsexual's problems. Life is far too complex for anything as simple as a mythical "magic pill," it just doesn't happen like that.

Although this may be stating the obvious, it still seems to come as a surprise to many transsexuals who expect that their surgery will somehow solve a significant portion of their problems. The fact that the problems are still there, patiently waiting for them, following their surgery seems to come as a surprise.

In fact, some of the other issues that a transsexual faces can actually become *more* acute immediately following the surgery. Money issues. Relationship issues. Employment issues. Self-Image or life-direction issues. There is sometimes a significant reaction to the permanence of the surgery; by spouses, by children, by parents and family. The realization that this person has actually done it, and any faint hope that they will ultimately change their mind and go back is now gone, slowly sinks in.

For the transsexual, the question often becomes, "Now what?" SRS had been a lifelong goal that had been achieved; a realized dream. Suddenly, the transsexual may find herself facing a life devoid of goals. She may have deluded herself into thinking that she would feel different once she had the surgery, and be dismayed to learn that she still actually feels the same.

To top it all off, post-op care can become very tedious very quickly. Some post-ops have ongoing complications, ranging from minor pain and bleeding to significant infection requiring hospitalization. There was a time when I dilated first thing in the morning, went home at lunch to dilate again, did my third dilation as soon as I got home from work, and did a final dilation just before bed. I have heard of gals who have actually set their clocks to wake them up in the middle of the night for a fifth dilation as instructed by their surgeon.

To many, the weight of it all can quickly cause a fairly serious, and sometimes fatal, bout of post-op depression.

JOURNAL ENTRY

I am a believer that reality is in the eye of the beholder. To some people, for all intents and purposes, I am female...mentally and physically. To others, I am a castrated man who has breast implants and an inverted penis, and that does not make me female. Which of those is reality? Take your pick. Also, in my own mind, there is a difference between knowing your reality, and feeling the pressure of it. I am so well aware of the facts and details of my existence that it isn't funny. If I let the weight of that pressure get to me, I have no idea how I would function. I am very good at forging ahead despite my encumbrance...trying to solve the issues at hand in bite size pieces...one at a time. And so far, I always seem to be able to find a solution. Right now, however, the pressure of it all is beginning to seep in. I am feeling the weight of it. I think about it. It keeps me awake. It concerns me. It affects me. And although it has certainly always been here...it has not bothered me so much until lately. The financial picture, and divorce picture, and relationship picture, and job picture.... in its entirety it is a depressing and harrowing and daunting "reality." It IS upsetting. But it is my life right now. If I had no resources at my disposal to climb out of this, I have no idea what I would do. Desperation is not my forte. If I got to that point, I think I would shut down like a toy whose battery has died. But I am not there yet, so I'll deal with these realities one by one, as I always have, and hope to climb back to the light of day. I will get there, eventually, but I have never had so many fires blazing at the same time, so it will be quite the recovery.

Some people mistake this depression for regret. That's not to say, despite all of the safeguards to prevent it, that there aren't post-ops who don't regret what they've done (to one degree or another). But those who realize that a post-op depression is waiting for them usually handle these situations well.

I had no regrets. I was content. I felt loved, and peaceful, and over the next several months I continued to become comfortable in my new role, and my new routine. I took joy in the simple firsts that I found confronting me every day: my first visit to the woman's restroom at a Buffalo Bills game, my first time swimming in a woman's bathing suit, my first time making love as a woman, and my first birthday where I didn't need to wish that this would be my last one as a boy. In those simple firsts and simple pleasures I found the joy that had eluded me for so many years, and that so many people seem to take for granted: the simple peace that comes from being comfortable in your own skin.

My life as a man suddenly seemed as though it had happened so long ago. All the pain, and frustration started to fade in my memory, although the ongoing rigors of my divorce, of the pain of separation from my son, and of continued anger, bitterness, and rejection by my wife, kept some wounds constantly fresh. I did my best to dwell on the future, rather than be sucked back into the past, and my eyes were firmly planted on the road ahead, wherever it was to lead.

In the months following SRS I would find myself back in Neenah for the second of the two operations. I would eventually leave Rochester, and move to a place where nobody knew me or my unique pedigree, and I was totally and unquestioningly accepted as Donna. I would face continued rejection by people I once loved. I would continue to learn and grow, and become more and more comfortable in my skin. I would fall in and out of love. And, as always, I would test the boundaries of myself and my world, my head held high and my eyes wide open.

In Closing

Each year, my mom writes a Christmas letter to all of her friends. While some people may find these kinds of letters cheesy and impersonal, my mom's annual letter chronicles our family history to everyone that is special to our family. She has written her letter since before I was even born, and continues to send it to well over a hundred people that have touched her life in some capacity. She has not actually seen many of these people in 20 or 30 years, but they faithfully acknowledge the strength of the friendship bond by reciprocating, sending letters of their own back to my mom.

As 2000 drew to a close, my mom asked if she could include something about my journey in her letter. She usually adds a paragraph for each of us kids, giving updates on families and careers and current events, and was hoping to be able to explain, in her own way, what had happened and how she was feeling about it. Of course, I told her that it would be fine.

Mom wrote and included a heartfelt addendum that was dedicated to my story.

12/25/00

DEAR FRIENDS:

Dave has asked me to send this information to those I thought would want to know. He came to me in July of 1999 and said he was Transgendered.

That he had felt he should have been a woman since a very early age. He has been having psychological counseling for several years, had been on female hormones for over a year, and was soon going to start living as a woman. This kind of thing only happens to someone else. My immediate reaction was, "What did I do wrong?" And my second reaction was, "How could I have missed it all these years?"

It has taken me a year to come to terms with this. I was finally able to work it through to realize this was an accident of nature and to establish my priorities. This is my kid!

In October of 1999, Dave became Donna Gail, legally on her Social Security, Driver's License and eventually on her Birth Certificate. She came out at work, had some plastic surgery on her face to look more feminine, and had a lot of electrolysis.

After living as a woman for a year Donna had the genital surgery to become a woman. Donna has changed jobs and now lives in Texas. She seems more at peace with herself.

There is a book entitled *True Selves—Understanding Transexualism* by Mildred L. Brown and Chloe Rounsley. It has helped me a lot. There have been several programs on TV about being transgendered. Oprah had one, and Dateline another. They were mostly sympathetic depictions of the situation.

I am very proud of Judy and Jay and their families. Here is a paragraph from Judy's letter which explains, perhaps better than I have, what has happened:

"A few months after Dad died, David told me a secret he has been keeping all his life. It's a situation that has meant enormous changes over these past two years for all of us who have loved him, especially his estranged wife and son. It turns out that David was born with a birth defect that nobody could see. He became aware of it very early on but also realized he couldn't tell anyone—not even Mom. It's called "gender dysphoria" and basically means that a person's gender identity is different from one's body.

It left Dave trapped and isolated, dealing with a situation that many people consider freakish or worse—all by himself. I don't know how he survived. He did the only thing he could: Make the best of things and live up to the expectations everyone had of his apparent gender. As it happened, Dave succeeded so completely and thoroughly that nobody could quite believe it when he came out with the truth. But as we all worked to learn as much as we could about this condition, we began to understand. David had decided to make a complete break with the life he had built for 40 years and start over with the correct gender. It's been a long, involved process with many steps, all medically supervised and legally documented. It has been painful, expensive, and harrowing but finally, at the end of it, David managed to correct the birth defect. The way I look at it is that he's given birth to himself the way he should have been…or should I say SHE. David doesn't legally exist anymore. I now have a sister, Donna Gail Rose. We have welcomed her into our lives with open arms and open minds. As you might imagine, this has forced all of us to look inside at our own value systems and beliefs, our prejudices, our definitions of love, our expectations of ourselves and the people around us…in short, a lot of thinking, soul-searching and discussion. I'm happy and proud to say that our extended family is stronger and closer than ever because of all this. I'm building a far richer relationship with my sister than I ever had with my brother. And my kids have been truly amazing in their ability to accept and love the person inside their uncle/aunt without judgment."

Donna Rose has a remarkable story. For her first 40 years she lived a successful and seemingly full life as a man. She was a world-class collegiate athlete, a husband, a father and a successful businessman. That world imploded under her need to explore and reconcile vexing gender confusion that had plagued her since childhood.

Donna's transformation has been extraordinary. Very few who meet her today have any clue about her unique pedigree. She is a noted speaker and educator, as well as an advocate for transgender and diversity issues. She actively promotes the power of the human spirit, and the ability that each of us has to define and manage our lives.

Donna currently lives in Texas with her son, and two dogs.